★BERLIN
▪LITTLE WANNSEE

N

0   25   50 MI

0   25   50 KM

GERMANY

CZECHOSLOVAKIA

▪ULM

▪MUNICH

AUSTRIA

A Guest of the Reich

A GUEST OF THE REICH

The Story of American Heiress
Gertrude Legendre's Dramatic Captivity
and Escape from Nazi Germany

Peter Finn

PANTHEON BOOKS, NEW YORK

Copyright © 2019 by Peter Finn

All rights reserved. Published in the United States by Pantheon Books, a division of Penguin Random House LLC, New York, and distributed in Canada by Penguin Random House Canada Limited, Toronto.

Pantheon Books and colophon are registered trademarks of Penguin Random House LLC.

Grateful acknowledgment is made to Special Collections, College of Charleston Libraries, for permission to quote from the materials held in the Gertrude Legendre collection, and to Stephanie E. Phelan for permission to reprint "New Year's Sonnet" by Larry Phelan.

Endpaper map by Mapping Specialists

Library of Congress Cataloging-in-Publication Data
Name: Finn, Peter, [date] author.
Title: A guest of the Reich : the story of American heiress Gertrude Legendre's dramatic captivity and escape from Nazi Germany / Peter Finn.
Description: First edition. New York : Pantheon Books, 2019. Includes bibliographical references and index.
Identifiers: LCCN 2019002112. ISBN 9781524747336 (hardcover : alk. paper). ISBN 9781524747343 (ebook).
Subjects: LCSH: Legendre, Gertrude Sanford, 1902–2000. World War, 1939–1945—Secret service—United States. Women spies—United States—Biography. United States—Office of Strategic Services—History. Women prisoners of war—Germany—Biography. World War, 1939–1945—Germany—Prisoners and prisons. Socialites—United States—Biography.
Classification: LCC D810.S8 L516 2019 | DDC 940.54/7243092 [B]—dc23 | LC record available at lccn.loc.gov/2019002112

www.pantheonbooks.com

Jacket photograph of Gertrude Legendre, 1938, by George Platt Lynes. Used with permission of The George Platt Lynes Estate. Print: College of Charleston Special Collections, Charleston, South Carolina
Jacket design by Kelly Blair

Printed in the United States of America
First Edition
2 4 6 8 9 7 5 3 1

For Nora

Contents

1 Paris *3*

2 Luxembourg City *12*

3 Wyoming *23*

4 Addis Ababa *30*

5 Hanoi *40*

6 Washington, D.C. *50*

7 London *62*

8 Wallendorf *72*

9 Limburg an der Lahn *81*

10 Diez an der Lahn *89*

11 Naples *99*

12 Diez an der Lahn *104*

13 Berlin *111*

14 Cologne *126*

15 Bad Godesberg *133*

16 Königswinter *146*

17 Kronberg *152*

18 Constance *161*

19 Bern *167*

20 Brandenburg *176*

Epilogue *191*

Acknowledgments *199*

A Note on Sources *201*

Notes *205*

Selected Bibliography *225*

Index *229*

A Guest of the Reich

Paris

On the afternoon of September 22, 1944, Gertrude Legendre strolled into the bar on the rue Cambon side of the Hôtel Ritz. Outside the street was lined with U.S. Army jeeps, and inside the place was already crowded, mostly with Americans, a mixture of military officers and war correspondents, their volubility rising amid whorls of cigarette smoke. White-jacketed barmen mixed cocktails behind a dark mahogany counter, and the hotel's patrons consumed the signature drinks in clusters around the small tables. Just one month after the city was liberated from the Nazis, this was the Paris a certain kind of American remembered: exclusive and jolly and alcohol-soaked.

The forty-two-year-old Legendre—known all her life as Gertie—was perfectly at ease in the legendary watering hole, a magnet over many years for wealthy Americans and Hollywood stars, as well as assorted European aristocrats, diplomats, spies, oligarchs, and, until recently, Nazi grandees. Field Marshal Hermann Göring had taken over the imperial suite after Paris fell to the Germans.

Gertie knew the head barman, Frank Meier, from previous visits to the Ritz, including a stopover in the winter of 1928, when she was twenty-six and on her way to a big-game hunting expedition in East Africa. Meier, inventor of such cocktails as the bee's knees, the royal highball, and the sidecar, was still managing the room in 1944, his eyelids and jowls heavier, but with the same slicked, center-parted hair, groomed mustache, and pince-nez. He had worked in the bar during the occupation but surreptitiously helped the Resistance, ensuring that he kept his position after liberation.

The two reminisced about Gertie's prewar stays at the hotel, and she talked about the 1928–29 hunt in the highlands of Abyssinia. Meier had told Gertie that when she reached Addis Ababa, she should drop in on his friend the head chef to the emperor Haile Selassie; she later dined with the Lion of Judah in his palace and ate a fourteen-course meal, alternating between European and African dishes, off dinner plates encrusted with gold coins. Gertie recalled that the local honey wine, called *tej*, was "especially potent. It went straight to my head like champagne."

In 1944 Paris, Gertie was wearing the uniform of a first lieutenant in the Women's Army Corps (WAC), though, as she was the first to acknowledge, she was no soldier and couldn't salute properly. She did, however, know how to dress. After arriving in the city, she had her khakis tailored by Madame Manon, her longtime dressmaker, who "couldn't wait to fit my uniform properly—taking it in here, and lifting a bit there." Her helmet, three sizes too big, stayed as is.

"I must send you a picture of me in my Khaki. You would be so amused," she wrote to her husband, Sidney, who was serving in Hawaii, a navy lieutenant commander in the intelligence center of the U.S. Pacific Fleet. They had not seen each other for two years and expressed their love—and the distress of being apart so long—through their almost daily letters. "Do you ever cry because you miss me?" wrote Gertie. "I do so much. I wonder if time is rubbing off the edge and you are now accustomed to the separation. I find it an incurable heartache, and I don't suppose I would want it any other way."

Gertie was a civilian employee of the Office of Strategic Services (OSS), the U.S. spy agency created in 1942 by President Roosevelt and led by William "Wild Bill" Donovan, whose charisma and daring transformed what had been a bureaucratic stepchild—despised by the FBI and sections of the brass—into a global organization that won grudging respect from the U.S. military. (J. Edgar Hoover, director of the FBI, never came around.) By war's end, more than twenty-one thousand men and women would serve in the OSS.

Gertie had until recently headed the cable desk at the London branch, overseeing the distribution of all top secret communications in and out of a building that ran European operations. The office was a key point of contact for the governments in exile in Britain; it ran agents into occupied Europe, managed relations with the prickly British services, which resented the growing independence of the OSS, and formulated plans for operations against the Reich after D-day.

Communications about many of these matters passed through Gertie's hands, and she was privy to some of the OSS's most secret plans and personnel. She was an administrator, not a spy, but her position gave her unusual insight into OSS operations and post-invasion planning. London was at the heart of the agency's espionage in Europe, and Gertie sat at the center of all communications about that work, giving her an almost accidental font of knowledge about the war effort.

Now she was among the flocks of Americans descending on Paris to set up shop behind the advancing Allied armies. Everyone entering the European theater of operations fell under General Dwight D. Eisenhower's command, so Gertie, unlike in her previous posting, was required to wear a WAC uniform. In Paris, it carried the mark of the liberator, a feather that had yet to lose its plume among the French. It also got you into U.S. mess halls.

Gertie wasn't classically beautiful, describing herself unkindly as a "moon-faced, buxom girl." But she radiated confidence and resolve, and her brown eyes and laughing smile were immediately winning. Her grandfather nicknamed her Spunky, and the moniker captured something essential about the girl, and later the woman, with the sometimes fierce mien. Her face, quicksilver in its expressiveness, could open in sparkling enthusiasm or crease in sour distaste. When she was five or six and her governess swept her hair up in a blue taffeta bow that held a corkscrew curl over her forehead, Gertie cut off the twirl of hair with scissors, infuriating the household.

Gertie was self-possessed, impatient, charming, and courageous and appeared to those who met her in London and Paris to be an archetypal American woman endowed with a kind of bullying certainty, as if she had just strolled, cigarette in hand, out of a celluloid frame. "When Gertrude felt strongly about anything all opposition died a quick if not graceful death," her husband said. Another less forgiving observer said, "I have to leave my personality at the door. There's no one in the room but her. She fills up all the space."

She was, in fact, the inspiration for the character Katharine Hepburn played in the movie *Holiday*, based on the 1928 Broadway play by Gertie's friend Philip Barry. Hepburn's character is an amusing, cocky, sometimes abrasive society girl who wants to escape the confining expectations of her family's fabulous wealth. The play, with a light, comic touch, captured some of the undercurrents of dissatisfaction with the materialism of the Jazz Age just before the crash, but without ever probing the theme too deeply.

Gertie's desire for escape, too, was more intuitive than the result of any great introspection. "I look ahead. I always have," Gertie said. "I don't contemplate life; I live it." It was a philosophy that would steer her and others toward tragedy.

Just a couple of weeks before her visit to the Ritz bar, Gertie got her orders to leave England and join the new office the OSS was opening on the Champs-Élysées, where she would also run the communications office. She also agreed to take on the added, volunteer duty of helping to organize a Paris club for the Supreme Headquarters Allied Expeditionary Force (SHAEF), the command of General Eisenhower. The club was to be located in Paris's Grand Hotel, with a cafeteria, a dancing hall, a bar, and an information bureau. She was to serve as the American representative on the organizing committee with the wives of Anthony Eden, the British foreign secretary, and Marie-Pierre Koenig, military governor of Paris.

Since D-day on June 6, Gertie had been pining to get across the channel because London seemed "dead as a doornail."

"Life has moved to Normandy, and it makes me want to go too," she said. Gertie felt overlooked because many of her male colleagues, including the head of the London branch, Colonel David K. E. Bruce, had already made it to France. "I only wish I could be jeeping my way in on their cloud of dust," she said, complaining that "a female civilian is the worst thing you can be in a war."

There was lots to envy. Bruce entered Paris, still occupied by some German forces, in the company of Ernest Hemingway and his band of irregulars. "Everyone thrust drinks at us that they had been hoarding for this occasion," Bruce wrote in his diary. "It was impossible to refuse them, but the combination was enough to wreck one's constitution. In the course of the afternoon, we had beer, cider, white and red Bordeaux, white and red Burgundy, champagne, rum, whiskey, cognac, armagnac, and Calvados."

Gertie's boss and Hemingway raced through side streets until they emerged behind the Arc de Triomphe, which they ascended at the invitation of the French captain guarding it. They looked out over "the golden dome of the Invalides, the green roof of the Madelaine, Sacre-Coeur." The air shook with the sound of tank fire, and the arch itself was under attack from snipers, but the view "was breathtaking." Back on the street, where they hid behind a tank during a gun battle, a man dove in beside Bruce, asked if the Americans would like to drink some champagne, and led the group through a confusion of gunfire—"every side street seemed enfiladed"—to several iced magnums at his luxurious apartment on the avenue Foch.

The ultimate goal, especially for Hemingway, was the Ritz, which was almost completely deserted when the writer's ragtag group of fighters strode through its doors on the Place Vendôme. Claude Auzello, the "elegantly unruffled" manager, asked what he could do for them. "We answered we would like 50 martini cocktails,"

Bruce wrote in his diary. "They were not very good, as the bartender had disappeared, but they were followed by a superb dinner"—soup, creamed spinach, raspberries in liqueur, and Perrier-Jouët champagne.

Gertie feared that the adventures would all end before she could witness the U.S. Army on the march. "Her obsession was to see the battle," recalled a friend, who described her as "completely fearless" and with "the vitality of ten men."

Gertie finally took off from Croydon in south London on September 17, with seven other OSS employees transferring to France. It was a country she knew well from before the war, remembering, apart from the Ritz, "summers in Biarritz, St. Jean de Luz, and Cap Antibes, the color and odor of Riviera flowers and the deep blue of the Mediterranean." They flew low over the countryside, and the France that greeted her was a vista of flattened villages, toppled spires, and fields pitted by shells. Outside her port window, a formation of B-17 Flying Fortress bombers swept by, heading back to England after another mission in the relentless pounding of Germany. The pilot came in low over the Paris rooftops, circling the city center to allow a view of the iconic and intact landmarks, before descending to Orly Airport, where a newly repaired runway was still a gouge of red dust.

Gertie had arranged to stay with a friend from their days in London, Marian Hall, who worked with the Red Cross and had recently rented a flat on the rue François 1ᵉʳ, near the Champs-Élysées. Gertie also planned to volunteer with the Red Cross, as she had in the United States right after Pearl Harbor.

Electricity, heat, and food were all in short supply, but Paris crackled with a "great gaiety of spirit."

"I am getting used to cold baths, candles and no heat," she wrote to her husband.

The OSS building was still being renovated, so the arrivals from London were free to roam. "During the day, I walked around Paris, amazed at how beautiful it still was," Gertie recalled. "The Parisians looked exhausted, although less shabby than Londoners. Always alert to fashion, young girls were painting their wooden heels to match the hue of their lips. Pedestrians and cyclists filled the streets." The shops, although largely empty of goods, were decorated with red, white, and blue flags and ribbons. "It's really gay and stimulating and I'm sure the GIs love it."

As she walked down the Champs-Élysées, an approaching American, also in uniform, saluted her. "I looked around to see who was behind me," Gertie recalled. "Then it dawned on me—the uniform." Everything was a little disconcerting. With almost no cars on the streets, Paris seemed strangely serene, as if it were awakening, not yet restored to its old noisy bustle.

Gertie checked in each day with the OSS, but the renovations were slow going, and her boss decided to give some of the staff a formal five-day leave. It was her first official break in more than a year, and she "decided to chance luck to turn up something interesting to do" with the free time.

That Friday afternoon in September, her first stop was the Ritz, where she soon found herself in the company of a group of American reporters. They were leaving the next day for Luxembourg, near where elements of the Third Army under General George Patton were headquartered. Gertie knew Patton from London and they had had dinner and attended the theater together. "It is always fun to meet the guys who run the war, and though less attractive than some, we had a good evening," she recalled.

The chattering reporters prompted a stab of envy. "I wanted so desperately to see troops on the move, to actually feel the urgency of war, and to know more of what it really meant," Gertie said.

She could not get that feeling in Paris. The city, now well behind the front lines, was a playground for officers and GIs. Eisenhower, at first, had considered leaving Paris in German hands for the short term, concerned about bloody street fighting and then feeding a vast civilian population when his troops could be better deployed chasing the retreating Germans across northern France. Better, the military initially calculated, to "bypass and encircle it, then await the inevitable capitulation of the isolated garrison."

General Charles de Gaulle, the leader of the Free French Forces, objected strenuously and argued that Paris would be razed by vengeful Nazis, which had happened in Warsaw earlier that month as Soviet troops stood by on the opposite bank of the Vistula River. There must be no such cold-bloodedness by the Allies. Through his characteristic hauteur and bluster, de Gaulle got his way. Eisenhower moved up the attack on the city, which swiftly fell.

At the liberated Ritz, Gertie spotted Bob Jennings, a wiry, sandy-haired navy officer and World War I aviator. He was a friend of her husband's; Gertie also knew him from London, where they had met socially several times at cocktail parties. Originally from Michigan's Upper Peninsula, the forty-nine-year-old Cornell graduate had prospered in the Texas oil industry and in investment banking during the interwar years. His security background check for the OSS noted that he had "accumulated a comfortable fortune in the oil business and is worth four or five hundred thousand dollars."

After Pearl Harbor, Jennings reenlisted and served in the Aleutians, the Alaska islands seized by the Japanese in June 1942 and retaken by the United States after some bitter fighting the following year. Jennings, a lieutenant commander, had been transferred in 1943 to the London branch of the OSS. His assignment was to help the spy service with its air operations; OSS relations with the U.S. Army Air Forces were often strained as the spies battled to secure planes to conduct their work.

Jennings was also at loose ends. He was scheduled to leave for London early the following week and from there to return to the United States. He had promised his mother he would be able to spend Christmas with her. Listening to the reporters, he, too, was soon infatuated with the idea of getting closer to the western front, though one of the reporters also discussed the risks. Bill Hearst of the International News Service, the agency founded by his father, William Randolph Hearst, told Jennings that three correspondents had recently been captured. Edward W. Beattie Jr. of the United Press, John Mecklin of *The Chicago Sun,* and Wright Bryan of NBC and *The Atlanta Journal* had stumbled into German hands while driving near the French city of Chaumont. The front lines were dangerously fluid.

Jennings, undaunted, said he could borrow an old Peugeot convertible, originally German property but now with "USA" tags and an American flag sticker on its bumper. The car was a little dilapidated, Jennings confessed, but it would get them there and back. Gertie said she could possibly arrange for them to say hello to Patton at his headquarters near Luxembourg.

At the last minute, the trip became all the more urgent for Gertie. She had gotten a letter from her husband, Sidney, telling her that he had finally been granted permission to travel home from Hawaii for a break—the first leave he had received since he was commissioned after Pearl Harbor. "The impossible has happened," he told her, "a months duty on the mainland and a months leave, making a total of two months on the mainland . . . It will be such heaven to pick up our lives again."

He said he would leave Oahu on October 1 and suggested they meet in New York City, where their two young children, Landine, eleven, and Bokara, four, had been in the care of their longtime nanny. Gertie and Sidney both missed their girls, but with none of the fervor they felt for each other. Children, in their milieu, were to be enjoyed, but in small doses; the quotidian work of parenting was best left to maids and governesses. "Watching their lives," their youngest daughter commented, "was like looking at a movie in installments—most of which I never saw."

Gertie now knew that the trip to Luxembourg might well be her last chance to get close to the front in order "to smell the fighting." She could get up and back for one last adventure before flying home to Sidney; she felt sure Bruce would sanction her reassignment.

"Just received this minute the great news about your return to the States on leave. Hooray! Hooray! How marvelous," Gertie wrote back to her husband. "Of course I can return and *will* . . . beat it home in all speed . . . a little shooting, a bit of sea and sun life and Oh what fun together. [Here's] to our happy future darling—I too can't wait."

Luxembourg City

Paris was overcast when Gertie and Jennings set off early on the morning of September 23. "We rode along straight roads of richly plowed fields that looked the same as in peace time," Gertie observed. "Only the occasional remains of a burned out truck or tank gave one the feeling of war." By noon the rain was pouring through the Peugeot's rotted canvas top; Gertie tried unsuccessfully to patch it with band-aids but the water kept pouring down their necks. It was just the first portent that the trip was ill-fated.

At Compiègne, about fifty miles northeast of Paris, they blew out a tire. After much discussion with some locals, they eventually found a junkyard and a replacement that fit the rim; they continued undaunted in sheets of rain another fifty miles to Saint-Quentin. The town was packed with soldiers, and they wandered fruitlessly from hotel to hotel in the fading light until a local resident took pity and found them accommodations in a pension—but only after the owner had been assured they were not regular GIs, who to his mind would break his furniture and burn cigarette holes in his carpet.

The next morning, after a breakfast of K rations—the daily food package for troops on the move—and Nescafé, Gertie and Jennings continued toward the Belgian border, fording a series of rivers on ferries that had replaced bombed bridges. By a farmer's cottage in a small village near the Belgian town of Arlon, the Peugeot wheezed and died. The local mechanic's diagnosis was dispiriting—a broken water pump and fan. He said the car needed to be taken to a bigger garage for repairs.

The hapless vehicle was hauled into Arlon, where Gertie and Jennings spent another rain-soaked evening trudging through the streets in search of a hotel. The next morning the pair pushed and steered the car, which had been deposited on the street, to a mechanic who said the parts could only be obtained in Luxembourg City. At a nearby military barracks, the sight of two distraught Americans was sufficient passport to secure a tow.

Along the way to Luxembourg City, the emboldening effects of liberation were evident. A "stuffed effigy of Hitler, dressed in a tattered German uniform and complete with helmet and black boots," hung from a tree, and the "grotesque face above the noose somehow caught the agony of strangulation." The tow truck driver stopped at Gertie's request so she could jump out and snap some photographs.

At a garage in Luxembourg City, the mechanic said he needed twenty-four hours to fix the car. A visit to Patton's headquarters seemed out of the question; time was running out, and soon they would have to return to Paris. The pair dolefully explored the city. The Grand Duchy of Luxembourg, which was incorporated into the Reich by the Nazis, had survived the war largely intact, and there was an air of prosperity to the place. Also, a heavy American presence: "Convoys rumbled through the streets incessantly. Soldiers on the march, our countrymen going to battle, were everywhere. Their faces were so young, so full of eagerness and spirit," Gertie said. This was some of what Gertie had hoped to see, but the following morning at the Hôtel Brasseur, over coffee and cigarettes, she and Jennings rued "the failure of our trip."

At that moment, Jennings spotted two U.S. officers entering the dining room and exchanged a grin of recognition with one of them—Jerry Papurt.

Major Maxwell Jerome Papurt was in X-2, the counterintelligence branch of the OSS. He was part of an OSS detachment with

T-Force, a joint U.S.-British intelligence mission designed to seize key German technology as the Wehrmacht retreated and root out and flip any agents the Germans had left behind. T-Force was under the Twelfth Army Group, commanded by General Omar Bradley, and Papurt's small unit was based at the Hôtel Brasseur.

A thirty-seven-year-old native of Cleveland, Papurt had a PhD in psychology, specializing in the rehabilitation of young criminals. He had taught at Ohio State University and worked in various corrections systems before enlisting in 1942. The son of Austrian Jews who had immigrated to the United States, Papurt spoke German, as well as some Italian, French, and Spanish. He had served first in the U.S. Army's Counterintelligence Corps (CIC) before joining the OSS. Prematurely gray and wearing glasses, Papurt in uniform still looked like a slightly doughy academic. But he was also a charismatic and daring veteran of army counterintelligence in North Africa and Italy, where he "had controlled important enemy agent operations."

The photographer Margaret Bourke-White, who met Papurt in Italy when she was on assignment to cover the Italian campaign for *Life* magazine, recalled that Papurt's comrades—who called him Pappy—admired his smarts and bravery; he always accompanied his men on the most dangerous missions. "If they gotta, I gotta—that's my code as an officer," he told Bourke-White.

"He was a dead shot with a pistol, had great moral as well as physical courage, and commanded intense loyalty from his staff," said Bourke-White. The two had begun an affair in Naples. "One soon forgot his ugly face for his kind eyes," she said.

Though his wife in Columbus, Ohio, was awaiting his return, Papurt had fallen hard for the photographer. He proposed shortly after they first met in October 1943. Bourke-White, recently divorced, had yet to respond when Papurt met Gertie and Jennings.

Because of his mission and position in the X-2 branch of the OSS, Papurt knew of one of the Allies' most closely held secrets: British cryptanalysts and mathematicians had broken German codes and were able to read large portions of the German armed forces' top-secret communications—a bounty of intelligence that was distributed to Allied commanders and select personnel under the code name Ultra from Bletchley Park, north of London. All military personnel briefed on Ultra were under strict orders to avoid any risk of capture by the Nazis. Papurt was expected to stay well behind the lines.

Jennings explained what he and Gertie were doing in Luxembourg.

"We had a little extra time and thought maybe we'd mosey up to the line so the lady could hear some gunfire," he said.

Papurt flashed his oversized grin and lit a cigarette.

"I know where there is some gunfire. Think you could spare the day for a little trip?" he asked.

"That's all you have to say, Major," said Gertie. "That's what we came up here for."

"Where is it?" Jennings asked.

"Wallendorf," replied Papurt. "Forty kilometers from here, just over the border . . . It's the first German town we took."

Wallendorf was to the west of the Siegfried Line—Westwall to the Germans—a constellation of border fortifications that stretched from the Netherlands to Switzerland. Through the first half of September 1944, the Germans were on the run, retreating through the northern French countryside, but the Wehrmacht was now digging in to defend the fatherland.

The Allies faced the forces of the Reich in an arc along the Dutch, Belgian, and French borders. Eisenhower's troops were far ahead of where they expected to be when the invasion had been planned, and had suffered relatively few casualties in the drive up to the German frontier. Their supply lines, the lifeblood of all armies, were stretched thin, however, and a general pause was under way.

The Westwall was made up of bunkers, gun pits, antitank ditches, and pillboxes—some with eight-foot-thick walls—that were connected in places by tunnels to facilitate mobility in battle. "Planned with a shrewd eye for terrain and interlocking fields of fire, the pillboxes were most numerous where approach avenues seemed especially vulnerable; as many as fifteen big bunkers might be found in a single square kilometer," wrote one historian.

Adolf Hitler had ordered the barrier built in 1936 to protect against a ground assault from the west. It had been neglected over the course of the war, but as the German army retreated, there was a desperate effort to rehabilitate these defenses. Beyond lay the Rhine and Germany's industrial heartland. For all its disrepair, the Westwall remained a formidable barrier, immune in some early probing to bazookas, flamethrowers, and small explosives.

The 5th Armored Division, assigned to V Corps, protected the city of Luxembourg and was responsible for thirty miles of the front, including the area facing Wallendorf. Major General Lunsford E. Oliver, the division commander, instructed Combat Command R—CCR—to probe the Westwall and be ready to attack, if ordered. The initial reports back from these surveillance forays were encouraging. Some parts of the wall were unmanned; at others, the Germans seemed to be just arriving and getting set up. And the wall itself was not as stout as in other sectors, because its German builders had relied on the area's rugged terrain to form a natural barrier. On September 13, CCR conducted a reconnaissance by fire and "failed to provoke a single return shot." In the face of this apparent weakness in the German lines, CCR was ordered to advance through Wallendorf and take the high ground beyond.

On September 14, CCR forded the Sauer River, about forty yards across, and entered Germany. Those defending Wallendorf, though they had only small arms, "defended with tenacity" and were only forced back with artillery fire and flamethrowers. The village was left gutted and smoldering. Nazi propagandists seized on this early attack into the fatherland as evidence of "the Allies' will to destroy all Germans together with German culture and history."

By the night of September 15, CCR was five miles inside Germany beyond the Westwall. But just a day later, Oliver called off the offensive. "The explanation for the halt appeared to lie . . . in the decisions that had emerged from the meeting of General Eisenhower and his top commanders on 2 September at Chartres and in a critical over-all logistical situation," according to one history of the campaign. The advancing forces, in short, could not outrun their supplies.

CCR now sat in a soft bulge just over the German border, and the inevitable counterattacks by infantry and panzer units followed, beginning on September 17. The Americans held and "sent the enemy armor and infantry reeling," but with some serious U.S. casualties in the effort. Oliver pulled CCR back to a smaller perimeter around Wallendorf on the nineteenth, protecting two tactical bridges across the Sauer. But late on the twenty-first, orders came from V Corps to abandon the village. Oliver's troops fell back, blowing up both bridges as they left.

Wallendorf was back in German hands.

Major Papurt, Gertie's new acquaintance, didn't know any of that despite his role in the OSS. He had recently checked the status of the village on a situation map at a nearby army headquarters, and Wallendorf "appeared to be close to the lines but in American hands." He was also told at headquarters that "the situation north of Luxembourg was fluid and that persons traveling there had to be on the alert." Papurt informed his commanding officer about the trip, but without specifying that the mission was little more than a joyride.

At the Hôtel Brasseur, a visit to Wallendorf that September 26 seemed like a daring but safe enough jaunt. Papurt said they could be back in time for lunch and Jennings and Gertie could return to Paris later in the afternoon, after picking up the Peugeot.

"Let's go," said Jennings. "Why talk about it?"

Still, Papurt stopped by headquarters once more "to check the situation map again and verify that Wallendorf was safe to enter." The maps still had not been updated. As he emerged, he gave an all-okay sign with his thumb and forefinger. Papurt, Jennings, and Gertie took off at 11:00 a.m. in a jeep driven by Doyle Dickson, a twenty-year-old private from Los Angeles who was assigned to the OSS.

The rain of the previous days had cleared, and they drove in brilliant sunshine past fields and woodland. They saw army convoys traveling in the opposite direction, and Gertie could hear the distant boom of cannons and artillery fire. The war she had helped prosecute, albeit as a key administrator in an office across the channel, was now thrillingly close.

Dickson had a heavy foot, and they raced through small villages, scattering ducks and geese. They headed north to Ettelbruck before turning east toward Wallendorf. As the trip progressed, other traffic disappeared. Jennings, experiencing a frisson of unease, asked Papurt if he was sure they were on the right road. Looked like a good spot for an ambush, he said.

Papurt spoke in German to the next farmer they passed, and he seemed quizzical about the presence of Americans but told them they would be able to see the village when they got around the next bend. He also said the front was close to two miles away.

All was quiet. "There were no signs of convoys, no sound of gunfire," Gertie noted. The sound of artillery had receded. They were in the well of a valley with the village on a slight elevation above them. It lay across a large field cut by a river. For the first time, images of the war began to intrude on the pastoral setting. A cow lay bloated in the field, its legs stiff with death. As the houses in the village came into focus, they noticed they had no roofs. There also didn't seem to be any American presence.

"Well, here's Wallendorf, according to the sign," said Gertie. "But I don't see any . . ."

The whistling crack of a single shot cut her short. A bullet had hit the front fender.

Gertie experienced a long moment of disbelief before she heard Papurt shout, "Sniper, he's mine."

The major grabbed a rifle and ran behind a roadside hedge. As he crawled on the ground, he lined up his sight on a distant copse of trees from where the shot seemed to have come. Gertie thought he looked faintly ridiculous; he reminded her of the actor Tom Mix, a cowboy from the silent film era. Still oblivious to the possibility they were actually in danger, Gertie, Jennings, and Dickson remained sitting upright in the jeep "watching the major's performance." Gertie even pulled out her camera and took Papurt's picture as he wriggled about in the dirt.

There was no second shot, and after several minutes Papurt stood up. The group considered what might have happened: "An enemy sniper, who perhaps had eluded our occupying forces; a stray shot not intended for us at all; a diehard German civilian putting up a token defense of his pitiful property; even the possibility that one of our own men had mistaken us for a party of the enemy making an escape in a stolen jeep."

Papurt shrugged his shoulders. "If there's anybody up there I can't see them," he said.

Against all common sense and training, they decided to push on.

Dickson started the motor, and Papurt climbed in, placing the rifle between his legs.

Dickson hadn't even gotten the car into second gear when a burst of machine-gun fire raked the ground in front of the jeep. Dickson braked and all four jumped out. Gertie, Dickson, and Jennings lay in a "cowering bundle" on the side of the jeep by a shallow ditch that provided some shelter from the attackers. Papurt was on the exposed side of the vehicle. The Germans were firing a portable machine gun that could unleash over a thousand rounds a minute.

"Geysers of dirt fairly exploded from the hard earth" as the gunner sought his range.

Papurt, in a quiet, unemotional voice, whispered, "They got me through the legs."

As Gertie tried to look around the tire to see him, bullets whipped by her.

Papurt called out, "Turn the jeep around. It's our only chance."

Dickson jumped into the driver's seat, but the vehicle wouldn't start. "It's kaput, sir," he shouted.

A fresh round of fire erupted, and Dickson was hit as he tried to scramble from the vehicle. Jennings raced around and pulled the young driver back to the sheltered side. The private had been shot in the legs and shinbone, and his right hand had been shredded, leaving three of his fingers barely attached. Jennings urged Papurt to try to drag himself a little closer to the vehicle. "This way, man, so I can bring you over here."

Gertie was peering under the car, watching Papurt's slow and painful crawl, when bullets hit the front axle, ricocheted into the engine, and sprayed her face and tin helmet with oil. Around her it puddled in the mud, soaking into her coat. Jennings suddenly rushed out from behind the car and dragged Papurt back.

"I take Bob's revolver, Bob takes Papurt's carbine," Gertie recalled.

Dickson's wounds were bleeding freely, and he seemed "ghastly" to Gertie. She thought his lips looked faintly blue and his face was ashen, but he managed a weak smile as Papurt was placed close to his side.

"Don't worry, son," Papurt said, assuring the young private that he'd get home to tell his war story.

There was, however, no obvious escape route. Around them was only open ground with no cover within even sprinting distance. Gertie was too stunned to be frightened but did, in that moment, experience stomach-churning sensations of regret and guilt: that she wouldn't see her husband again; that the OSS would be compromised; that she had been so damn stupid to get herself—someone, she thought, who should have remained an office drudge—into this jam.

When Papurt smiled at her and said he'd been in tougher spots than this, she snapped, "The hell you have."

The four knew their OSS IDs were deeply incriminating and could lead to their being branded as spies, tortured, and possibly shot. Gertie's hand trembled as she burned the documents with a cigarette lighter. She ground the ashes into the mud and oil by the disabled jeep, scraped earth over them with her toe, and tamped the pile down. Gertie kept her U.S. passport. She likely had been issued a new one after her arrival in London, as the one she had originally traveled to England with noted that she was "on special private business for the Office of Strategic Services."

"Isn't that a laugh," Gertie said. "I love those sorts of things. They are so ridiculous."

Pinned down, the group held what Gertie called a war council. Jennings was afraid the constant barrage of fire would lead to either the jeep's gas tank exploding or someone being hit by a ricocheting bullet. "The Germans continued to give us bursts of heavy machine gun fire and we realized the situation was hopeless," Jennings said. They decided to surrender. Jennings pulled a white handkerchief from his pocket and raised it on the barrel of Papurt's carbine. The firing from the German position eased and then stopped. Gertie took the moment to sprinkle some sulfur powder from the jeep's first aid kit on Dickson's right thigh, left ankle, and fingers. He was shivering and wet, and Gertie pulled a blanket from the vehicle and put it over him.

American artillery now began to rumble, hitting a ridge near the village, kicking up spouts of dirt. U.S. planes circled overhead. "We wished they could look down and see our predicament," Gertie recalled.

Waiting for German soldiers to arrive, the four OSS members lined up their stories.

"What about you, Gertrude?" asked Jennings.

"I'll claim to be an interpreter loaned to you by the American embassy," Gertie replied. "My job can be . . . file clerk. File clerk with the embassy in Paris." That was what she had been told to say at a security briefing in Washington in 1943, just before she left for London. At the time, she had thought it ridiculous that she would need a cover story, but now her training flooded back.

"Sounds reasonable," said Jennings. "I guess I'm a Naval observer on a mission to the front."

"What mission?" Gertie asked.

"I was to be told on arrival," he said.

They looked at Papurt.

"I'm just an ordnance officer," he said.

"Can they catch you on that?"

"No, I know all about ordnance."

It was thin stuff, hardly likely to survive interrogation, but would have to do. As to why they were in Wallendorf, the best explanation was the truth: they thought it was in American hands and took a ride to see a small piece of Germany.

Gertie turned to the young driver and smiled at him. All the color had drained from his face. He continued to tremble as he lay on the ground.

"Just a GI, I reckon," Dickson said. "Nothing to hide."

An eternity seemed to pass before the German soldiers emerged from the trees.

"Here they come," Jennings said, standing to face them, issuing a snort of disbelief.

Gertie lit cigarettes for Papurt and Dickson and placed them in their mouths. Then she too stood up.

The soldiers came at them from two directions, guns leveled. "Hands up," said one in English.

The four were prisoners of war.

And Gertrude Legendre had just become the first American woman in uniform captured by the Nazis.

Wyoming

One afternoon in the summer of 1920, Gertie sat on a log along a ridge in the Teton Range. The sun fell in bright shards through the treetops, but it was cool high up in the mountains, and the air was sweet with the smell of pine, fir, and spruce.

Gertie—in full western-gal mode—was wearing a Stetson hat, kerchief, lumberjack shirt, sheepskin chaps, and boots. Her rifle lay across her lap, gripped tightly at the trigger guard as she waited in the vast silence for the sound of hoofbeats.

While most of her contemporaries were celebrating their high school graduations with debutante parties in New York City, eighteen-year-old Gertie instead insisted on an adventure out west with an old friend and a chaperone sent along by her father. Shooting had been a part of her life since she'd picked off birds as a young girl in South Carolina; she was an excellent markswoman before she reached her teens. Later, at the all-girl Foxcroft boarding school in Middleburg, Virginia, she foxhunted, went beagling after rabbits, and tracked raccoons at night under the tutelage of the principal. It was an education in which "outdoor life . . . was as important as the 'finishing' touches that we were receiving," Gertie recalled.

In Wyoming, Gertie's party picked up their hunting licenses in Jackson, a dusty backwater with a post office and a few houses, before heading to a dude ranch at the foot of the Tetons that catered to wealthy visitors from back east. They hired a pack train of ponies and with a young cowboy as a guide started to climb. Nights were spent in sleeping bags by log fires at base camp. They passed their days hiking and looking for game in the farther reaches of the range.

Several days in, they spotted a group of five elk through field glasses and took off at a trot to intercept them. As a doe, a bull, then some more does crossed in front of Gertie's party, the animals sensed their presence and began to lurch away in panic. Gertie fired and the bull stumbled and crashed into the brush, still running but mortally wounded. They found it some distance away, a not very big animal, lying on its side, with "neither great points nor heavy horn, but it was my elk, my first, on my first real hunt—shot with a bullet through the heart," Gertie said. "I was filled with pride and the exultation of success . . . I strode in to camp—all five feet five of me, every inch the successful huntress."

Over the next seven years, Gertie would continue to hunt in Alaska and Canada—black and Kodiak bears, moose, caribou, mountain sheep, and goats. "If I hadn't gone on that first trip to the Tetons, I might never have known the thrill of life in the wilderness," she said. Gertie enjoyed what she described as her "own safe extravagant world" gilded by great wealth but felt that she "wasn't going to be like most of the girls I knew. I wanted something different, something more than the social whirl."

She found her vocation in hunting expeditions, the purview of the very wealthy, breezing across the world with her crisp calling cards, American spunk, and license to kill. The animals she felled were brought back to major U.S. institutions such as the American Museum of Natural History in New York and the Academy of Natural Sciences in Philadelphia. Gertie "was a real 'let's get cracking, let's get the show on the road' kind of girl," her daughter recalled. "She just wanted to taste everything, and try everything, have a ton of fun."

Gertie came from New York and New England stock, stretching back many generations on both sides of the family into colonial

America, where one ancestor had been governor of Connecticut. Among the more famous of her relatives was her grandfather Henry Shelton Sanford. He served as President Lincoln's minister to Belgium and ran secret operations on the continent to disrupt supplies to the Confederacy. "In my view, it is most important to prevent a thousand arms or hundred weight of powder going home to the enemy than to secure ten times that amount for ourselves," said Sanford, a polyglot who had previously served as an American diplomat in Saint Petersburg, Russia, and Frankfurt, Germany. He set up a network of informants at key European ports and in factory towns to monitor Confederate agents while tirelessly promoting the Union cause.

At a diplomatic reception in Paris in 1864, he met Gertrude DuPuy, a Philadelphian. They wed, and their daughter Ethel, born in 1874 and educated in Europe, was Gertie's mother.

Much of the family's fortune was built by Gertie's paternal grandfather, Stephen Sanford, a West Point graduate and distant relative of Henry's. He oversaw the growth of a family carpet company, founded in 1842 in Amsterdam, New York, into a major brand. He also developed a Thoroughbred farm—called Hurricana—in the Mohawk valley, a pursuit that began as a hobby but became its own thriving venture.

Stephen Sanford married Sarah Jane Cochran, from New Orleans, and their son John was Gertie's father. Both father and son would represent upstate New York districts in the House of Representatives.

John and Ethel were married in 1892 in the central Florida town of Sanford, founded by Ethel's father, Henry. John was forty-one; Ethel was nineteen. "Father was a businessman, forthright, blunt, an athlete, not particularly interested in the arts," Gertie said. "Mother was quiet, thoughtful, sensitive; absorbed by music, art, literature and the theater." She spoke French to her children.

The difference in age and temperament would eventually make itself felt. The couple became estranged and stopped speaking to each other; they communicated through notes sent back and forth on the elevator in their Seventy-Second Street mansion in Manhattan. Gertie gingerly said there was "less companionship" as they got older.

John and Ethel had three children: Stephen, known as Laddie, who became an international polo player; Jane, who would marry an Italian diplomat and confidant of the Italian dictator Benito Mussolini; and Gertrude, the youngest, born in Aiken, South Carolina, on March 29, 1902.

At Stephen Sanford's death in 1913, Gertie's father inherited an estate estimated at $40 million—close to $1 billion in today's dollars. Under John Sanford, the family business continued to grow, becoming a booming national enterprise that sold flooring from New York to San Francisco and generated enormous wealth for the family. Sanford, like his father, was a major figure in horse racing, and the sport—along with golf and watching his son play polo—was one of his few indulgences. "Horses, my mares, my stable . . . [keep] me out in the air, it keeps me active and among my friends," he said, dismissing other pursuits of the wealthy as pointless. "To put me on a yacht is like putting a man in jail, with the additional risk of drowning."

Sanford's colt George Smith won the Kentucky Derby in 1916, and in 1923 the family became the first American owners to win the English Grand National with the horse Sergeant Murphy. Gertie's mother, Ethel, and her brother, Laddie, were in Liverpool to watch the grueling steeplechase; only seven of twenty-eight starters finished the thirty-fence course. The American winners were congratulated by the king.

Gertie's family moved with the seasons between Amsterdam and Aiken, the family's winter home about twenty miles northeast of Augusta, Georgia. "My memories of those early days in the South are happy ones," Gertie recalled, "of ponies, picnics, costume parties, the smell of wisteria and jasmine." As she got a little older, and the family's social ambitions grew, summer brought vacations in

Newport, Rhode Island, or Maine, and trips to England and France, where John Sanford also kept racehorses at a farm he had bought in Normandy. The Sanfords—along with a governess, a tutor, two cars, and a chauffeur—were in France in the summer of 1914 when World War I broke out. Near the French coast, while attempting to reach a ferry to England, they had their Rolls-Royce and chauffeur requisitioned by a French general; both eventually turned up in London unscathed.

By 1918, the Sanfords were living at 9 East Seventy-Second Street, just off Central Park—a palatial town house built in 1896 with oak and iron entry doors and "giant French windows with garlands, cartouches, scrolls and other details applied in profusion." The same architects had designed the New York Public Library on Fifth Avenue. An elevator took guests to the sitting rooms of Ethel Sanford, where she frequently entertained. There were also six bedrooms on the upper floors. The broad main hall and library were on the first floor and the kitchen and servants' quarters on the ground floor, and below them a large wine cellar extended out under the street. It was a mansion fit for an industrial titan.

Gertie moved to New York City after graduating from the Foxcroft School. In her senior year, only one classmate planned to go on to college. "We probably thought that she was a little strange," said Gertie. For most of her peers, a career was not deemed necessary if even considered. Life in the 1920s was "a blur of parties, dances, theater and music," facilitated by the Rolls-Royce and chauffeur that Gertie and her sister, Jane, shared to move around Manhattan. A Broadway professional taught the girls how to sing and dance. Each day the butler placed theater tickets on the hall table in case anyone had a hankering to go to a play or musical. Gertie never lost her taste for skits and adored hosting costume parties. One of her more famous events was baby themed, with everyone carrying rattles and wearing bonnets. At another of her galas, with the circus as a motif, Gertie arrived on the back of a baby elephant.

Gertie's mother died from cancer in November 1924; she

was only fifty-one. In her writings, Gertie dwelled little on Ethel's death—"It seemed that she was sick only that month, but perhaps it was longer." Shortly after the funeral, "Father decided Janie and I needed to go away on a trip that winter, and he sent us off with Doctor Coffin, who had been with me to Wyoming and Canada, as chaperone on my various fall hunting trips. Now he was to take us to Syria, Palestine and Egypt." The highlight of the journey was a cruise up the Nile from Cairo to Edfu on a chartered *dahabeya*. At Luxor, they entered the recently opened tomb of the Pharaoh Tutankhamen. Little had yet been touched or removed, and "the treasures were piled high."

In late 1927, Gertie—whose hunting exploits in North America were occasionally chronicled in the New York papers—was invited, along with her brother, Laddie, to go on a safari in East Africa. Harold Talbott, a director of the Chrysler Corporation and a future secretary of the air force, and his wife, Peggy—"one of those twenties top-drawer charmers"—came by the Sanfords' box at the Saratoga racetrack to ask them to come. For Gertie, it was the fulfillment of a long-held wish, and, to her delight, "Father agreed."

After crossing the Atlantic, they took an old Italian ship, the *Giuseppe Mazzini*, from Naples, passing through the Suez Canal to Port Sudan, where the visitors swam in the Red Sea—in a "sheltered spot away from the barracudas." The ship stopped again at Aden, in southern Yemen, where Gertie found the water "blue as the Mediterranean and hot as Antibes in summer." The passengers spent their days on deck chairs reading and their evenings watching movies and drinking. The group celebrated Christmas Eve aboard. "We drank scads of champagne," Gertie said, describing a "free-for-all roughhouse at the ship's bar." Someone poured beer over her head. "It was an epic evening," she concluded.

At the port of Mogadishu, Gertie remarked to her diary on the "wonderful build" of the "naked wiry black people" ashore. She was genuinely curious about native peoples but also infused with a racial superiority endemic to the globe-trotting white Americans of the time. Africans were hired to serve and obey. During the expedition, Harold Talbott felt entitled to give a "public whipping" to a porter for an alleged infraction.

Gertie rejected some of the racist characterizations of Africans by the New York newspaper reporters who later interviewed her, telling them of Ethiopians, for instance, that "they are called savages, but they are not savages. They live a quiet life, subsisting on the cattle they raise and rarely become hostile."

But she could also describe the port workers at Port Sudan as "black little natives (resembling animals more than anything else)." Ugandans she found to be "terribly stupid and half-witted," and she was equally contemptuous of the Western missionaries who converted them to Christianity.

Every expedition that followed brought similar, racially charged assessments in her diaries, no matter the location. After arriving in Baghdad in 1937, a stop before hunting in northeastern Iran, Gertie remarked on the "swarthy, dark-skinned, bandit-looking faces of the East, dressed in long white nightshirts, bare feet and Arab headgear." Her thesaurus was a stockpile of the jejune.

4

Addis Ababa

The last stop of the *Giuseppe Mazzini* was Mombasa, a port city of whitewashed homes on the Indian Ocean alive with the colors and scents of mimosa, bougainvillea, pawpaw, and mango. From there, the hunting party traveled in the British governor's private railroad coach to Nairobi, drinking iced champagne and admiring the abundant game along the tracks. Nairobi catered to wealthy adventure tourists, and under the guidance of two "white hunters," a South African and an American, the Talbotts and Sanfords bought two trucks, two box sedans, and the food, medicine, clothing, and camping gear needed for the months-long trek into the interior. "We are all one inch ahead of a fit with excitement," Gertie said.

Britain was the colonial power in most of East Africa, and under its game-licensing system fees were charged for animal kills, including elephants, the most expensive, though the shooting of cow elephants and small bulls was barred. Big cats such as lions and leopards were considered pests and cost nothing.

The Americans hired a large group of Africans, including individual gun bearers and "personal boys," who acted as servants—preparing Gertie's bath in a tin tub, putting the toothpaste on her toothbrush, unlacing her shoes, and washing her underwear. Her gun bearer, called Simba, wore "a wig of baboon hair, which gave him a savage look."

Africa struck Gertie as a playground so full of wildlife that "no one thought there could be an end to it." The Americans rumbled across the plains like medieval lords, their gun bearers hanging off the sides of the open trucks and looking to the horizon for game their employers could shoot—ostrich, warthogs, dik-diks, giraffes, roan, gazelles, rhinoceroses, impalas, and zebras. "I was ready with the 20-gauge shotgun to plug anything that came along," Gertie wrote of the small game she targeted from her windowless car. She shot a cheetah and chased him into the long grass and finished him off as he snarled at her. "And then we had our usual round of press photography," Gertie wrote, anticipating the publicity that photos of her standing over her kills would generate when she returned to the United States.

Gertie and Peggy Talbott shot zebras "to get enough skin for a summer sports coat. We shot four yesterday and we each need six." Near Lake Natron, south of Nairobi, Gertie and Laddie killed a rhino with six shots, and the animal let out "high shrill shrieks" as it was struck. "It wasn't as exciting as I either expected or hoped for," Gertie confessed to her diary. "In fact, we both felt almost sorry for killing such a huge, happy beast who didn't seem to be disturbing anybody and looked so peaceful and harmless." She was astonished by the thickness of its skin, like "steel plating on a battleship." She had a big strip taken off the animal's back "to make a table top."

The white hunters cured the heat with drafts of beer. In the evenings, they gathered around fires at their base camp, drinking whiskey and soda and passing around a bottle of quinine to prevent malaria from mosquitoes "big as moths." The smell from baboons lurking on the nearby rocks hung in the air. For dinner, they ate what they had killed, "steak, spur fowl or cold guinea," before retiring to the cots in their tents, where exhaustion brought deep sleep. "Nothing could wake me except the grunt of a lion or the eerie, mocking laugh of a hyena."

· · ·

On the morning of January 10, 1928, Gertie's gun bearer spotted a large lion with a black fuzzy mane about 600 yards from their position. The animal was standing over a zebra kill with his pride—three lionesses and about six small cubs. Gertie crept through the grass until she got within 150 yards of the lion, which was standing at an angle to her. She aimed and fired, the bullet entering from rear to front. The lion ran about 50 yards before collapsing. Laddie finished him off with a .476 through the backbone. Back in camp, Gertie was carried on the shoulders of the gun bearers, and the party had champagne for dinner. "As far as I was concerned, it was a gala, red letter day," she wrote in her diary.

"He was my first. The first of anything is exciting," Gertie wrote. She killed several more on that trip. A picture of her posing over another slain lion, a rifle across her knee, made *The New York Herald* with the caption "His majesty bites the dust. This beautiful specimen came to an ignoble end when it came within range of Miss Gertrude S. Sanford's gun, in the lion country of Tanganyika, before she left to stalk elephant in Uganda."

Gertie, reflecting later in life, found it all too "staged, like a still from some adventure film. I was twenty four when they took that picture and the thrill of the kill was paramount. Today I wouldn't pose like that for anything, nor would I shoot a lion."

The expedition continued into Uganda, where Gertie killed her first elephant on February 25. She had tracked a herd for twelve miles, beginning at around 7:00 a.m.; six hours later, she found the herd by a river in the shade of two big trees. The elephants were "fanning themselves with two big ears and throwing water over themselves with their trunks." Catching the scent of intruders, a large bull turned to run and everyone fired. "I put a shot right into his heart," Gertie said. "We all put several more shots into him when he was down and screaming."

It took three hours using axes and knives to sever the tusks from the head. They weighed sixty-nine and seventy-four pounds. Locals took the meat.

The expedition now turned for home, eventually heading north for Khartoum on a riverboat, where Gertie recalled that they "sat on cheetah and leopard skins, played the Victrola, rolled dice, laughed a great deal, and drank beer, sherry and cocktails before dinner."

The trip, so long anticipated, had by the end left Gertie dissatisfied. Seeing so much game was the "greatest thrill in the world," but escorted by white hunters, pampered by African servants, she found it all too "deluxe" and easy when she had wanted to be challenged. "We never lift a finger. Everything is done for us," she complained. "Hunting by motorcar is not one-half as sporting as struggling over the mountains on foot as it is done in Alaska." She resolved to come back to Africa on her own terms. "This trip solidified my desire . . . not [to] collect for personal trophies but for a cause—collecting for the American Museum."

The expedition ended with a flight back to Cairo along the Nile valley in an airplane with double-decker wings and an open cockpit—past Aswan and Edfu and onto Luxor, the land lush green on either side of the river before giving way abruptly to endless desert. At Luxor, they landed for lunch, all arranged by their travel agent; printed menus offered beer, hors d'oeuvres, cold meat, salad, and peaches. Approaching Cairo, the pilot feared they might not have enough fuel and would have to make an emergency landing. Gertie and Peggy, fighting nerves, "decided to manicure our nails. When there is nothing to do, you can do something silly, and it makes you feel better." In the end, red flares pointed out the landing strip, and they came down safely.

That summer of 1928, Gertie traveled to England, where her father had rented Osterley Park, a large mansion and grounds in London. Visiting Oxford, she met two young Americans, Morris Legendre, a Rhodes scholar at the university, and his brother Sidney—both former football players at Princeton. The brothers, who shared "a killing sense of humor," later visited Osterley Park for a weekend of lawn tennis, and Gertie was immediately smitten. With both of them.

That first encounter was fleeting because Gertie and her sister, Janie, left for the South of France at the invitation of Gerald and Sara Murphy, the American couple at the center of a glittering circle that included Pablo Picasso, Ernest Hemingway, F. Scott and Zelda Fitzgerald, John Dos Passos, Igor Stravinsky, Serge Diaghilev, Somerset Maugham, and Harpo Marx. Also in the South of France that summer were Gertie's friends Ellen Barry and her husband, Philip, the playwright who had made a study of Gertie for *Holiday*.

The poet Archibald MacLeish said the Murphys were "masters in the art of living" and became a sort of "nexus with everything that was going on." Mornings that summer were marked by dry sherry and sweet biscuits on the beach, followed by swimming, picnics, tennis, and croquet. "Life was carefree, uncomplicated and fun," but Gertie also wanted to see more of the Legendre brothers and arranged to have them hired as lifeguards at the Hotel du Cap, immortalized by Fitzgerald in *Tender Is the Night*, his novel that drew on the life of the Murphys.

Gertie brushed up against this bohemian set of artists and their patrons but was never a part of it. Away from her expeditions, she could be firmly conventional, preferring a rigid social hierarchy and norms of behavior dictated by tradition and class. And like any outsider on the edge of an exclusive party, she resented the spectacle on the Riviera: Hemingway and Scott Fitzgerald were bad drunks. Maugham was a complainer and not very likable. Zelda was sweet but distant. Harpo, at least, was amusing; he played his harp in the back of Gertie's Renault convertible, always the first to join in the silliness.

"As far as company is concerned, I've had the good fortune to have known far greater men," Gertie harrumphed. "I never thought of myself as belonging to any special milieu that summer."

She only had eyes for the Legendre brothers.

After arriving in Antibes, Morris Legendre had a local carpenter make a kind of wooden water ski that he called a "free board." The brothers, sometimes with Gertie on their shoulders, rode the waves in the harbor with ropes attached to a small motorboat. One evening at a party, someone dared Gertie to ride the free board in her evening clothes. She took off her white satin high heels, and with Morris on another board beside her they circled the harbor twice before Gertie let go of the rope and glided ashore "bone dry and slightly incredulous" that she had pulled it off. *Vanity Fair* recorded the moment, describing her as "a rebel finding in the strange mutinous craft with which she rides the night waters a more magic carpet than her grandpa's looms turned out in Amsterdam."

Maugham, unimpressed, called them "crazy show-offs."

The summer ended with Gertie still infatuated with both brothers and unable to choose between them. "I have always enjoyed the company of men, and Morris and Sidney Legendre were the most attractive men that I have ever met," she said. That fall, she invited the brothers to travel with her on her second safari in Africa—clearly intending to capture one or the other as a husband.

"There was some question about whether it was going to be Morris or Sidney," Gertie's daughter later recalled with some bemusement.

Her plan for the expedition was to kill and mount a group of giant mountain nyalas—known as Queen of Sheba's antelope—that would be staged among a series of planned dioramas in the new Hall of African Mammals at the American Museum of Natural History in New York. The existence of the animal had not been recorded by Western scientists until 1908. The museum said such a permanent exhibition—along with a perfectly represented backdrop of the landscape where the antelope lived—would cost $30,000. That was separate from the expense of the expedition to East Africa. Gertie's father gave her the money.

The public flocked to see these dioramas, which drew observers into the close study of a three-dimensional depiction of a slice of Africa and its animals—a combination of taxidermy, painting, and flora. They were designed "to bring a vision of the world to those who otherwise can never see it," said Henry Fairfield Osborn, the museum's president when Gertie pursued the nyalas.

Hunting in exotic locales to acquire specimens for the museums being built and expanded with the country's bourgeoning industrial wealth was becoming more and more popular with rich Americans, who were lauded by *The New York Times* as people with the "indomitable will of true explorers." In 1930, the American Museum of Natural History had thirty expeditions in the field, many of them headed by amateur explorers accompanied by museum scientists. In Gertie's case, T. D. Carter, assistant curator of mammals at the museum, was along to oversee the skinning and preservation of specimens for the nyala diorama. Unflappable, with a sense of fun, he was also "the gyroscope that kept our tempers on an even keel," according to Gertie.

The journey was previewed by *The New York Times,* which reported, "Many dangers face the members of the expedition. Outside of Addis Abeba, the capital, on the wild highlands and on the frontiers, the real authority is exercised by feudal lords. These hereditary chieftains . . . and their wild followers are dangers to be faced by the Sanford-Legendre expedition in addition to the constant perils of the jungles."

In late 1928—after rendezvousing with Morris and Sidney at the Ritz bar—the party left for Marseille and embarked on a seventeen-day boat trip to Djibouti, on the Horn of Africa.

A slow train to Addis Ababa followed—and eventually dinner with the emperor Haile Selassie. Gertie found the Abyssinians "the most beautiful people I'd ever seen. They were tall and elegant looking, with sharp chiseled features . . . They weren't like anything I'd expected. The men wore white jodhpurs with a white cloak and they carried long spears." The emperor gave Gertie a silver mule from the royal stable with a silver bit, red embroidered reins, and a hand-stitched green velvet saddle. She gave him a white polar bear skin.

Many of the supplies, including the tents and a portable toilet, had been shipped in advance from David Abercrombie's store in Manhattan to Djibouti. It took nearly a month to hire all the trackers, skinners, and cooks before they headed to the Ethiopian highlands. It was a hard expedition. Smallpox broke out, forcing the party to burn some tents and blankets, and some of the young Africans came down with malaria, as did Carter, the museum scientist.

Gertie never got ill, on that or any other trip.

"This couldn't be a more perfect life," she decided. "One exercises all day, sleeps well at night. The weather is perfect. We have a lot of fun—a lot of laughs, and it's all delightful, so different. So much more fun than being in a crowded city or a hot stuffy restaurant. When we eat a cold partridge in our fingers it tastes better than any fancy partridge cooked at Larue or any other swell place." She celebrated her birthday that March with a bottle of champagne cooled with a damp cloth and ate a cake Morris made with Aunt Jemima pancake flour and apricot jam. They had run out of cigarettes but instead smoked green Abyssinian tobacco bought at a local market.

Museum officials back in the United States were thrilled with reports from the field. "I am looking forward to seeing the specimens here in New York," wrote Harold E. Anthony, curator in the Department of Mammalogy, "for I imagine from the measurements you sent back that you have several unusually fine bulls . . . Since the region where you are working is completely unrepresented in the Museum collections, everything that you bring back will be desirable."

Sidney, having lost a coin toss and nursing an infected finger, returned to Addis Ababa with the first of the nyala specimens, separating him from the hunting party for a month. His absence focused Gertie's mind. Morris was the bigger personality, but Gertie missed Sidney's humor "and the thoughtful quality he had about himself, some unknown side of him that he protected. Maybe it was that vulnerable quality that is so attractive to women, especially in strong men. Maybe that is all it was. But Sidney was also gentle and not afraid of his gentleness."

Back in Addis, Gertie and Sidney were able to spend some time

alone as they stayed behind in the residence of the Italian ambassa-
dor while Morris and Carter went north to do some more collecting.
"I suppose we started to know then," Gertie said of this interlude in
Addis, though there are hints in a letter written during World War
II that she had all along favored Sidney and the two kept it a secret
during the expedition.

After leaving Ethiopia, Gertie and Sidney traveled to the South
of France and rented the Villa Les Cèdres, a mansion with stables,
an Olympic-sized pool, and a botanical garden on the peninsula
of Saint-Jean-Cap-Ferrat near Nice. The romance deepened. "We
knew that we were in love," Gertie said. Sidney proposed.

Carter told *The New York Times* on August 10, 1929, that the expedition had collected 300 mammals and 120 birds, as well as insects and
reptile specimens. Eleven nyalas were killed for the diorama at the
museum, including four shot by Gertie. A live cheetah was brought
back for the Bronx Zoo.

Gertie held her own meeting with the press a couple of days
later. *The Brooklyn Eagle* wrote that she received reporters "curled
up like a nymph in the luxurious drawing room of her home near
Central Park and 5th Avenue. She described the trip in crisp, vivid
phrases, while she smoked an exotically scented cigarette. She was
dressed in jungle green silk that stood in contrast to her dark, sun-
tanned complexion, red lips and straight black hair, like the verdure
of the jungles she had just left."

Sidney and Gertie were married the following month, on September 17, 1929, at Manhattan's St. James' Church, which was decorated with white dahlias and Australian fern. The bride, carrying
a bouquet of white orchids and lilies of the valley, wore "a gown
of cream-colored satin with a close-fitting bodice and long tight
sleeves," *The New York Times* reported.

Morris—the brother not chosen—was the best man. The reception for several hundred was held at the family's Seventy-Second

Street mansion, where Emil Coleman and His Orchestra played in the ballroom filled with pink roses. The newlyweds spent the night at the Waldorf.

Hot-cheeked with delight at her catch—the tall, square-jawed, gap-toothed, tanned, and handsome Sidney—Gertie said, "I must confess that I was rather proud of myself."

The honeymoon, inevitably unorthodox, was a camping trip to British Columbia's Cassiar Mountains, where the couple waded through snowdrifts and had to sit out a blizzard for several days. "It was glorious," Gertie said.

Hanoi

Gertie and Sidney were still in Canada when the United States experienced the Wall Street crash of October 29, 1929, the harbinger of the most devastating economic crisis in the nation's history. But the financial shock and the hardships of the Great Depression largely passed the couple by. "Father had very little money in stocks," Gertie explained. "The misery of much of the world was unknown to us."

On their return to the United States from their honeymoon, the couple decided to forge a new life, away from both New York and New Orleans, where Sidney's family lived. They took a leisurely drive through Virginia and the Carolinas looking at property. Friends near Charleston asked them to a picnic at a plantation called Medway that was up for sale. The old estate had a large but simple brick house, built at the beginning of the eighteenth century. The dilapidated structure stood in the shadow of great oaks covered with dripping moss and was surrounded by an area rich in forest, swamps, wetlands, ponds, and wild game, particularly quail and duck. The front lawn swept down to a black lake. There were miles of riding trails through longleaf and loblolly pine woods. The place was derelict, even eerie, but Gertie was attracted by "a sense of remoteness and serenity . . . the slight decay of everything and the deception of timelessness."

Gertie's father had at first insisted the couple reside in Manhattan or Palm Beach. Gertie couldn't abide the idea of living in a city, and Florida, with "the thrashing of those damn palm trees," seemed equally disagreeable. Her father relented and provided $100,000 for the purchase of the house and 2,500 acres in South Carolina's Low Country. By 1934, they had acquired a total of 7,110 acres around their new home, about twenty-five miles outside Charleston.

The Legendres tried, with mixed success, to turn Medway into a working plantation, experimenting with rice, wheat, corn, hogs, cattle, and chickens before settling on marketable pine trees. Gertie remembered Sidney falling asleep in the evening as he read *Farming for Profit* or *How to Farm Timber*. To bolster their skills, they attended some courses at the Cornell Agricultural School, where Gertie studied nutrition and car mechanics. "We learned enough theoretical knowledge to run any farm successfully," Sidney noted in his plantation diary. "Unfortunately farms are not run on theoretical knowledge but on experience and hard work. Neither of these two virtues are inherent in me, neither do either of us know them except by hearsay."

Sidney, at times, considered selling and moving north. "Virginia has so much to offer compared to South Carolina," he decided. "There was no fever. It was a year round place, [one] to which we could return at any time . . . There were no mosquitos, ticks and we hoped not as many plantation worries as besieged us at Medway. We could have a smaller place, [one] that would be relatively inexpensive, and one that would not give us that frustrated and desperate feeling that we have so often here." But he also admitted that one of those "startlingly beautiful" days that Medway produced could dispel their doubts, pulling them back into the plantation's embrace until the next crisis soured them again.

Medway was staffed by black field hands and servants, some of whom lived in cabins on the grounds. Gertie built a two-room schoolhouse for black children in the neighboring community of Strawberry, after consulting her old principal at the Foxcroft School. The Promised Land School was named after a church of the same name that had burned down. "I have found in my long life that nothing makes one love a place more than being a constructive part of it, and if you can give those colored people 'a leg up' and get them trained for some future job, you are doing something real for your South Carolina and something that will make Medway a real part of your life," Charlotte Noland, the founder of Foxcroft, wrote to Gertie in 1941.

Medway was a world of master and servant. Gertie treated her staff well, feeling genuine affection for them, but also maintained an aristocratic distance from all but her society friends. The plantation, despite the best efforts to make some money off the land, became the center of Gertie's life as a hostess. "She loved to entertain," her grandson recalled.

Guests arrived for a week of hunting, and the plantation staff addressed every need for the large parties—preparing the guns, marshaling the horses and dogs, serving lunch in the field, then cocktails and dinner. Medway was staffed around the clock. One guest remarked on the "breakfast trays every morning for the ladies, high tea [and] finger bowls at supper."

Sidney described one meal after a morning of dove shooting in December 1940: "Luncheon was laid under the pines and tables covered with yellow cloths and set with crude pottery plates . . . Everyone was seated and then sherry was passed . . . Gertrude had ordered a marvelous meal. Hot bean soup, chicken mushroom and rice all mixed together. Sweet potato pie with marshmallows on top, and succotash . . . a heaping plate full of corn bread sticks . . . and beet . . . And then to end, we had apple pie and cheese, finished with coffee." Sometimes a nap followed on Gertie's zebra skins in the grass.

Gertie and Sidney continued to go on expeditions—Gertie said she had an almost physical need for them—beginning with French Indochina in 1932 for both the Academy of Natural Sciences in Philadelphia and the American Museum of Natural History. They left San

Francisco on July 30, 1931, stopped for two weeks in Hawaii, where Gertie took a "terrific beating" learning how to surf, before continuing on to Japan. After visiting Tokyo—"an ugly brawling city"—they took a boat to Shanghai, followed by a fifty-four-hour train ride to Peking. "The city breathed antiquity, charm, intrigue," Gertie wrote in her diary, also noting that it was "filthy. I have seldom seen filthier."

As they waited for their hunting licenses to be processed, they played polo and tennis, went to the races, partied at foreign legations, and spent weekends in Peking's western hills. Merchants flocked to Gertie's room at the Imperial Hotel. "I recline in bed like an oriental princess, with a breakfast tray, and yards of brocade hang over the bedroom door. The bed is strewn with jade and figurines, and earrings and the walls are covered with scrolls, paintings, Ming, Sung."

The expedition, again including T. D. Carter from the American Museum of Natural History, was planned to find mouflons—wild sheep—and other specimens. After arriving in Vietnam, they stocked up in Hanoi for a six-month trek: "saddles, zinc-lined chop boxes, tents, folding chairs, cots, mosquito nets, medical supplies and pounds and pounds of tinned food." Evenings before their departure from the city were spent on the terrace of the Café Metropole, sipping gimlets out of champagne glasses as they watched the rickshaws pass by.

The party traveled across the northern part of what is now Vietnam and passed into Laos before continuing along the Mekong valley, sometimes by canoe, to Cambodia, then returning to Vietnam. It was a tough trip, with backbreaking hikes in sometimes scalding heat through thick jungle and across mountainous terrain. They frequently stopped at the French army posts that dotted the countryside, attending formal dinners with the local commanders. Otherwise, they ate what they killed—goat, partridge, pheasant, deer, and monkey, which Gertie "did not like the idea of" and "did not enjoy."

Gertie reveled in the adventure, fascinated by the forbidding physicality of the jungle and spellbound by the ancient civilizations of the region. Approaching the city of Angkor "in full moonlight for the first time is almost indescribable," she wrote in her diary, "the thick dark walls, the high narrow doorways, the flight of stone steps; the bats coming out of the tower, the pillars etched against the velvet sky—impression of grandeur, beauty, symmetry of ancient splendor."

It was an enthusiasm and wonder she brought to every expedition, whatever the hardship. After sleeping under a rocky outcrop in Iran in 1937, with a freezing wind blowing off the Alborz Mountains, she made her way back to base camp, where a warm bath and a hot supper—antelope roasted in a gasoline tin, blackberries, and the local yogurt—"seemed equal only to the Ritz."

Sidney, on the other hand, never seemed quite as enamored with the rough life and surprises of their foreign trips. "It was very fortunate that [Gertie] did feel strongly, because I never did," he said. "I never expected camp food to be marvelous, nor did I think that sunrises or full moons were extraordinary. I am not what you would call a vital person."

Beginning with the Indochina trip, Sidney wrote a series of books about the expeditions. He was a lively travel writer who could re-create in confident prose the landscapes through which he passed, but his work was also infused with smugly racist assertions. He characterized the Annamites, as he called the Vietnamese, "the most despicable race of people I have ever had the misfortune to deal with. Cringing, lying, thieving, sneering and cruelly treating those weaker than themselves are their main characteristics." He called the offspring of French colonists and local women "half-castes." As they "become more and more numerous," he wrote, "the government becomes weaker and weaker. This is because the strength of a Colonial Government is based on the natives' recognition of the superiority of the white race."

By late February, the hunting party had reached Saigon—a chance to catch up on news from home and relax "in the wickedest city in the world." Gertie was determined to visit an opium den. Accompanied by Carter, she and Sidney went to a restaurant in the Chinese section of Saigon, and after dinner a long reedlike pipe attached to a bowl was delivered to the table. A server heated the brown liquid opium until it hardened into a small ball, then it was placed in the pipe. Gertie, lying on a couch, inhaled deeply four or five times before the opium burned out. "Two pipes had no effect on me whatsoever," she complained. "I had no dreams or feeling of elation." Carter said he felt intoxicated, and Sidney, who had smoked before, complained about "the bitter foul flavor of an old uncleared pipe." He described the sensation of smoking opium as being at complete ease, "so that you look down as from a great height on the trials and tribulations of the world and wonder why they should have troubled you." But on this evening that kind of high proved elusive.

Before they left Vietnam, there was one last excursion: a tiger hunt in Di Linh, about 150 miles northeast of Saigon.

The group set up camp by a small lake where Gertie saw fresh tiger prints on the beach when she went to take a bath. Carter and some of the local hires began to build blinds—wooden boxes covered in long grass and tied with rattan vine. A hunter could sit but not stand in these small enclosures—called *bomas*—which had peepholes to shoot out of. Four of these hunting boxes were placed along jungle trails, near where the tigers tended to hunt. Large bait—recently killed buffalo or sambar deer—was tied to a stake just thirty feet from each *boma*.

Returning to inspect the bait, they found one of the buffalo had been eaten, its hind quarters ripped off, and the tears were so fresh they feared they had interrupted the tiger during its meal. The local guides beat on the bamboo and talked loudly to keep the animal at bay while Gertie slipped into the *boma*. Then the rest of the party withdrew, leaving her alone with her rifle, a shotgun, a camera, and a wooden case to sit on. She had brought some chocolate but threw it out because the blind was soon crawling with ants.

"I sat and waited," Gertie recalled. "It was hot. The odors of the decaying carcass blew in my face at frequent intervals."

Ten hours passed and dusk came. Gertie could just make out

the dead buffalo in the fading light. And then she heard "a bound and the tearing of flesh." She could barely see the tiger but distinctly heard the "rip and tear," the crunching of bones, and a licking sound as he savored the blood. "Suddenly, I saw his two red eyes, far apart, staring at me." Spooked by the noise of people returning to get Gertie before it got too dark, the tiger turned and ran.

Gertie was up at 2:00 the following morning, gulping down breakfast and preparing for another day in the blind. Sidney tried to persuade her to stay. "If you take my advice you'll come back to bed and get some sleep," he said. "Then we can buy a nice skin in Saigon and no one will know the difference."

"Don't you ever do anything for the sport of it?" Gertie replied.

They arrived at the blind with the usual noisy fanfare to keep the animal at a distance while Gertie entered the box and the guides retreated. And then suddenly the tiger was there, racing out of the semidarkness, standing broadside to Gertie as he tore at the buffalo's entrails. Gertie pushed her gun through the peephole. The animal turned, looked at Gertie, and spat loudly before vanishing into the undergrowth.

But he wasn't gone. He was behind the blind, prowling and continuing to spit, just thirty or forty feet from her position. "I could hear him just outside the door through the slits of my grass hut," Gertie said. "I could see his shadow pass by me . . . I sat transfixed." Tigers have been known to charge blinds when disturbed or wounded, and "there is nothing but a shield of straw between you and the most powerful beast in the jungle."

Gertie's gun was pointing in the wrong direction. Her heart was pounding. Her mouth was dry. And she wondered if the cat would smash through the flimsy cover to reach her. And then he was gone again. "I was saved, but I also felt I had lost my chance to shoot him for if a tiger is frightened he rarely returns," Gertie wrote ruefully.

But she couldn't leave the blind until the guides returned. She passed the time killing ants or being bitten by them. "Flies buzzed around the half-eaten carcass in a black cloud. Vultures circled overhead; the heat was intense." At about 4:00 p.m., a monitor lizard climbed on the buffalo and tore at the flesh, its pointed face quickly smeared with blood. The minutes continued to tick by slowly, the ants continued to bother Gertie, and, very quietly, she tried to shift her position so she wasn't overcome by stiffness and cramp. "It is often said that hunting from a boma over a kill is poor sport," Gertie said. "Maybe it is, but it is not all as soft as a bed for roses . . . One must have colossal patience." And nerve.

The light was fading when Gertie heard the rush of the tiger returning—a swift, almost stealthy arrival. She pushed her gun through the hole. The tiger had its two front paws on the kill, its head facing the blind. Gertie fired and the tiger fell. Still alive, he lifted his head. Gertie fired again. She threw down the shotgun and grabbed her Mauser rifle, pushing the blind aside as she moved. She raced to the animal. Its feet and tail were still moving. "I gave him a bullet in the head for good measure and he became motionless."

Summoned by the gunshots, Sidney and the guides hurried to the *boma*. "I broke into a run cursing myself that I had ever let her sit alone," Sidney said. "And then we arrived and I cursed myself for running. There she sat smoking a cigarette on top of an enormous tiger. I should have known it, everything always ended this way."

The tiger was carried back to camp, its feet suspended from two long poles. The animal weighed six hundred pounds and was eight feet, eleven and a half inches from his nose to the tip of his tail.

The expedition was over. After nine months away, it was time to return home.

The dismal condition of the United States, mired in depression, and a world steadily marching toward war rarely intruded into Gertie's concerns—at least as they were reflected in her diaries. While in Indochina, she noted that "business is evidently as blue as ever in America—unemployment no better . . . and the news of the world is certainly gloomy and depressing."

There is a detachment to her sporadic political observations. When Hitler threatened Czechoslovakia, Gertie, hunting in Iran at the time, couldn't "imagine war being declared over something so hopelessly small and pathetic as Czecho."

"I do hope the U.S. is able to keep out of it somehow. (I doubt it though)," she said, noting that Hitler would probably have to be stopped before his power got too great.

Gertie, unlike most Americans, had seen Nazi Germany first-hand. In early August 1936—just as the Summer Olympics began in Berlin under the führer's gaze—she and Sidney landed in Bremer-haven after an Atlantic crossing that was as calm as "a mill pond." Their ultimate destination was Hungary, where they planned to shoot partridge. "With German efficiency, we went from the gang-plank into our Plymouth convertible." They passed through customs without opening a bag, and drove south to Düsseldorf. Over the next two days, they continued on through Frankfurt, Wiesbaden, Heidel-berg, and Nuremberg—shopping, eating, and sightseeing—before crossing into Austria.

The most remarkable aspect of Gertie's journal of traveling through Germany is the lack of any reference to the Nazis. Granted, the regime hid some of the visible signs of its extremism during the Olympic Games. The fascists were on their best behavior with the influx of foreigners: signs banning Jews from public places were tem-porarily taken down, and party thugs were ordered not to harass Jews in public.

Gertie's diaries and letters contain occasional flashes of her own anti-Semitism. In one instance, after getting a ride from Washington to Middleburg, Virginia, from Larry Lowman, a vice president of CBS before the war and chief of communications at the OSS, and his wife, Eleanor Barry Lowman, a former *Harper's Bazaar* editor, Gertie wrote to her husband, "Larry is sweet. Very nice, very amus-ing and I like him. He is smart as a whip and has an important job in our outfit. Barry is alright though certainly nothing special to be admired . . . He is not cheap. She is. You know how I hate jews so that is quite a statement from me calling a jew alright." Low-man and Gertie became friendly in Washington, but time with the OSS's eclectic mix of characters didn't change her private attitudes. Discussing where they might live after the war, Gertie told Sidney that "I feel the future and the new horizons are going to be out [west] . . . I think the east coast is too crowded, too full of jews and too confined."

For all her swashbuckling, Gertie was in some of her attitudes a creature of her country and class—casual with her prejudice in her private correspondence, comfortable in a segregated America where Jews, blacks, and other outsiders knew who sat, and who didn't, at the head table.

The fabulous world she inhabited—precious and exclusionary—was finally upended with the advent of war.

Sidney was reading the newspaper in the gun room at Medway on December 7, 1941, when the phone rang.

"Have you got your radio turned on?" his brother Morris shouted.

"No," said Sidney.

"Then turn it on, the Japs are bombing Honolulu and have sunk some of our boats."

There were bulletins on every station.

"Gertrude," Sidney called out. "The Japs are bombing Honolulu."

The news was a gut punch. Like much of the country, Gertie was dumbstruck, even though the flames of war had already been consuming Asia and Europe. The American idyll was over.

Washington, D.C.

Sidney was commissioned as a lieutenant in the navy reserve in early April 1942. In his application for an appointment, which was supported by Undersecretary of the Navy James Forrestal, Sidney had emphasized his world travels, including two Atlantic crossings in a schooner. He was assigned to intelligence duties. Initially Sidney worked at an intelligence center on the Battery in Charleston, occasionally going on operations along the coastal waterways of South Carolina, Georgia, and Florida to look for signs of enemy activity. In the early months of the war, there was genuine fear on both coasts of imminent attack. J. Edgar Hoover told the White House that the Axis powers planned to invade along the East Coast. The bombing of Los Angeles was expected to quickly follow the attack on Pearl Harbor, and some feared that the Japanese might even come over the border from Mexico.

Gertie joined the Red Cross Motor Corps in Charleston—taking first aid classes, greeting troop trains, and feeding soldiers embarking from the city's port.

The future of Medway was uncertain as "one by one the plantation Negroes were drafted," Gertie recalled, until only three men, who didn't meet draft requirements, were left.

Sidney was ordered to report to Washington for a course in foreign intelligence, and the house at Medway was closed, the furniture covered in sheeting, and mothballs scattered everywhere. Sidney, Gertie, and their two children left in the family station wagon, "our three faithful Negroes waving a last farewell."

The family found a short-term rental in Georgetown.

It was only a matter of time before Sidney had to ship out to Hawaii, his next assignment. Gertie also wanted to contribute to the war effort and first approached the Red Cross, which rejected her because she had two young children, and the Library of Congress, which told her she didn't meet the requirement of a completed college education. Gertie decided to draw on her society connections to secure a position.

In June 1942, she wrote to F. Trubee Davison, a former president of the American Museum of Natural History who knew Gertie from her expeditions on behalf of the institution in the 1930s. Davison was a decorated aviator in World War I and a former assistant secretary of war; he had also supported Sidney's application for a navy reserve commission. In her three-page résumé, Gertie noted the number of countries she had visited, that she could shoot a rifle and a shotgun, spoke French fluently, and had considerable experience with outdoor photography, including the ability to develop and print her own work. "I am physically fit. Can walk 20 miles a day. Have unusual endurance and exceptional health."

In an accompanying letter, Gertie wrote that "possibly due to my traveling experience I might be of some assistance working in a foreign country in either intelligence or some other type of work. I would be willing to go anywhere or remain in America."

Davison wrote back that he had one possible lead for her. That was the new spy organization headed by Donovan. (In 1932, Davison had run for lieutenant governor of New York when Donovan stood for governor at the head of the Republican ticket; they lost in a landslide.) Within two weeks, Gertie was writing to David K. E. Bruce, an old acquaintance and the husband of Ailsa Mellon, daughter of the banker and industrialist Andrew Mellon. Bruce was head of the Secret Intelligence branch of the OSS. Gertie told him in a letter that she was already providing his agency with information on Iran and southwestern Africa—locales where she had hunted. "I would stick at a job for the duration," she promised.

Bruce, one of Donovan's senior lieutenants, would prove to be Gertie's most important patron during the war. "He was the most marvelous man—a connoisseur and collector, a charmer, polished in manner and looks, smooth in every way," Gertie recalled.

A prominent "internationalist," Bruce had advocated support for Britain when the United States remained deeply isolationist. He traveled to England in the summer of 1940 as a special representative of the American Red Cross and witnessed the Battle of Britain from the white cliffs of Dover in the company of American reporters. "All around you anti-aircraft guns were shuddering and coughing, stabbing the sky with small white bursts," the correspondent Virginia Cowles wrote. "You could see the flash of wings and the long white plumes from the exhausts; you could hear the whine of engines and the rattle of bullets. You knew the fate of civilization was being decided fifteen thousand feet above your head in a world of sun, wind and sky."

In October 1941, Bruce had joined the Office of the Coordinator of Information (COI), the fledgling spy service that Roosevelt had created by executive order that July 11 over the objections of bureaucratic rivals at the army, navy, State Department, and FBI. The COI, led by Donovan, had a vague mandate to "collect and analyze all information and data, which may bear upon national security," and began with a payroll of thirteen employees. But it—and its successor, the OSS—quickly grew, becoming creatures of Donovan's personality: "intrepid and madcap."

"Woe to the officer," wrote Bruce, "who turned down a project because, on its face, it seemed ridiculous or at least unusual."

There were several attempts to kill the new organization by its political enemies, but Donovan, the most decorated American soldier in World War I, had also become an astute Washington infighter. And, ultimately, he had the backing of the president, whose discretionary funds underwrote COI. In July 1942, that organization was reinvented as the Office of Strategic Services, evolving into five branches: Research and Analysis (R&A), Counterespionage (X-2), Special Operations (SO), Morale Operations (MO), and Secret Intelligence (SI), under Bruce—the section that would hire Gertie.

Her background security check was completed by early August. The investigation report noted that "subject's family have always been prominent socially and are reputed to have been extremely wealthy." It stated that Gertie was "married to an American (who was born in England) but whose family like that of the Subject are of old American stock" and described her as being "100% loyal to her country." The report said she was "a person of unusual ability, energy, courage and resourcefulness. It has been said of her that she can 'hold her own with any man, in shooting or riding.'"

But there was one caveat. Gertie's older sister, Jane, was married to an Italian diplomat—and no ordinary one at that. Mario Pansa had been close to Benito Mussolini since his early years in power, when the Italian leader descended on Rome untutored in the social graces, to the horror of the city's high society. Pansa, according to one Mussolini biographer, took Il Duce in hand and "instructed him in what to wear and how to behave in polite society. Mussolini owed a great deal to this man and gained much in self-confidence."

Mario Pansa and Jane Sanford had married in Palm Beach, Florida, in February 1937, despite some qualms within Gertie's family. They had met through Jane's brother, Laddie, who had played polo with the Italian. The OSS security review concluded that Jane Sanford "is said to be more American in her sympathies than she is Italian, and is really a victim of circumstances in the sense that she is technically an enemy of this country."

A final interview was waived, and Gertie was told to report to an OSS office on the National Mall in early August. Her salary was $150 a month—not even pin money for Gertie. The desire to contribute to the war effort had finally brought Gertie into the ordinary world of work—a place she otherwise would never have experienced.

The appointment came just as Sidney, along with his brother Morris, received orders to ship out to Hawaii, where they would join the intelligence staff of Admiral Chester W. Nimitz.

Gertie and Sidney savored their time together before he boarded a military flight out of Washington. "The last day with you seemed so extraordinary," Sidney wrote on August 10, 1942. "We talked about the war . . . and other things when we both knew that all we really wanted to say was how much we loved one another and how we dreaded the parting. But I knew if I once let myself go and did, I would remain in tears for the rest of the day. I thought you were wonderful to be able to wave to me as I entered the plane, and to wish me good luck. My throat was so choked and my eyes so full of tears that I could not say anything and only waved and then plunged into the plane."

Washington was a city transformed by the war. It brought hundreds of thousands of new residents, eventually doubling the District of Columbia's population, including bankers, lawyers, businessmen, academics, scientists, inventors, hucksters, and draft dodgers who would form a new ad hoc ruling class atop the existing bureaucracy. Washington was also flooded with foreign emissaries—diplomats, spies, and exiles—adjusting to the unbearable summer humidity and winter freezes just as they were to the emerging preeminence of the upstart United States.

"Wartime Washington, in the view of those most experienced in the field, was socially the most aggressive and most tireless city in the western world," the journalist David Brinkley concluded in *Washington Goes to War*. It all gave the American capital a febrile atmosphere, and Gertie dove right in, one of the many thousands of women who were suddenly needed to make the machinery of government turn.

Gertie found a house on Thirty-First Street in Georgetown for herself, two-year-old Bokara, the child's nurse, and a housekeeper. Landine, Gertie's nine-year-old daughter, was sent to the Foxcroft

School, Gertie's alma mater, about fifty miles away in Virginia. Gas was strictly rationed, and public transportation was overwhelmed by the influx of new workers, so Gertie either walked or rode her bike to work. The main OSS campus was on Navy Hill, just off E Street in the Foggy Bottom neighborhood. The agency also occupied offices in a series of large temporary wooden structures built early in the war. These drab buildings, thrown up hastily, lined Constitution Avenue and the Reflecting Pool and surrounded the Washington Monument as the government attempted to accommodate its small army of new workers.

The OSS buildings were soon teeming with recruits. Donovan hired what he called his "league of gentlemen"—the wealthy, the blue-blooded, and the well connected, including President Roosevelt's son—but he would also consider anyone with a skill he coveted, regardless of background, which gave the OSS much of its daring and creative energy. Safecrackers, burglars, forgers, Mafia enforcers, and madcap inventors were as welcome as scientists, linguists, chemists, historians, and mapmakers. Those who failed to get into the military and those who didn't want to get into the military also turned to the OSS. "We get all the crocks working for us eventually, high blood pressure boys, grey bearded professors, young draft dodgers and tired business men," Gertie told her husband. "It's quite a group when en masse."

Donovan, unorthodox but single-minded and surrounded by competent administrators, was slowly forging an effective espionage service, one that would add a critical, if never decisive, element to the war effort and lay a foundation for the postwar Central Intelligence Agency. Simultaneously, the OSS could be disorganized and harebrained, sanctioning bizarre schemes, including, for instance, a proposal to make Hitler's mustache fall out and turn his voice soprano by having agents inject his vegetables with hormones.

At first, Gertie was excited by her work and described her agency as "hot stuff." Her job was to route all cables in and out of the Secret Intelligence branch, which gave her a broad if glancing view of OSS operations. On her desk was a battery of rubber stamps: "RESTRICTED," "CONFIDENTIAL," "SECRET."

"My Western Union office life, if you get me, is plenty rushed," she wrote, not mentioning the OSS by name so she would not fall foul of military censors who might read her letters before they reached Sidney. "It is quite exciting and growing in leaps and bounds."

But the struggle ahead still seemed hugely daunting in the summer and early fall of 1942. The Nazis had taken France. They were deep inside Russia, and Soviet troops had not broken out at Stalingrad. German and Italian forces were still ascendant in North Africa. U-boats trawled the Atlantic. Japanese troops had seized Hong Kong, Singapore, and Manila, though U.S. forces were buoyed by the bloodying of the Imperial Navy at the Battle of Midway in June, even if the decisiveness of that engagement was not apparent to everyone back in the United States.

"We don't seem to be doing anything anywhere—but then it is hopeless to know what is really going on or what the plans are. I hope there is a plan," Gertie said. A month later she could only rue that "there are so many damn islands to conquer and so damn many japs to kill. I hope we are equal to it. I bet it takes years." She confessed that "those sinking burning ships just make me curdle inside."

Casualty lists began to be published and with them names they knew. "We heard yesterday that young George Meade had been killed in the Solomons," Sidney wrote in September. "Terribly sad. He was just 22." A few weeks later, he told Gertie about meeting an aviator who had fought at Guadalcanal and the man, he said, looked "haunted. He could not have been more than twenty four and yet his face was drawn up like an old man's . . . Now he will have to go through a period of nightmares and terrible fits of depression before he will forget and be himself again. He had just arrived and wanted only one thing, a bottle of whiskey. That is all they want, a bottle of whiskey so they can get drunk and forget."

Sidney and Morris, on the other hand, landed cushy jobs as essentially uniformed office managers at the navy's intelligence headquarters in Hawaii. "I know more about paper clips than I do about the armed forces," Sidney confessed. For all his self-deprecation, Sidney was an excellent officer. At the Joint Intelligence Center in Hawaii, he was the head of an administration section that assembled and disseminated intelligence material to various commands. In his quarterly officer fitness reports he was consistently rated an exceptional officer by his superiors and was described in one as having a "zealous, aggressive and unceasing devotion to duty" and an "intelligent, cooperative leadership." In April 1944, he was promoted to lieutenant commander.

Phone calls to and from Hawaii had to be booked in advance and often had to be limited to three minutes because of high demand and the cost—nearly $4 a minute—so the couple wrote to each other almost every day. Sidney's letters tended to be paeans to the quality of his life in Hawaii, which, he said, "flows along very pleasantly."

"I already have the clear eye and pink skin of a monk," Sidney wrote, describing days of tennis, swimming, and surfboarding interrupted only by his eight-to-five work schedule. He also noted that the "food could not be better and I am fat as a pig." Rationing was beginning to pinch on the mainland, but Sidney, describing one day's meals, feasted on a breakfast of "two fried eggs, three pancakes, bacon, papaya, pineapple, juice, coffee, three pats of butter, totaling about a pound of the latter, a pitcher of maple syrup over the cakes"; a lunch of "chicken a la king mixed with lots of green pepper and vegetables, ice tea, cake, butter, bread"; and a dinner of "steak, cauliflower, potatoes, fruit cup and ice cream." Alcohol flowed at private gatherings. "Not a worry in the world," he informed his wife.

Gertie threw herself into the social life of Washington: cocktail parties where nearly every shoulder boasted gold braid and tony Georgetown dinners with senior advisers to the president. "I sat between Harry Hopkins and Nelson Rockefeller the other night at Bill and Anne Vanderbilts," she told Sidney. "After dinner, Col. Donovan came and sat next to me. He is very dynamic and most attractive."

Gertie also hadn't lost her ability to snarl when the nightlife

paled. "Sat beside John D. Rockefeller Jr. (Not so hot)," she noted
of another evening. A supper evening at the 1925 F Street Club
involved "masses of dreary old people" and "frothy nitwits." The
first blush of her new life began to fade and with it Gertie's zest for
life in Washington. She was desperate to join Sidney in Hawaii and
plotted at every turn to make it happen. The issue came to dominate
her letters to her husband. But the navy didn't allow the wives of servicemen to live on the islands, threatening to court-martial anyone
who secretly brought his spouse to Hawaii.

As Gertie realized that her separation from Sidney was likely to
last a very long time, her unhappiness grew. "I never realized anything could be so hard and frightful as this separation," she wrote. "It
is really torture." Sidney's blasé descriptions of his days only fueled
her sense of grievance. "When I hung up the telephone last night I
burst into a flood of tears. I realized you are having a wonderful time,
you are terribly happy, you do not really care whether I get out there
or not. You do not miss me the way I do. You are content. It all came
over me like a flood . . . never in any of your sixty letters have you
told me you missed me, maybe you really don't."

Sidney did tell her he missed her and loved her, and to little avail
he invoked the sacrifice of others to help her cope with the distance
between them. "Many women's husbands will never come back," he
wrote. "They are buried on some foreign island, or drowned at sea.
Others will find themselves married to a man without legs or eyes."
He reminded her that for the twelve years after their wedding they
had "a life that was almost mythical," full of "travel, shooting, tennis
in Palm Beach, swimming on the Riviera etc. and there must be a
certain amount of bad with the good."

There was also, occasionally, an undercurrent of suspicion in
Gertie's letters, a discreet probing of whether Sidney was being
faithful. Recalling an old conversation, she said to her husband,
"You said I did not understand men's point of view about liking to
go with women just for an affair and no other reason. I am afraid I
still don't when one loves as we love, but I suppose some still do and

always will. How does Morris fair in such a celibate life?" She said the temptation must be terrific to take up with an attractive woman. "I am afraid I selfishly hope there is none," she added.

Sidney professed his devotion repeatedly. "Every night I kiss your lovely eyes and lips and hold you in my arms. Then I put my head on your shoulder and with a last good night drop off to sleep hoping that in the morning I will find you by my side, so that your kisses will not only be dream ones." But while Sidney's letters gave Gertie no reason to doubt him, family lore suggests he wasn't a faithful husband in Hawaii.

Gertie's unhappiness began to bleed into the rest of her life. Washington, once exciting, became unbearable—"purgatory pure and simple. The crowds, the noise, the grey grim atmosphere." She also bristled at the glass ceiling for women. Gertie earned half the salary of her male supervisor and noted, "I do all the work and he does all the talk."

"What burns me up the most is the unbelievable lack of confidence in a woman's ability," she said. "Men cannot bear to have their world encroached on by more efficient women. They hate to give way, they hate to admit they are good, they hate to give them power. It fairly drives me nuts. Gee, I would love to speak my mind on that subject every now and again."

The vast majority of women who worked at the OSS held clerical positions in Washington. Only a small number went overseas, and smaller still was the number who operated behind enemy lines. Donovan, in a remark that would have raised Gertie's hackles, described OSS women at home as the "invisible apron strings of an organization which touched every theater of war."

Gertie continued to do an excellent job, according to her supervisors, despite her growing disenchantment. One of her bosses said she "has energy and initiative as well as a pretty good knowledge of the workings of this organization." And by February she had been promoted to head of the cable desk with a monthly salary of $210, a $60 bump from where she had started.

Terribly allergic to the word "no," Gertie continued to seek a way out to Hawaii. In February, she wrote to the head of the OSS on the islands asking for a job. She noted that she had traveled extensively in Japan, China, Malaya, and Indochina and said she was "entrusted with the responsibility of handling most secret material." She also asked Donovan for his help, but another OSS official, while sympathetic to the request, told the director, "I should also add a doubt as to just how easy it is for wives of officers to go into theaters of command." Gertie, in the end, could not inveigle her way to the Pacific theater.

With Hawaii closed off, she turned her attention to getting another posting. In late March 1943, Donovan came to her house for dinner and told her that if she stayed with the OSS, he would see to it that she got a foreign assignment, possibly to London or Cairo. "I told Col. D that London was OK and I would like to go," Gertie wrote to her husband. "I was really thrilled because my darling if I can't get to you I would rather be 'in the war' close to things than stay here in this dreary town for the duration." Her patron Bruce was already in London as the new head of the OSS branch there, and the United States was rapidly building up its forces in anticipation of an invasion of the Continent. Bruce agreed to request Gertie's transfer to run his communications office—essentially the same job as she held in Washington. But Bruce was not above having some fun at Gertie's expense, cabling Donovan, "Would like Legendre to handle crèche we have started for Polish babies during the day and teach English to the unmarried mothers in the evening."

Sidney was generally supportive of Gertie going to London but asked her to consider what it would mean for their children, particularly the two-year-old, Bokara, who was growing up to be an amusing fireplug, Gertie reported. Both Sidney and Gertie were unhappy with the development of their older daughter, Landine, thinking that she lacked an independent spirit and "craves affection."

"I do believe that the lonely hotel life of nurses, boarding houses, and never seeing her parents had a profound influence on [Landine's] life," Sidney wrote. "You may not think that BoBo is affected by what you say and do, but I am certain that she is, and the fact that she has a mother with her makes an enormous difference . . . Please do not feel that this is a suggestion that you stay with the children, because it is not. It is simply an idea that may be based on an entirely wrong premise and as a result worthless."

Gertie noted in letters back that the girls would summer in Rhode Island without her in any case and she was signing up for only six months; the separation might be short-lived. She said she would arrange for her daughters, accompanied by their nanny, to stay in New Orleans with her sister-in-law in the fall. Gertie was intent on leaving Washington, and parental responsibilities would not hold her back. As her daughter Bokara said, she "didn't much like children around." Later in life, she asked Gertie about it. "Mummy," she said, "I would like to get one thing straight. When I was a little girl and later growing up, was there some reason you didn't—well—include me in your life?"

"I wasn't around," Gertie replied.

That was partially true. But even when Gertie was at home, she didn't want to live with her children. Depending on their age, they lived separately in rented cottages and apartments with their nanny or at boarding school, visiting their parents on holidays and occasional weekends.

Gertie told her husband that mothering was not her priority. She had "worlds to conquer type of thing always appeals to me, change, motion, new possibilities, new heights . . . it's my restlessness, my wander lust, my desire not to stay put forever in the same spot with the same scene, the same people and the same everything."

London

On August 16, 1943, after months of delays, Gertie boarded a Portuguese liner in Philadelphia for the trip across the Atlantic. Portugal was a neutral country, and Gertie reassured her husband, "NO Portuguese boat has been sunk—so far so you don't have to worry a bit. It's very safe." Even without the protection of a neutral flag, conditions in the Atlantic had changed significantly from the treacherous crossings in the first years of the war, when German U-boats hunted the merchant shipping that kept Britain alive. By mid-1943, the United States and Britain had effectively won the Battle of the Atlantic through technological advances in decryption, radar, longer-range aircraft, and the ability of the United States to produce more and stronger escort craft as well as cargo ships.

Gertie's crossing was smooth. The forty to fifty passengers passed the time playing gin rummy over whiskey and beer. They watched flying fish and schools of whales off the side of the ship, and Gertie read Antoine de Saint-Exupéry's *Little Prince*, which had just been published. "It's full of charm [and] imagination." She slept on the deck some nights, waking one morning to the sound of an airplane overhead, probably from a nearby U.S. carrier. The ship stopped in the Azores to take on coal and more passengers, but those already on board were not allowed ashore. Boats glided out from São Miguel Island to sell them fruit. "War seems so far away," Gertie thought.

On September 4, she cabled Sidney from Lisbon. "Fine trip. Love Gertrude Legendre." Gertie spent the next week in and around the Portuguese capital, visiting the beach and "stuffing myself on the good food and making the most of unrationed things for it will be a different picture when we get to" London.

Sidney, reflecting on her arrival in Lisbon, said he felt "certain it is impoverished and a rather unhappy city filled with the refugees from neighboring countries. It is extraordinary to think that tomorrow the refugee of today may be the conqueror and the conqueror in turn may be [fleeing] for his life as a refugee. From out here the ultimate war in Europe appears to be following the plan. The Russians will press from one side and we from one or two sides towards Berlin. Both of us know whoever arrives there first will take the situation in hand and any peace terms that follow will be at the dictation of the winner in the race."

On September 15, Gertie boarded a blacked-out British flying boat, which flew in a wide arc over the Bay of Biscay to avoid attack from German fighter planes based on the west coast of France. The plane lost power in one of its engines over the channel and was forced to make an emergency landing in the port of Southampton. A Royal Navy motor launch took the passengers ashore.

Gertie, with her usual measure of drama, had arrived in England.

Two years after the Blitz, London's scars were camouflaged, with bombed-out sections of the city hidden behind walls and fences, and Gertie remarked on how little destruction was readily visible. The people struck her as quietly determined but wan from the poor diet and shabby in their frayed clothes. She initially took a room at Claridge's hotel before chancing on a town house a couple of blocks from her office near the U.S. embassy on Grosvenor Square—nicknamed Eisenhower Platz because numerous buildings in the immediate area had been taken over by Eisenhower's command as well as by the army and the navy.

Gertie's job was similar to the one she held in Washington, but she now handled cables for all OSS sections in London—the agency's largest overseas station with more than twelve hundred staffers. Clerical help was promised but slow to arrive, and Gertie sat for several months at the end of an otherwise empty room behind an expansive desk beside large French windows; she was more potentate in pose than civil servant. Her colleagues took to calling her Mussolini.

As each afternoon waned, a bell rang to draw the curtains when a nightly blackout descended on the city; London was still being bombed with air raid sirens blaring. Negotiating her way home with the help of a small faint torch in the pitch black was a challenge. She marveled at the cats' eyes of London taxi drivers. Bruce, her boss, broke his nose when he walked into a lamppost after leaving the office without any light to guide him. "I am about to flounder out into the night with my torch and wend my way home," Gertie told her husband. "It's black in the morning, black at night, and we live like moles all week." She also carried a blackjack in her purse amid reports—much exaggerated—of rampant violent assaults in the darkness.

London still entertained behind its closed doors and heavy curtains. Gertie enjoyed the city's nightlife. Her wealth and society connections from the States allowed her to socialize with senior officials and other celebrities who would ordinarily have been beyond the station of someone who ran the cable office. She dined out most evenings at the flats of friends or at restaurants—the OSS provided a list of three dozen decent places—or her surly Swiss cook prepared dinner for small parties. "Mademoiselle Renaud was . . . sixtyish, stocky, extremely neat, primly spinsterish and all-work-and-no-play," Gertie said. "If the latter attribute can be considered a prized trait in servants, it can also serve as a warning that disapproval of all manner of light-hearted fun is lurking in the kitchen."

Gertie explained that "one cannot entertain more than about three people twice a week," because of the food coupon system. There was a meager weekly allowance of meat, bread, margarine, sugar, milk, coffee, and tea. Fish, chicken, fresh vegetables, and fresh fruit were next to impossible to find. "I remember the delight occasioned when Admiral Glassford ceremoniously presented me with two lemons," Gertie recalled. "No one had seen fresh oranges and lemons for over two years. We fell on those two lemons like hungry wolves—we smelled them, carved them, squeezed them, sucked them and what rind was not slivered for cocktails was used to make a pitiful dash of marmalade."

As an American, Gertie was provided a weekly allowance of treats from the PX, or military post exchange, including seven packs of cigarettes and chocolate, and she also received care packages from home. "We made provident use of the angel food cake mix, orange and lemon crystals, dried prunes and figs, Klim milk and chocolate pudding powder," she said of the parcels from her relatives and friends. For ordinary Britons, wine and liquor had all but disappeared, but for the wealthy and well connected the alcohol was still being poured—sometimes Algerian wine, instead of French, but wine nonetheless.

Gertie had a somewhat Churchillian capacity to consume alcohol while maintaining her poise. Her daughter noted that "Mummy was able to have a daiquiri before dinner, wine with dinner, and liqueurs afterward. By the end of the evening she was not only upright but not at all drunk." She also smoked incessantly and was frequently photographed with a cigarette hanging from her lips.

Weekends Gertie spent playing golf or shooting, sometimes at some of the most exclusive homes in England, including Ditchley, which Winston Churchill had used early in the war instead of Chequers. At Ditchley, she went bird hunting with Edward Murrow, the CBS correspondent, and brought home two partridges to cook. "Life here is very exciting and as you can imagine I eat it up with a spoon," she told Sidney, all the lassitude of Washington having dissolved. "It is very stimulating and I am ashamed to say I enjoy it."

When Sidney suggested some months later that Gertie end her tour and return to the United States to be with the children, she rejected the idea. The limited six-month tour she had first spoken about was forgotten. Gertie was in for the long haul. "Why don't I go back to Virginia and be with the kids? No doubt that is what I should do, and maybe that is my duty—but I just couldn't go back and live in the country alone without you. It would be frightful . . . I far prefer Europe to Washington (which is my idea of the worst place on earth)."

There were regular trips to packed movie houses, dance clubs, theaters, and a drafty Albert Hall, where she saw the African American singer Roland Hayes with "a choir of 200 Negro soldiers." The singing reminded her of Medway when the plantation workers would serenade her and her guests with spirituals at Christmastime.

The black soldiers in and around London were a challenge to American racial mores. The British, for the most part, refused to accept the segregation their U.S. allies wished to impose in bars, restaurants, and other public places, and British women freely dated black servicemen. The British military issued a note advising "white women not to go out with black soldiers and, in general, suggested that people should watch how white Americans treated their compatriots." It was advice British civilians took pleasure in defying, much to the consternation of some Americans in Britain, including Gertie. "The Colored Troops are much argued about as you can imagine," she told Sidney. "We are going to have a time with them when they get home, as they go over big here in the worst way. It's quite something."

The war seemed much closer to Gertie—the streets packed with soldiers and the skies full of planes. "You can sit in the Ritz and eat a big lunch and hear the planes going over to bomb the hell out of the continent." But for all her exhilaration, she hadn't lost her acid tongue: "The streets are full of [British] girls in uniform [and] I must say they are a grim looking lot—cotton stockings, low shoes, toting brief cases and looking terribly masculine. The U.S. gals don't look too chic either. Think they picked a poor looking bunch to send over as I haven't seen any beauties."

Conversation was dominated by the expected invasion of the Continent, when and where it would happen, how quickly Eisenhower's forces would reach Berlin, and whether the Red Army would already be there. "The Russians are going to be the first to make them realize just how it feels to be the conquered. I'm all for Stalin going right into Berlin and carving them up a bit. We might be too soft-hearted to do a good job of it—but THEY WON'T," Gertie told Sidney. The ultimate defeat of Germany was widely assumed, and in the fall of 1943—with the Allies largely dominating the skies—the threat to London seemed to have receded despite persistent rumors that Hitler was about to unleash a secret weapon.

In January 1944, however, in a shock to Londoners, the Luftwaffe returned in numbers to the skies above the city in what became known as the little Blitz. "It's quite like old times again," said Winston Churchill, in a quip that the tired population resented. Many of the bombs were incendiary devices, sparking fires across the city, and hundreds more Londoners died in their homes.

Gertie wrote to reassure her husband: "I suppose you read in the papers about the air raids—but don't give it a thought. They are noisy sometimes but that's all. I generally sleep right through them." In reality, it was hard to sleep because nearby explosions were followed by tremors that shook the house and the flak barrages "fell like stones" on her roof. But Gertie mostly stayed at home rather than seek shelter underground. "I preferred, if I must, to die in bed, tucked in my blankets. The thought of being trapped in a gloomy cellar was by far the grimmer worry." When the all clear was sounded, she sometimes went up to her roof and watched the glow of the flames as sections of the city burned.

In March, after some of the heaviest bombing of the Luftwaffe's campaign, she told Sidney she was issued a tin hat. "It is the biggest, bulkiest, thickest . . . affair I ever saw. So becoming! A real Easter bonnet—you would laugh yourself sick to see me swimming under it. I am so afraid it will slip and biff me over the nose which would surely break it."

Gertie's good humor vanished the following month when Colonel Tommy Hitchcock, an old friend and the air attaché at the U.S. embassy, was killed while flying a fighter-bomber in southern England. "It was a military funeral and I marched in the honorary escort with thirty officers (I was the only civilian) and it was a shattering experience."

She despaired of the human toll of the war, and—with some pre-nuclear prescience—wondered at the level of death that would occur in future conflicts. It is "all so sad and frightful, it makes you shudder . . . think of the destruction there will be if another war follows in another 25 years. You will probably just press a button and everything will blow up."

By May 1944, the belief that an assault on France was about to happen was ubiquitous in London. "Although we are on the threshold of invasion, I believe we are all far calmer and less jittery than elsewhere," Gertie said. "I only wish we could go in with the army and not get left behind. That's the depressing side—getting left behind. Everyone in uniform will get over before the civilian."

On D-day, Gertie was struck by the composure of the British, offering Churchillian V signs to the planes overhead but unwilling to rejoice until the early battle reports were in.

A month later, London felt deserted and Gertie was restless. "Not a soul in the streets," she said. She had been practicing her French with her Swiss cook since the previous year and as early as November 1943 had contacted an American friend about renting her apartment in Paris, all in anticipation of the liberation and her part in it. But Gertie wasn't able to cross the channel as quickly as she wished. "Every big shot I know is over there in the thick of it and I do feel so left out on the outer fringe of it all," she told Sidney. "Gee I wish I were a man so often—because then I wouldn't be relegated to the sidelines."

The invasion of France was followed by a new threat to London when the Nazis began attacking the city with pilotless, low-flying missiles, which looked like small planes when in silhouette against the sky. The Germans called the device the V-1—the *Vergeltungswaffe,* literally the "revenge weapon." Londoners called them buzz bombs or doodlebugs, among other names, and dreaded the stuttering sound of the engine cutting out because that meant the cruise missile with its eighteen-hundred-pound warhead was dropping.

Between June and September, when the Allies began to overrun the launching pads in the Pas de Calais in northeastern France, more than three thousand buzz bombs reached London, hitting large sections of the city and killing more than six thousand people. "The pilotless plane, flying bomb, or whatever its correct name may be, is an exceptionally unpleasant thing, because, unlike most other projectiles, it gives you time to think," George Orwell wrote at the time. "What is your first reaction when you hear the droning, zooming noise? Inevitably, it is a hope that the noise won't stop. You want to hear the bomb pass safely overhead and die away in the distance before the engine cuts out. In other words, you are hoping that it will fall on somebody else."

One bomb fell so close to Gertie's home that the house shook, blowing out glass and creating long cracks in her walls. Londoners, although exhausted, coped with the onslaught, as they had with previous German bombing campaigns. "One is apt to sleep anywhere, on the floor, under the table, or stretched on the concrete floor of a shelter," Gertie told her husband. "My camp life is standing me in good stead. I can sleep almost anywhere including under a truck, as we used to do in Persia. Do you remember?"

Also in London that summer as the newfangled bombs fell was Jerry Papurt, the OSS major Gertie would meet in Luxembourg in just a few weeks. He had been transferred from Naples to England for counterintelligence training before being deployed to France and was staying in a flat in central London. Papurt also brushed off the

German gambit. "The new development of the Germans is interesting as hell," he wrote. "I've watched quite a few of them and it's a fascinating sight. I'm quite sure they're of little or no tactical value but they're devilishly ingenious. Naturally they'll not have the effect on the people here that the Germans hope they will. These people are tough and it will take more than a scientific toy to make a dent."

On the night of August 25—the day Paris was liberated—Gertie and some friends hosted the grandest soiree of her time in London, an event to honor veteran fliers of World War I with a dinner in the garden of her home. The guest list of twenty-eight included Donovan; Lieutenant General Carl Spaatz, commander of U.S. air forces in Europe; John G. Winant, the U.S. ambassador to Britain; and a group of senior officers.

The army supplied the food—melon, lobster, filet mignon, salad, ice cream, and cake, an almost unimaginable feast in the city's exiguous circumstances. There were songs, skits, and toasts on a buoyant evening, made happier by the news from France. Gertie later wrote to her husband, "Those Big Shots are all really swell men, and it gives one quite a kick to know the war is being carried out by such able good fellows."

In a slightly macabre touch, Gertie had decorated the large U-shaped table she had assembled in her walled garden with a miniature buzz bomb amid the model Mustangs and Hurricanes that were also used for decorations. One of the generals mentioned that he had never witnessed a V-1 attack. Hardly had he spoken, Gertie recalled, than "we heard the faint putt-putt of a deadly doodlebug approaching. It flew low over us and carried its sputtering power into the distance. With a sigh of relief, I looked around the table at the illustrious gathering. To think that one buzz-bomb could have destroyed most of the American high command."

After coffee, there was a screening of a short documentary titled *When Next I See Paris* that began with shots of the city before the war and ended with footage of the D-day landings. The party wound down with renditions of "April in Paris" and "Lili Marlene," a song loved by Axis and Allied troops alike:

> *My love for you renews my might*
> *I'm warm again, my pack is light.*

It was an appropriate farewell to London. Gertie's orders to report to Paris were on their way.

Wallendorf

In the early afternoon of September 26, 1944, Gertie sat on a pile of rubble and broken plaster outside one of the few largely intact buildings in the German village of Wallendorf. Chickens ran around in front of her, pecking the ground beside an American caisson left behind by the U.S. troops that Gertie's party had expected to find upon their arrival. Instead, Major Papurt and the driver, Doyle Dickson, lay wrapped in blankets on bedsprings in the building behind her, shivering from their wounds and, in the case of the young private, drifting in and out of consciousness. He was badly wounded in the right thigh, part of one of his heels had been shot away, and Gertie was worried about gangrenous infection. "He was such a nice looking boy," she thought, who should be at home thinking about football.

Their German captors told them no one could be moved until the American shelling eased.

Gertie and Jennings, the navy lieutenant commander, along with two German soldiers, had carried the wounded men from the destroyed jeep across a great meadow to the burned-out village, fording the Sauer River on a small flatboat. Gertie toyed with escape, ludicrously informing a soldier through sign language and her badly broken German that she was just off to get some medical help. As she walked away, he yelled at her to get back, pointing out German positions in the hills where soldiers would happily fire on her; as if dealing with a recalcitrant child, he took her by the arm back to her comrades. U.S. planes circled overhead—frustratingly oblivious, Gertie thought, to her ordeal. Suddenly she was, as another American prisoner of war put it, "a nonentity in the huge business of war."

"I felt a dreadful sense of guilt," Gertie said. "Why had I been so keen to plunge into such an adventure which common sense would have forbidden. But adventure that was it! . . . Danger and adventure, they quickened the pulse and challenged me. I wondered why I was made that way."

Exploring the building on her own, Gertie found some unexpected loot: two or three dozen bottles of wine, loaves of coarse bread, American flour, and granulated sugar—the detritus of both former German residents and retreating American troops. With their German guards, the prisoners drank a little and feasted on pancakes made on a portable brazier. The German soldiers seemed to regard their American prisoners as more of a nuisance than any great capture or threat and moved around them with disinterested ease.

At four in the afternoon, a German medic arrived to administer tetanus shots to Papurt and Dickson and dress their wounds. He was followed two hours later by another soldier leading a scrawny horse hitched to a farm wagon. Papurt and Dickson were loaded onto the wagon. The soldier pulled so harshly on the horse's bit that Gertie itched to chastise him but restrained herself for the sake of the wounded men; she wanted them to get medical care as quickly as possible.

With the horse and wagon leading the way, Gertie and Jennings immediately behind on foot, and two soldiers following, the group began a steep climb through the woods leading out of Wallendorf. On the way up the hill, Papurt, who had largely remained alert throughout the ordeal, slipped Jennings some papers that he had found on himself, and the navy commander managed to crumple them up and toss them away without the guards noticing. Dickson occasionally moaned as the wagon bounced roughly in the dirt.

Gertie, whispering to the others, again contemplated escape, but Papurt warned her not to, running a finger across his throat. "You'd better forget about it," he whispered. Too many Germans in the woods. They arrived, drenched in sweat from the climb, at a farmhouse and stable. Gertie and Jennings were taken to a nearby two-room bunker, and a hush fell over the soldiers inside as the Americans were brought in.

An officer looked Gertie up and down and, speaking in French, asked her, "How long will the war last?"

Gertie shrugged. "Not long."

"What were you doing in Wallendorf?"

"Oh . . . just riding," Gertie said, briefly explaining their visit to Wallendorf.

The officer feigned a smile: "Such a pleasant pastime during war."

"We thought Wallendorf was in American hands."

The officer shuffled some papers. "Do not worry," he said. "You will probably be exchanged as soon as higher authorities are contacted."

Gertie and Jennings glanced at each other in surprise. For Jennings, this was a fanciful notion, but for Gertie a distinct possibility, though one she had not really considered until now. Throughout the war, the Allies and Nazi Germany had exchanged noncombatants in deals brokered by the International Committee of the Red Cross.

The officer pulled down a bottle and some glasses from a shelf that also held cans of American corned beef hash and tomatoes, more abandoned food happily swept up by the covetous Germans.

Gertie tossed back the drink—Jamaican rum.

Another officer decided to try out his English.

"It is a nice day, is it not?" he asked.

"Yes, a lousy day," Gertie replied.

There was something oddly relaxed about these exchanges— even as the bunker occasionally trembled when the constant shelling got closer. These soldiers and many others Gertie would encounter already carried the faint dishevel of defeat. Retreat had been unexpected and humiliating. Nazi Germany was back inside its western border, and the next push of the Allies loomed; on the eastern front, the Russians ground forward with a bloody inexorability.

Gertie asked if she and Jennings could check on Papurt and Dickson. The two men were still in the open air on the back of the wagon, and at Gertie's insistence they were carried into a cellar beneath the stable, where fifteen or twenty soldiers lay about, some snoring loudly. They had barely settled the men on some straw when two German officers descended the steps—"dull black boots and then dark faces under the black visors of high-grommetted caps." One wore a monocle, and the second waved his Mauser pistol around with a theatricality Gertie thought should be reserved for B movies. She was treating the debacle as another adventure to be observed with a kind of detached insouciance.

"Madame," said the first officer in French, "you and this man are to go with us."

"But what about our friends?" Gertie asked.

The monocled German explained that they would be taken to a hospital in the morning, and with another wave of his pistol the second officer dismissed Jennings's entreaties that he and Gertie be allowed to stay with the wounded men.

"One moment," Gertie said, "please."

As she turned around, Papurt told them they had better leave. "I'll take care of the boy," he said.

Gertie dropped to Dickson's side. "It looks like we have to go with them. Are you all right?"

"Yeah . . . yeah," he said.

She turned to the first officer and asked for cigarettes, lit them, and placed them in the mouths of Papurt and Dickson.

As she left the bunker, she cast a final glance at the two men, queasy as to their fates.

Gertie and Jennings were placed in a large open troop carrier, armed guards on either side of them, with the two officers up front.

They came down the other side of the hill and then turned southwest along the Westwall—in the moonlight, parts of its fortifications looking like rows of giant concrete teeth protruding from the ground. The flash and boom of cannons convulsed against the night sky, and Gertie felt as if she were driving through a dry electrical storm back in South Carolina.

Around midnight, they arrived in Trier, a small city on the Moselle River. There were few people on the street, and Gertie was ushered into a dark, brick building where she immediately tripped over the feet of a sleeping soldier. The soldier barked at her in German until he sat up in alarm when he saw the officers following behind. Gertie and Jennings were separated, and she was led to a room where she was asked to sit opposite "a wizened little man in military uniform wearing spectacles" who reminded her of a predatory animal and a second soldier, an overweight sergeant who spoke French and seemed to Gertie as if he should be running a restaurant in Austria. The questioning was perfunctory, and Gertie for the first time rattled off her cover story about being an embassy file clerk without serious challenge.

"Why did you come so far forward?" the German asked.

"I wanted to see what it was like near the front," Gertie replied.

The interview over, a second officer, who had questioned Jennings, walked in and began to chat amiably with Gertie in perfect English.

In a strange interlude, they briefly discussed people they knew in the horse business in Ireland before he said, "I'm sorry but we have no accommodations in this building. You are to continue your journey."

They left in a small sedan accompanied by two new soldiers who argued violently about directions between stops for beer at various taverns. By dawn, they had reached Wittlich, about twenty-five miles northeast of Trier. On the edge of town, they passed a formation of young boys with small wooden guns over their shoulders, singing a marching song. They were led into a large barracks-like building and directed to sit on wooden benches in the hallway. A soupy meal of meat and potatoes followed, and Gertie was allowed to wash in a large communal shower—a privilege that became farce when the water turned scalding hot and she had to flee with soap suds still caking her hair and her uniform soaked from the steam. "Nearly fried to a crisp," she recalled.

Jennings and Gertie spent the day in a small room chitchatting but restless, because the German soldiers had told them they could be moved again at any moment. They were being bounced from unit to unit deeper into Germany, but without being told their ultimate destination. When they emerged onto the street in Wittlich that evening, a German Messerschmitt and a U.S. plane were engaged in a dogfight right over the city, swooping like feuding birds of prey. The two Americans were whisked to an air raid shelter packed with German officers, soldiers, and civilian staff who greeted them with stares. "I was struck by the silence," Gertie said.

The all clear sounded after fifteen minutes, and Gertie and Jennings were led to a truck camouflaged with pine boughs. A young, sheepish GI sat in the back. He explained that he had gotten separated from his unit and eventually fell asleep in a pillbox where he was discovered by German soldiers. They had taken his overcoat, and he was cold. The truck, with its lights dimmed to a pinpoint, crawled along in the darkness for several hours before it rendezvoused with a second vehicle. Gertie was moved into the cab of the truck, and Jennings and the GI were put in the second vehicle. "I hope this is not goodbye, pal," she said to Jennings as he left.

A guard stood outside on the running board of Gertie's truck watching the sky for enemy planes—standard practice, she soon realized: "The reaction [to] our terrific might in the air is evident when you realize that automobile traffic is almost always made at night, except in cases of extreme emergency," she noted. "The majority of people I observed were intensely nervous and jittery."

On this night, the bitter cold overcame nerves, and the guard eventually climbed in. Attempts at conversation failed, but the two

Germans and Gertie spontaneously burst into song, giving rousing renditions of "Wien" and "Lili Marlene." "We shrilled away in the night," Gertie said. "They had good voices and in the communion of song, I felt relief."

At one in the morning, the truck pulled up to a pub in the village of Flamersheim, about thirty miles southwest of Bonn. A group of German officers sat around one table. Gertie was parched from the raucous singing. Along with the driver and guard, she was on her second round of beer when an officer in a green overcoat and heavy gun belt walked in, drawing everyone in the room to their feet to issue stiff-arm salutes with the clicking of heels. "At last, here was my typical Nazi," Gertie thought. "Prussian, pompous and over-bearing."

In French, he ordered Gertie to follow him and the two soldiers accompanying him, and they proceeded—Gertie scampering to keep up—along a street to an old stone building. For the first time, she was carefully searched and the contents of her shoulder bag emptied for examination. Her camera, film, and an army identification card, which made no reference to the OSS, were seized. Her U.S. passport, cigarette lighter, lipstick, and shoulder bag were returned.

The officer asked the familiar barrage of questions but quickly announced, "It is quite possible that you will be exchanged." He asked if she wished to sleep in one of the bunk beds or preferred to be taken to a nearby prison to be with her compatriots. Gertie chose the prison, hoping to see Jennings or at least some other Americans. Again, she followed the German officer through the streets, a guard some paces behind, until they reached an imposing door in the side of a long wall. A bell was rung, and eventually a cadaverous figure opened the door a crack and held up a lantern. Gertie was guided to a small cell about eight feet by ten with three wooden bunks. The nauseating stink of an open latrine wafted in from the yard outside. But after nearly two days without sleep, she was too tired to care and collapsed on a bunch of gunnysacks filled with straw.

Gertie awoke to the delivery of ersatz coffee—the artificial brew that American prisoners called "mucker fuck"—five slices of coarse bread, a small blob of margarine, and fleas. What began as a tiny itch spread across her torso and down her thighs. As she tore open her tunic, she found small red welts across her stomach. She was infested. The prison, she learned, had only recently been used to hold Russian forced laborers, and they had been kept in crowded, filthy conditions.

Standing on tiptoe, looking out at the courtyard through the narrow bars of her cell while scratching continuously, Gertie saw Jennings pass by.

"Bob!" she shouted.

"My God, where have you been?" he asked.

"Right here in this pesthole," Gertie replied. "I thought I had lost you."

"How are you making out?"

"Marvelously," Gertie said. "Wonderful people. Treat me like a queen."

A guard intervened, shrieking at them to stop talking, and Jennings moved away with a wink. Returning from the latrines, he indicated with a glance skyward that he was in a cell above Gertie's. A short time later, she heard scratching in the ceiling of her cell; the building was old and crumbly. Some plaster fell away, and a hand emerged to drop a folded piece of paper. It read, "As you will probably get out of here before we do, here are the names of the airmen who came in last night. Several are wounded and have been taken off to a hospital. Tell their families that they are okay." The paper contained a list of names written in a blunt blue pencil. Gertie tucked it inside her bra.

The notes continued to arrive for the eleven days Gertie was held at Flamersheim, including addresses back home and requests that she send gifts to the sweethearts of the airmen and soldiers— perfume, stockings, and chocolates. "I tried as best I could to dispose them about my person and into crevices among my effects," Gertie said. "Had I kept them together in my original place of concealment I felt sure my new buxomness might invite attention." The communications and camaraderie were a boost but couldn't disguise Gertie's new reality. "Have no cigarettes, no books, no toilet paper. No toothbrush, no soap, no nothing." She was a POW in a German camp.

Limburg an der Lahn

On the morning after Gertie and the others were captured, the OSS sent out an officer to retrace their probable route; Papurt had informed his commanding officer where he was going but without specifying his mission. At the Luxembourg village of Reisdorf, about a mile and a half from Wallendorf, the officer searching for the missing group was stopped at a U.S. military roadblock and forced to turn around—belated recognition that the German village down the road was back in enemy hands. The search continued through the following day in hospitals throughout the area, but by September 28 the military had concluded, "The party was missing in action, presumably either captured or killed by the enemy."

Consternation—and fear—about the potential implications of their capture ricocheted across the OSS as Paris, London, and Washington were informed of the disappearance. Donovan paced in his office in a rage, calling Gertie a "loose cannon." He was "concerned that Legendre might talk," according to Edwin Putzell, one of his aides. Gertie had highly sensitive information about operations in North Africa, Italy, and occupied France. Most recently, she had seen reports on French Resistance teams working with the OSS following the invasion of southern France. "Her knowledge of these activities could have been vital to Nazi planning at the time German forces were being ambushed and scattered by the French resistance," one OSS veteran concluded.

A letter to John J. McCloy, the assistant secretary of war, captured some of Donovan's alarm when the OSS chief wrote of Gertie that she "has acquired a tremendous fund of information concerning OSS operations in the European theater. Any discovery by the Germans that she possesses such information would have grave consequences not only for her personally but also for this organization." He urged the military to see if it could arrange a prisoner exchange. "Ample justification for an urgent request, it seems to me, lies in the fact that Mrs. Legendre is a woman," he wrote.

The OSS ordered that any news stories on the capture of Gertie and the others be suppressed by the War Department. The families of the four POWs were eventually informed about their status as missing in action—the standard first notification—but not until news had begun to break publicly about a month after the capture. The families were warned not to discuss the OSS service of their loved ones. Donovan personally called Sidney, but Gertie's husband was angry it had taken so long to let him know what had happened. "Naturally, I had gone over to [the OSS] to ask where you were when you did not show up as you had promised," Sidney said. "All the time the louses knew you had disappeared."

Much of the alarm at the OSS focused on Papurt. After serving in army counterintelligence during the Italian campaign, Papurt was attached to the OSS and transferred to England just before D-day. He was trained in running agents by Britain's Secret Intelligence Service, better known as MI6, and also took courses in traditional special forces skills, including jump school, which he loved. "I don't know when I've gotten such a kick out of anything," he said. At thirty-seven, he noted, "I'm one of the oldest active jumpers in the U.S. Army."

Papurt moved to France in late August, first for a brief stint in Paris and then in operations just behind the advancing troops. "This is one of the most thrilling assignments of the war," he wrote. "I've been everywhere—on all fronts—and beyond and it's been a terrifically fast moving job. I'm in command of a completely self-maintained detachment and we really get around and see things and do things."

Military censorship prevented him from getting into any more details in his letters to the war photographer Margaret Bourke-White. He was even enthusiastic about the routine deprivations of being in the field. "I feel wonderful right now," he wrote in one letter. "We hit a town where there was water and I actually had a bath—my first in three weeks that wasn't out of a helmet. Also had a chance to change underwear so feel terrific."

By late September, as the Allied advance paused, Papurt's unit was ensconced in the Hôtel Brasseur in Luxembourg City—the spot where he would cross paths with Gertie and Jennings. Papurt's SHAEF pass said he was involved in the "detection and prevention of the enemy's espionage and sabotage"—information that would have been a stunning gift to German interrogators had the four Americans not burned their most incriminating identification. (The capture prompted Papurt's deputy to urge the OSS to produce "passes bearing wording of a less specific nature.")

Papurt was part of what was called a Special Counter-Intelligence (SCI) detachment—joint British and American units that accompanied Allied regular forces and exploited intelligence from top secret British intercepts of German communications. Papurt's unit used the intelligence—code-named Ultra—to find enemy agents and any abandoned German matériel that could benefit the war effort. Ultra—so named because it was regarded as even more sensitive than the top British classification, Most Secret—gave the Allies immediate insight into the resources and plans of the Germans on multiple fronts. Its existence was among the most closely guarded secrets of the war and was not publicly revealed until the 1970s. The British severely limited access to Ultra intelligence, and Papurt was one of a select pool of OSS personnel who knew about the program. If the Germans learned about Ultra, the Allies would lose a critical edge over the enemy.

As a result, the issue of Papurt's capture reached the level of

General Stewart Menzies, the head of MI6, as well as General Kenneth Strong, the British chief of staff for intelligence at Eisenhower's headquarters, and his American deputy, General Thomas J. Betts. It was a matter of acute embarrassment for the OSS and a validation in some British quarters of their disdain for American tradecraft.

Senior officials at the OSS, with little more than wishful thinking about Papurt's resourcefulness, tried to assure themselves that he—and they—could survive the blunder. Norman Holmes Pearson, the head of X-2, told the acting chief of OSS London, Russell Forgan, in a memo, "My general feeling is that of all our SCI personnel, Papurt stands the best chance of bluffing his way out of his embarrassing situation. He possesses a certain natural instinct for this." Papurt could draw on his experience with the U.S. Army's Counterintelligence Corps in Italy to provide the Germans with some limited information if they associated him with intelligence work, while keeping his knowledge of OSS and Ultra secret. Divulging information about CIC procedures "would be much the lesser of two evils," Pearson told Forgan.

After his wounding at Wallendorf, Papurt had been moved to a hospital in Limburg an der Lahn, a town on the Lahn River between Bonn and Frankfurt and a major transit point for American and British prisoners of war. At some point, he was searched, and the Germans found a sheet of paper on him under the heading "SCI" with a list of at least fifteen people, including several French names. One was Lieutenant Pierre Haas, a Free French liaison officer to T-Force. Some came with ranks, others not. The Germans were immediately suspicious of the document, but uncertain what it meant—a list of intelligence officers and agents, or something more innocuous?

The Papurt document became an increasing focus in the questioning of Gertie and Jennings at Flamersheim. A constant flow of American POWs moved in and out of the prison—interviewed and assessed before being transferred to another facility—but Gertie and

Jennings continued to be held. At one point during Gertie's detention in the town, there were eighty American officers and men in the prison; at others only a handful. Gertie and Jennings remained the objects of special suspicion. Why was Jennings, a naval officer, so far from water? Why did Gertie, a civilian, have a "simulated" rank and a uniform? And what were they doing with Papurt?

In one interview, a plainclothes German, who Gertie believed was Gestapo, accused them of being spies.

"Madame Legendre, I have new information," he said. "You, Papurt and Jennings are a team. We have found incriminating papers on Papurt and it looks serious for all of you."

Gertie repeated her cover story and described their casual encounter in Luxembourg and trip to Wallendorf.

"I know nothing of Major Papurt," she said.

The Gestapo agent brought up the SCI document.

"Is it not true that [Papurt] is with your intelligence?" the Gestapo agent insisted. He demanded to know what "SCI" stood for.

Employing her best ditzy girl act, Gertie said she "told him I was not up on all the funny letters used by the government."

"Does not believe me at all," Gertie concluded after the interview. "Horribly suspicious."

Jennings, in a separate interview, said that as far as he knew, Papurt was in the Supply Corps and "SCI" "undoubtedly meant 'Supply Corps, Infantry.' I could not be sure of this because, being in the Navy, I was not familiar with the Army nomenclature," he told the interrogator.

The questioning eventually eased up; Flamersheim was not a location for the systematic interrogation of prisoners. That would come later.

Gertie was released from solitary and allowed to join other officers in a small common room during the day. Enlisted men were held separately.

The filthy conditions and meager rations were accepted without direct complaint until the arrival of an American captain who objected loudly and insistently, noting that German POWs slept between sheets and ate the same food as their U.S. guards—as required by the Geneva Convention. The Nazis reacted to the tongue-lashing. The building was fumigated, the latrines were cleaned and flushed, and the prisoners were given fresh straw in new sacking. The diet remained unchanged, but the "goons," as the prisoners called the Germans, could be moved to action, it seemed, if given a loud enough bawling.

Gertie benefited the most from the new regime. She was taken one evening without warning to a whitewashed cottage in the village, about a block and a half from the prison, and shown to a small neat room on the second floor with a feather bed, sheets, and a washstand with a pitcher of clear water. Her coat and shoes were taken by her escort—surety, apparently, that she would not try to escape. "I flung myself on the bed and let myself sink into the soft clean mattress." This became a new routine. Each evening at 7:00, Gertie was deposited at the house, and each morning she was picked up at 8:00 and returned to the prison.

An elderly man and his daughter lived in the cottage. One night, the daughter entered the room, pressed a finger to her lips, and pointed to a hand-carved wooden crucifix on the wall, as if to enforce an oath. She gave her American guest a slice of *Apfelstrudel,* which Gertie devoured, and a freshly baked pie, which she brought back to the prison hidden in her clothes to share with her fellow POWs. The next morning when she uncovered it, the "room instantly became hushed. Then little exclamations arose."

Gertie was generally treated as a curiosity by the Germans. One guard, an artist called Toni May, made a charcoal drawing of her, posing her one afternoon in a guardhouse with only lamplight for illumination. "I thought it quite excellent," Gertie said, and May gave it to her as a gift; she tied it up with string and kept it at the bottom of her shoulder bag.

Some of the Americans also regarded her as an oddity, so much so that some newly arrived GIs thought she might be an English-speaking stooge planted by the camp authorities to pick up information.

Days were passed playing checkers and sharing any cigarettes brought in by new arrivals; everyone took just one drag, the butts held with a pin to draw out the last hit.

The prisoners' happiest diversion was the sight of daytime American bombers overhead, drawing whoops from the cells and courtyard as the sky began to throb from the collective noise of their engines. "Come here, sister, and blow those buddies kisses," one GI shouted at Gertie. She happily obliged. The guards, cursing the absent Luftwaffe, told them that Bonn, about twenty miles away, was being pummeled. The Germans held their native ground, but the air above was increasingly British and American.

On October 6, without notice, Gertie and Jennings were led to the street and ushered into a Buick limousine. Gertie was seated beside the driver. Jennings was put in the back between two officers. They headed south along the Rhine toward Koblenz. Gertie was struck at how lightly guarded the city seemed, with just a few trenches and stockades, and she concluded the coming onslaught would crush these defenses.

They continued on toward Limburg and Stalag XII-A—a complex whose hospital already housed Papurt and Dickson. The camp held thousands of prisoners, including Russians, Poles, Italians, Indians, and French as well as increasing numbers of Americans, British, and Canadians.

In all, the Germans would imprison about ninety-five thousand U.S. servicemen over the course of the war. Many of the U.S. ground troops captured after D-day were first interned in Limburg in a section of Stalag XII-A reserved for Americans—the officers in barracks and separated from the enlisted men, who slept on the ground in vast tents. By the time Gertie arrived, there were already several thousand Americans inside the barbed wire. Almost immediately, the presence of a woman in an American uniform caused a stir among the men. "I stood there in the sunshine and realized what consternation and interest I was causing," she said. For the first time, she worried for her safety if she were held in a camp of several thousand men.

Conditions at the camp, never good, still varied depending on nationality. Some of the Russians, in particular, struck Gertie as "dirty and devitalized," moving about like robots. "My emotions were those of mixed sympathy and revulsion," she said. The Russians were treated far worse than the other prisoners, in terms of the food they received and their living conditions, and were forced into grueling labor.

Of the 5.7 million Red Army soldiers captured by the Germans, 3.3 million, or 58 percent, died in captivity; the rate of death for American or British POWs was 3.5 percent. Explanations for the vast number of Soviet dead include an overwhelmed detention system, prisoners who were already malnourished, extreme weather, and disease. "All of these things are partially true, but they fall well short of the whole truth," according to one historian of the Reich. "What is missing is human agency and intentionality within this exculpatory fog of contingent circumstances."

In short, the Russians were starved to death or worked to death or allowed to freeze to death.

Gertie's stay at Stalag XII-A was blessedly brief. This was not her destination. It lay just two miles away: the Wehrmacht interrogation center at Diez Castle.

Diez an der Lahn

Diez Castle in Germany's Lahn valley juts high above the village below, a fairy-tale pastiche of sheer slate walls, battlements, and turrets, parts of which date back to the eleventh century. Once owned by the Dukes of Orange-Nassau, the castle had been a penitentiary for many years before it was commandeered by the German army to interrogate prisoners of special interest captured on the western front; it had about thirty individual cells as well as several dorms.

As she approached the castle, Gertie thought the "forbidding towers looked like an ogre's lair" and "conjured up pictures of dungeons and thumbscrews." The German army used the castle's louring menace, followed by a period in solitary confinement high in its keep, to loosen the tongues of its occupants. The military facility was also staffed with fluent English speakers, German soldiers who drew on their prior connections with the United States to try to establish a rapport with their prisoners. One spoke of his time working at a gas station in Nebraska; another said he had lived in Washington when his father had served in the German embassy there.

One such officer, five feet eleven and trim in the gray-green uniform of the Wehrmacht, emerged from the shadow of an arched doorway as Gertie and Jennings stood in the courtyard. He crossed the yard, clicked his heels, saluted, and said, "Follow me please. You are my prisoners now." Jennings arched his eyebrows at the American accent. They followed the officer up a steep stone stairway, the steps grooved by centuries of use, to a parapet that provided them with a brief panorama of the valley below. Next, they stepped into a dimly lit hallway of steel doors, each numbered. The walls seemed a yard thick. "This is yours, Mrs. Legendre," the officer said, pointing to number 38 but continuing on without opening it. Gertie and Jennings followed him into an office where he invited them to sit.

"Please call me Bill," he said. He offered each of them a pack of Camel cigarettes, which they grabbed a touch too enthusiastically despite the unease they expressed in stolen glances: Who is this guy?

His name was Wilhelm Gosewisch; he was a forty-one-year-old lieutenant. He had immigrated to the United States in 1921 and married another German immigrant in 1925. They had two children in New York City, a son born in 1929 and a daughter in 1932. Gosewisch, by his own account, had worked as a confectioner, a longshoreman, and a piano tuner before opening a lunch counter in Brooklyn.

He described himself as a once "quite well to do" businessman and recalled vacations fishing for bluefish and kingfish off Southampton. Gosewisch told Gertie that he returned to Germany with his family in 1939 and over time offered a number of different explanations as to why: anti-German boycotts in New York had affected his business; his citizenship application was denied when he said he would not fight on German soil; he was showing his wife, who he said was an American, his home country; and finally, because he wanted to finish a German undergraduate degree he had nearly completed before first immigrating so he could use it to apply to St. John's University Law School. He also said he was still in Germany when war broke out and he was conscripted into the army.

Many of these complicated explanations were lies. Gosewisch later affirmed under penalty of perjury that he left the United States in November 1934 with plans to return and he applied to the U.S. Immigration and Naturalization Service for extensions of his right to reenter the country. He told U.S. officials he needed to complete his studies in psychology and pedagogy. While in Germany, he worked as an English teacher, joined the Nazi Party, in 1937, and the National Socialist Teachers League, as well as the National Socialist People's Welfare Organization, the Association for German Cultural Relations Abroad, and the Reichskolonialbund, which sought the restoration of colonies Germany lost in the Treaty of Versailles. There were about 850,000 Nazi Party members in May 1933, when the party itself suspended new registrations to control a surge of applicants. The suspension was lifted in 1937, when Gosewisch joined, and by the eve of war there were about five million party members—about 6 percent of the German population. Teachers had to swear allegiance to Hitler and follow the prescribed curriculum, but party membership was not mandatory and the majority of educators did not join.

The lieutenant, for all his apparent bonhomie and cultivated American accent, had been at the very least a Nazi sympathizer, and perhaps a committed fascist, albeit one who was now rapidly realizing the war was lost. He held valid reentry visas for the United States in the 1930s but chose to stay in Nazi Germany long after the country's direction under Hitler was abundantly clear. He didn't join the military until July 1941, trained as a military interpreter in Berlin in 1942, and served in occupied Belgium before his posting at Diez.

With Gertie and Jennings, Gosewisch was following a well-practiced script. He told them that he had to leave for a few days and that their questioning was scheduled to begin upon his return. In the interim, they would be held in solitary confinement.

"How long will that be?" Gertie asked.

"Are you impatient?" Gosewisch replied.

"Frankly, yes. We've been going from here to there and everyone tells us the same thing. They told me I'd be exchanged as soon as I reached high headquarters."

"I will return next Tuesday," Gosewisch said.

It was Friday afternoon, October 6.

Gertie was taken to her cell. Jennings was briefly taken back to the Limburg camp to be deloused—a blistering-hot shower followed by two hours of naked shivering while his clothes were run through a hot-air chamber.

The six-by-ten-foot cells, unlike the filthy barracks Gertie had been held in prior to her arrival at Diez, were clean. A Russian forced laborer cleaned out the cells every day. There was a wooden bunk with a mattress, sheets, a pillow, three blankets, a stool, and a chamber pot. A guard brought her a novel—Zane Grey's *Sunset Pass: A Western Story*—to help pass the time. The windows were unbarred; it was a steep drop to the ground below. From her window, Gertie could see a village street, a river, railroad tracks, and grassy areas where children played. She watched as the residents rushed home when the air raid sirens sounded. The sky seemed to pulsate almost every day as hundreds of American bombers and fighters passed directly overhead.

Gosewisch had also given Gertie a Red Cross care package. After days of bread and slop, she enumerated its contents with lip-smacking pleasure: six packs of cigarettes; Nescafé coffee; one chocolate bar; a can of powdered milk; some lumps of sugar; dried prunes; packaged cheese; fortified biscuits; tins of corned beef hash, roast beef, and salmon; grape jam; and soap.

Treasure. Unimaginable treasure! "If the Red Cross had no other function, the sending of such packages would have made its wartime services invaluable," Gertie decided, a conclusion shared by all prisoners of war lucky enough to get food parcels. Deliveries became more difficult as the war progressed, especially to camps in the east.

Gertie was learning one of the first truths of life behind bars: food—stale or rotten and always inadequate—was a persistent ordeal. The Geneva Conventions required that prisoners be given the same quantity and quality of food as their guards, a provision rarely honored by the Nazis. Most prisoners subsisted on a diet of sawdust-based black bread, soup, and potatoes, with foul, fake coffee or tea to drink. Rations were steadily cut as the war progressed, and men emerged from some POW camps as living skeletons.

Food, inevitably, was a singular obsession for all prisoners, both a daily deficiency and a recurring fantasy, a preoccupation that found amusing expression in a poem by Larry Phelan, a lieutenant from New York held at Oflag 64, a camp for American officers in Szubin, Poland:

New Year's Sonnet
(Written to the Loveliest Girl in the World—Who Won't Like It)

I dream as only captive man can dream
Of life as lived in days that went before:
Of scrambled eggs and short cake thick with cream
And onion soup and Lobster Thermidor;
Of roasted beef and chops and sirloin steaks,
And turkey breast and golden leg or wing,
Of sausage, maple syrup, buckwheat cakes,
And chickens, broiled or fried or a la king.
I dwell on rolls or buns for days and days,
Hot cornbread biscuits, Philadelphia scrapple,
Asparagus in cream or Hollandaise,
And deep dish pies—mince, huckleberry, apple;
I long for buttered, creamy oyster stew,
And now and then, my pet, I long for you.

The hours and days passed slowly at the castle. Gertie recalled in detail past expeditions, taking herself back through Africa and Indochina, remembering waltzes in Vienna and harvest time in the vineyards of France. "My mind never stopped daydreaming as I lay sprawled on my cot, fully dressed except for my boots, until stark reality intercepted my fancies."

Solitary confinement was a standard German tactic to unnerve and ultimately break a prisoner, and a U.S. military report noted that American airmen in bursts of relief often talked incessantly when they were finally let out.

Gertie also rehearsed her lines in her head and worried about what would happen to her. "Realization that this was the all-important interview at 'higher headquarters' put me into a cold sweat," she recalled. "I wanted to keep cool, appear unruffled and unconcerned. Often devilish voices would taunt me: 'You're OSS, you're OSS. You know what that means.'"

Gertie had reason to be concerned. The Germans still believed she and the others might be intelligence officers and that there was something "sinister" about their presence at Wallendorf. They planned a series of overlapping interviews of Gertie, Jennings, and Papurt. If one of the three broke and disclosed an intelligence connection, the case would be turned over to the Gestapo. And the Nazi secret police would prove ruthless with American intelligence operatives.

Several OSS officers who were part of an Anglo-American team were captured in Slovakia in late 1944 as part of a mission to evacuate Allied airmen and assess the needs of the local partisans. All were in uniform, but the Germans discovered orders on one of the men from OSS headquarters in Washington. "A great deal of interest was shown by the [Reich Security Main Office] in the OSS," according to Werner Müller, a Gestapo interpreter, who was one of the officials involved in the interrogations of both Gertie and the men captured in Slovakia.

The Reich Security Main Office was part of the Nazi security structure under Heinrich Himmler, the *Reichsführer-SS,* and it managed the Gestapo, the criminal police, and the SD, the intelligence arm of the Nazi Party. The organization—the Reichssicherheitshauptamt, or RSHA, in German—was headed by Ernst Kaltenbrunner, an Austrian Nazi who had succeeded Reinhard Heydrich after the latter's assassination in Prague in 1942.

Some of the Americans and British officers captured in Slovakia, as well as the Associated Press correspondent Joseph Morton, who was covering their mission, were taken to the Mauthausen concentration camp in Austria in early January 1945. They were tortured and then summarily executed under orders from Kaltenbrunner. Naked—ostensibly for a medical examination in advance of their transfer to a POW camp—they were shot without warning; their bodies were burned in the Mauthausen ovens.

Gertie's knowledge of the OSS, based on her reading of sensitive cables, might have been fragmentary, but she held vital information about the agency's personnel, agents, structure, locations, and means of communication as well as some of its covert plans. The almost blithe manner in which she had handled her captivity was about to undergo its most consequential test. Could she continue to play the unfortunate but harmless female prisoner?

Lights were out, and Gertie had already gone to bed, when a guard appeared at her door to take her to Gosewisch's office on October 10.

"Please be seated," Gosewisch said as she entered.

He sat, smoking, in semidarkness, his long fingers flipping through a notebook.

"There is no use mincing words," Gosewisch said. She was considered "a very dangerous, international spy."

Gertie didn't respond, but "an arrow of alarm shot through my spine."

"You might as well tell me the truth," the German said sharply. "There are certain questions I must ask you. If you don't [answer], well, we have ways of finding things out and, frankly, I would not like to force you to experience our methods."

Gertie felt her anxiety growing. Would she be tortured? In her head, she quickly ran through her rehearsed answers while feeling a "confusion of thoughts and emotions."

For the first time, Gosewisch appeared threatening, the facade of the benign American discarded for the countenance of the inquisitor. Gertie, with a chill, "noted the Germanic stiffness of his neck, as if the column were welded to his square shoulders." Gosewisch began by recapping summaries of her previous interrogations, running through the material in a manner that was "neither rough nor rude, only insinuating and direct."

Gertie steadied herself, drawing on her reserves of mettle. "I found myself listening to my own voice," she recalled. "It sounded alright and carried an air of confidence. I was perspiring, yet felt collected, and was not nervous in the extreme." It was the kind of controlled tension she had felt many times as she raised her rifle and listened to an animal crashing through the brush—coming toward her.

The Wehrmacht rarely tortured American POWs, but it did play on the prisoners' fears of Nazi brutality and the prospect of being turned over to the Gestapo. "Mental strain, psychological threats, solitary confinement and deprivation were all considered fair and used routinely," one historian wrote.

The questions from Gosewisch—issued with the snap of an impatient lawyer—first concentrated on her job.

"Where did you work before you came to London?"

"In the State Department."

"What were the names of the people in your office?"

"Is it absolutely necessary to answer that? According to the convention, I don't have to answer that."

"No. You don't. But, believe me . . . only what you yourself have to say can clear you."

Gertie pulled a name from nowhere: Edna Robinson, "a nicely rounded American name," and she added another, Sarah Elberfeld.

"German?" asked Gosewisch.

"I hardly know," replied Gertie. "The name is, I guess . . . come to think of it, she's Pennsylvania Dutch."

Gosewisch changed tack abruptly.

"Who was Major Papurt?"

"An ordnance officer. I met him that morning in Luxembourg."

"A prearranged meeting?"

"No. Just a casual one. I didn't know him before. I think you have the account there. Tell me, is he alright?"

"He's being well taken care of."

The interview circled through the same series of subjects for two and a half hours. Finally, in apparent exasperation, Gosewisch said, "You probably belong to the FBI." He ended the interview abruptly, and the guard took Gertie back to her cell.

Jennings was interrogated twice the following day. He was asked about his naval career, the trip to Wallendorf, Papurt, and Gertie, and he provided the Germans with the first indication that their female prisoner was a society heiress.

Gosewisch also probed the lieutenant commander with a series of questions about the OSS, without mentioning the organization by name. He was asked about Papurt's deputy, Walter Hochschild. "I gathered they knew something of the work Hochschild and Papurt did in Luxembourg," Jennings later said. He told Gosewisch that he knew Hochschild socially and believed he was "attached to some air corps doing liaison work."

Did he know what was located at 79 Champs-Élysées, Gosewisch asked. Jennings feigned ignorance about the address of the Paris branch of the OSS. And Colonel Walter Giblin? Jennings said he had met him socially in New York because they were both in the investment business, but said he knew nothing of his current role. Giblin worked with Bruce in the Paris office, focused on the penetration of Germany by OSS agents.

"Giblin was in a very dangerous business," Gosewisch said.

Jennings was shown the SCI document found on Papurt but persisted in his ignorance of it, though he recognized one of the names on the list. Gosewisch told him he had figured out what SCI stood for: "Secret Civilian Intelligence." He told Jennings that he and Gertie were "in a very bad spot."

But Gosewisch was working with shards of information, rather than more fully formed allegations, and his examination of his prisoners suffered because of it. He couldn't expose them as liars if he didn't already know the truth.

That night, Gertie was returned to Gosewisch's office. Without speaking, he immediately handed her the SCI paper found on Papurt.

"Read this please. Tell me whether you have heard of any of these names." He passed the list to Gertie and said, "Don't lie to me either."

Gertie had arrived feeling calmer than the night before, but when she first glanced at the paper, she felt her pulse quicken. She recognized some of the names from her time in the London office. To disguise how startled she felt, she leaned into the lamplight to hide her face.

"I have never heard of any of them," she said.

"What does SCI stand for?"

"It's a mystery to me," Gertie said. "The Army changes names all the time. I can't keep up."

Naples

At the hospital in Limburg, Papurt was also interviewed several times but parried the questions, as his superiors were confident he would. According to an American captain in a bed close to Papurt, the OSS major was the subject of two interviews and a visit from a Gestapo official who also seemed to lose interest in him. "Reports concerning [Papurt], though conflicting, show that little if any OSS information was made available to the [German intelligence services] through this prize capture," a postwar assessment concluded.

The Germans were also preoccupied with the fact that Papurt was Jewish. Both Wehrmacht and Foreign Ministry reports noted his religion, and it's possible the focus on Papurt as a Jew deflected attention the Nazis might otherwise have spent on the possibility that he was an intelligence officer. The issue was a worry for Gertie, who feared Papurt would be mistreated and hoped his American uniform would protect him. Most American Jewish prisoners of war—identifiable by the *H* for "Hebrew" on their dog tags—were not singled out for abuse, but there were instances where Jewish prisoners experienced horrifying treatment because of their religion. The commandant of Stalag IX-B at Bad Orb, west of Frankfurt, sent eighty Jewish POWs to a slave labor camp west of Leipzig, where 20 percent of them died.

The Allies were keeping a close watch on German wireless traffic to see if Papurt had revealed anything about Ultra. While there was some decline in the quantity of usable material being swept up in intercepts, it was attributed to a series of new security measures that Himmler had put in place after the July assassination attempt on Hitler at the Wolf's Lair, his military headquarters in Prussia. "So far as we can learn from monitoring there have been no ill effects traceable to the capture of Papurt," Pearson, the head of X-2, concluded in a letter to the London branch of the OSS.

Papurt, Jennings, and Gertie might also have been helped by the fact the Germans did not know much about the OSS. While Goebbels's propaganda machine had railed against Donovan and the OSS after the formation of the American intelligence service, the Germans had little hard information on the organization, its structure, and its missions. A postwar U.S. assessment, based on the interrogation of senior German military and intelligence officials, concluded that "German knowledge of OSS was fragmentary, uncollated, incorrect and diffuse."

Pearson of OSS counterintelligence wrote with an almost audible sigh of relief that the Allies' ability to keep intercepting German military communications was secure.

"It is possible to believe that we may escape what would have been one of the disasters of the war," he said.

As he lay in a German hospital bed, Jerry Papurt's thoughts must have returned to Naples a year earlier. In late October 1943, the photographer Margaret Bourke-White, on assignment for *Life* magazine, had arrived to document the heavily bombed city and the U.S. Fifth Army's Italian campaign—an experience she would record in the book *Purple Heart Valley*.

In Naples, Bourke-White needed a military pass from the commanding officer at the local army counterintelligence unit. Papurt was a little starstruck when she walked in, but his easy charm won her over and she agreed to a date.

Papurt fell hard for her. Between assignments, they "spent their evenings singing songs together off key, wrapped in overcoats in an unheated palazzo, or dancing in a ballroom where the rain dripped though the ceiling."

"From Africa and Italy the word has gone out—Papurt's got it bad," he declared.

By November 9, Papurt was writing to her, "I hereby solemnly swear that it is my unalterable intention to wed, espouse, marry and tie in bonds of wedlock the above-mentioned Maggie, the Bourke-White." He told her his marriage was troubled, though this would prove to be news to his wife back in Columbus, Ohio. Bourke-White, coming off a recent divorce and then a relationship with an officer in North Africa, was cautious. "Don't let your fear spoil a really great love," Papurt told her in a letter. "If there is one thing in this world you can count on, it is my love for you . . . Love me too."

The photographer's confidence and fearlessness struck a deep chord with Papurt. Just as he earned the fierce loyalty of his men through his willingness to share the risks of combat with them, Bourke-White was a frontline journalist, always daring in pursuit of the great photograph and remarkably calm in the heat of battle. She had survived the torpedoing of a troopship in the Mediterranean, flew on bombing missions during the North African campaign, and was also a veteran of the eastern front. Bourke-White had been in Russia when the Germans invaded and went on to photograph air attacks on Moscow and fighting at the front near Smolensk, a city in western Russia that had quickly fallen to the Germans.

In Italy, the United States flew unarmed, two-seater reconnaissance planes, known as Grasshoppers, over the front to spot enemy positions and call in artillery fire. Bourke-White went up in one several times to capture the bloody slog of the battlefield near Cassino. "I was struck by the polka-dotted effect of the valley, with hundreds of thousands of shell holes filled with rainwater and shining in the sun," she recalled. "It was as though this valley, in which so many had suffered and died, was clothed in a sequined gown."

As they were near the end of one flight, two German Me-109 fighters emerged from the sky. The slow-moving Grasshopper was an easy mark, and the pilot, Colonel Michael Strok, began "violent corkscrew dives" to evade fire from the German planes and reach the safety of American anti-aircraft guns. Strok recalled that as he looked back quickly at Bourke-White to reassure her, "she was calmly shooting rapid-fire pictures of the action."

Back on the ground, Strok asked her, "Peggy, you are either the bravest person I've ever met or a damn fool—what are you?" She gave him that "intense blue-eyed look and that mischievous grin" and said, "Which do you think I am?"

Like Gertie, Bourke-White could be seen—by the lights of the military and some of her colleagues—as demanding and imperious. As her assignment in Italy ended in January 1944, the military refused to renew her accreditation, saying she had at times been too independent-minded and difficult—fairly standard attributes for good journalists, but unwelcome to some of the bureaucrats in uniform. She returned involuntarily to the United States. For the next six months, Papurt wrote to her almost every day, sometimes several times a day, and implored her to reciprocate with the same epistolary intensity. He told her she had an "adolescent" on her hands, declaring he had "never really been in love before."

"I'd rather spend two months a year—or two nights—with you than a lifetime with any other woman," he exclaimed. He urged her to secure an assignment in England. "There will be millions of pictures to take on the continent that only B-W could really do—so hurry over and take them."

But Bourke-White's reputation was hampering her ability to get back to Europe. Among her hurdles was how high the animosity she generated reached. Eisenhower regarded her as a congenital rule breaker who had to be closely chaperoned because she would not be controlled. The army refused to credential her for the invasion of France. Bourke-White eventually wrangled a return to Italy, selling her presence there as a way to record a campaign largely forgotten after D-day. She hoped the assignment would eventually get her to the main event—the assault on Germany.

Five days before she docked in Naples, Papurt was captured.

"I was numb with worry lest the enemy should know this was no ordinary prisoner," she recalled, fearing that Papurt would be tortured to extract what he knew about U.S. intelligence operations. But she also believed that Papurt with his "quicksilver mind" was "a past master of this kind of game of chess."

Bourke-White learned that Papurt was in a POW hospital and that the Vatican could deliver messages to prisoners of war either on radio broadcasts or by other means. Messages had to be limited to ten words. Bourke-White needed just eight: "I love you. I will marry you. Maggie."

It was not to be. On November 29, Papurt was killed in Limburg when an Allied bomb struck the hospital in which he was being held during a raid on the city. He was already up on crutches but had not gone down to a shelter when the siren had sounded.

Bourke-White never learned if Papurt got the message that she would marry him.

Diez an der Lahn

At Diez Castle, after days of interrogation, the atmosphere had changed noticeably for Gertie and Jennings. By mid-October, Gosewisch had softened his approach, initially to see if it would elicit information his harsh demeanor had failed to. A German military report found that "interrogation of Allied POWs was most successful when the prisoner was unaware that the interrogation was going on, and instead felt he was taking part in a 'voluntary and pleasant conversation.'"

The lieutenant began to see Gertie not as a spy but as a potential propaganda tool. Gosewisch had attempted to exploit other prisoners in the same way for the regime. He suggested to Ed Beattie, a United Press correspondent who was also being held in the castle, that he could travel around Germany, "seeing everything you want and talking to everyone you want to meet, so that you can go out and tell the world the true story of Germany."

A fluent German speaker, Beattie was more than familiar with the Nazis, having first been posted to Germany as a correspondent in 1932. He was in Berlin on *Kristallnacht*—the Night of Broken Glass—in November 1938, witnessing Goebbels switch the anti-Jewish violence on and off. He was in Prague in March 1939 when the Nazis entered the city and heard "the hisses and catcalls of the people, who sang the Czech national anthem." And he was in Warsaw later that year when "German troops . . . smashed across the frontier from Slovakia to the Baltic." When Poland fell, he transferred to London, where he covered the Blitz before returning to the Continent after D-day. Beattie told Gosewisch that his offer was an invitation to commit treason.

Gosewisch began to focus on Gertie's wealthy background and her connections to senior U.S. generals, including Patton and Spaatz, the chief of the U.S. Army Air Forces, who had dined at Gertie's London town house. The conversation noticeably relaxed, and the lieutenant produced fine French wine and cognac to lubricate their exchanges, which sometimes ran from 9:00 p.m. until 2:00 or 3:00 in the morning.

Gosewisch expressed regret that he had ever left the United States and mentioned he had relatives on Long Island; he neglected to note—almost certainly as a matter of self-preservation—that his brother, who had immigrated to Long Island, was a GI fighting in the Pacific. He also had a nephew who was a German POW in the United States after being captured in North Africa.

Defeat, Gosewisch said, was inevitable. He told Gertie that after the Americans had toppled "Hitler's gang," he hoped they would build a new Germany. "Democracy," he said, "was the white hope now."

And Gosewisch promised he would do what he could to ensure that Gertie was transferred back to the Allies. He clearly recognized that this American woman, with her impeccable connections, was a potential ally for his own postwar survival.

Both Jennings and Gertie were allowed to write home in letters routed through the International Committee of the Red Cross. Jennings wrote a short note to his mother in Michigan telling her he was a prisoner of war. "I do worry about the distress it must have caused you! I so wanted to be with you for Xmas and I should have been except for just rotten luck," he told her.

Gertie wrote to Sidney, but he never received the letter. She also sent a letter to Marian Hall, her roommate in Paris, which got through; her husband did not learn about the Hall letter until January 1945.

"You see how my innocent little trip to Luxembourg has ended up!" Gertie told Hall. "Behind a double row of iron bars eating black bread and potato soup with plenty of time to catch up on my sleep. No alcohol or fattening foods to spoil the health regime and I shall come out a new woman (some day)."

But Gertie also managed to embed a message to the OSS, telling Hall that she was tired of being questioned over and over again about her job as a clerk at the embassy and her work for the Red Cross. This would provide some guidance as to the cover story she was using. "I seem to be very much under suspicion and am quite flattered to be considered smart enough to play the part of an international spy—No one has ever given one so much credit." She noted that Papurt and Dickson had both been wounded but believed they would be all right.

She signed off, "Your caged lion, Gertie."

While in solitary, Gertie had been allowed to exercise for an hour a day on one of the battlements above the castle courtyard. Her presence led to endless speculation among both the American prisoners and the ordinary German guards about who the "fair prisoner" was. The blue USA patch on a white triangle on the shoulder of her uniform designated her a civilian attached to the U.S. Army, but to many of those looking up at her, she seemed more apparition than real; women were not allowed anywhere near the front lines. How could she have been captured?

"Whoever she is, she has given both guards and prisoners a lively topic of conversation," Beattie noted in his diary. "The svelte spy theory has the support of most of the guards and a fair proportion of the prisoners."

Jennings eventually explained her situation when he was let out of solitary confinement, though he was careful to maintain their cover story, even in private conversations with other American prisoners. "One never knows whether the Germans have microphones planted in the camps, or what conversations reach their ears, through planted stool pigeons or by some other means," Beattie noted.

Jennings was transferred out of Diez Castle on October 22. Gertie was allowed to say good-bye. In an earlier conversation in the court-yard—on a day she had finally been permitted to mingle with other prisoners—they had quietly confirmed with each other that they had stuck to their cover stories. Jennings was taken to an interrogation center run by the Luftwaffe just north of Frankfurt. He was put back in solitary in a cell with painted windows and an externally con-trolled heating system, which was switched from stifling hot to shiv-ering cold. The Germans again insisted he was a spy and demanded that if he was a naval officer, he prove it by writing a report on anti-submarine warfare. Jennings refused.

The newest round of interrogations was followed by a bizarre trip to a hunting lodge, formerly owned by the family that founded the car manufacturer Opel, with two plainclothes agents, possibly Gestapo. Jennings was served a fine dinner and liquor. "They simply wait to see if you won't break down through a sense of relief and in this way obtain information from you," he recalled. One of the agents said he had been a jewelry salesman in North and South America; the other said he had worked in a New Jersey trucking company before the war. Jennings ate the food but otherwise kept his mouth shut. It was the last gambit before the Germans closed the book on the navy officer. He was transferred to a POW camp.

The capture of Gertie and the others, despite the best efforts of the OSS to keep it under wraps, was beginning to leak out. "Interna-tional News Service had the story on A who is obviously [the] only one with big news value," wrote the Paris office of the OSS in an October 13 memo to Donovan, referring to Gertie as "A."

"Story was killed and through censorship sources no story will be published on this side on any of the individuals involved," the Paris branch assured Washington.

But on October 20, the story broke—from the German side. The Transocean news agency headquartered in Berlin reported that Gertie, described as a "member of New York society circles," was "the first American woman to fall into German hands." The report said the decision to inspect Wallendorf had been taken "at a merry party in Paris," but Gertie's "craving for sensation received a sudden shock when together with her companions, she was caught in German machine gun fire."

Reports by Berlin radio and other outlets quickly followed, and Gertie was described as a WAC officer and interpreter who also acted as a liaison officer between the U.S. Army and the Allied Expeditionary Force Club in Paris. The reports named Papurt and Jennings and noted that Papurt and an unnamed driver were wounded. Berlin radio quoted Gertie describing their capture at Wallendorf with Papurt jumping out of the jeep when they were fired on. Papurt "jokingly pointed his pistol as if to pick off the sniper. He looked so funny I just had to take a snapshot," Gertie was quoted as saying. She also said her treatment at the hands of the Wehrmacht was "irreproachable," Berlin radio reported.

The Berlin correspondent of the *Aftonbladet,* a Swedish newspaper, added that Gertie believed that "after her escape she would get a Hollywood contract without difficulty." The stories were quickly picked up by British and American outlets that emphasized Gertie's "socialite" credentials. *The New York Times* described her as "a lover of adventure" and recapped some of her hunting expeditions.

Although OSS officials were upset the story was out, they also believed that the German reports meant "they do not regard her as connected with intelligence work of any significance or no release would have been given." Unspoken, and probably raising some eyebrows, was the clear implication from the German articles that Gertie had been yammering at quite a clip about her connections and social life. Gosewisch's late-night chats with Gertie were not just drinks and conversation; he was writing up everything she said. And with every word, Gertie was turning the key on her own detention. Gosewisch's reports were being read voraciously in Berlin, especially by the Gestapo and other senior security officials.

If Gertie had one regret from her interrogations, it was her statements—and those of Jennings—about her family, wealth, and important friends. Gertie came to believe that she would have been released from Diez had the Nazis not taken such an intense interest in her background. "I had a feeling later on it was entirely possible I was being kept in reserve as a means of contact, or as a courier, should certain negotiations be in order at a time of imminent collapse," she said. She was now seen not as a prisoner of war but as a "special prisoner" whose social standing and contacts could be exploited. The German high command and senior Gestapo and Foreign Ministry officials in Berlin began to debate how she should be handled.

While the Germans discussed what to do with her, Gertie spent her days in her cell, looking out at the village or reading. A Russian prisoner washed her floor in the morning, emptied her slop pail, and brought her a pitcher of water. Occasionally, she got to exchange a few words with a German guard. But mostly she was alone with her thoughts. Sidney, she imagined, was now back in the continental United States on the leave they had both longed for.

"There were so many things about our companionship I missed," she recalled. "Principally his never-flagging sense of humor. That, I decided, was the most charming thing about him." Sidney did make it home, and wrote to her—letters Gertie never received. "I do hope you are well and that you are receiving some of the things we send you," he told her in one of the copies he kept. "It all feels so hopeless somehow to write when I do not even know where you are or whether you are alive."

Gosewisch told Gertie he was attempting to arrange her release through Switzerland, a task beyond the powers of a lieutenant, but he might have been aware of discussions among more senior officials about repatriation. Both the Gestapo and the Foreign Ministry—the latter sent two officials to interview Gertie at Diez—became interested in overseeing her case. On October 1, 1944, Himmler had been given authority over all POW affairs, and the camps began to come under his control. The Foreign Ministry remained the principal intermediary with the International Committee of the Red Cross. Following the interrogation at Diez, the section of the Gestapo focused on the United States and Britain was asked if it "was interested in Mrs. Legendre." It was.

The high command of the Wehrmacht, the Foreign Ministry, and the Gestapo now began to jostle for control of Gertie. Some officials emphasized that the "sympathetic treatment" of VIP prisoners of war could be publicized to reduce the "hate propaganda" directed at the Reich and would ultimately spare the blood of German POWs.

One Foreign Ministry official "explicitly asked for [Gertie] to be treated as a lady," and another, noting that Papurt was Jewish, said "it would be completely wrong to connect her fate to the Jew because she was only with him coincidentally." Gertie, the ministry argued, should be exchanged quickly for "propaganda reasons."

But others in Berlin continued to suspect that Gertie was more than just an embassy file clerk and her connections to senior American officers and other dignitaries had to be examined further. One senior Gestapo official described Gertie as "an important American woman" and suggested she might in fact be Eisenhower's secretary.

Finally, the order came directly from Hitler himself: Gertie should be sent to Berlin and handed over to the Gestapo.

Berlin

Toward the end of October, three plainclothes security officials arrived at Diez for Gertie. She was told she was being taken to Frankfurt and then by train to Berlin. "And after that, perhaps Sweden," speculated the commander at the castle, toasting her possible transfer to a neutral country with a glass of cognac. "I am very happy for you," he said. "To be returning to one's own people is a wonderful thing."

The prospect of ultimate release made the trip through the German countryside a pleasant ride, and Gertie observed the farmers behind their plows and the late fall colors with a sense of optimism. None of her escorts spoke English, and the drive passed in silence. "Each kilometer was taking me closer to freedom," she thought.

They arrived in Frankfurt under moonlight, and the city rose before Gertie as a shadowland of destruction: "crumbled buildings, heaps of rubble, gaunt skeletons of towers" silhouetted against the night sky. This was Gertie's first sight of the damage wrought by the relentless Allied bombing of Germany—the phalanxes of planes that had flashed across the patch of sky visible through her cell window in the castle. The Allies, as well as targeting key military and industrial infrastructure, were sowing terror among the civilian population, driven by the principle "that in order to destroy anything it is necessary to destroy everything." To the captured United Press correspondent Beattie, who was separately transferred to Berlin just ahead of Gertie, the "wrecked cities made me realize how comparatively mild the old *blitz* raids were, terrible as we thought them at the time."

Allied bombers and fighter planes—growing in numbers far greater than the Luftwaffe as U.S. and British combat losses fell— rained down "well over one million tons of high explosives, incendiaries, and fragmentation bombs" on the Reich. "We had to climb over the dead to get away from the sea of fire," one German woman said. "I couldn't help thinking, 'We've been living through the day of judgment.'"

To Gertie, Frankfurt appeared mortally wounded—a shocking contrast to the vibrant city with its medieval center that she had visited in 1936. Her escorts drove to what appeared to be the only intact building for several blocks, and Gertie was immediately alarmed when she saw guards from the SD—the Sicherheitsdienst— the intelligence service of the SS and the Nazi Party. The offices had no electricity, and Gertie was brought to a third-story room lit by an oil lamp, where she was given a glass of Malaga wine and some potato salad.

Gertie's stay was brief, and toward 11:00 p.m. her escorts took her to the Frankfurt train station—its arched halls of iron and glass reduced to ribboned shells. The station was teeming with soldiers, and many seemed sick or lame as they hauled their equipment onto trains. Gertie buttoned her unmarked raincoat to her chin to cover her American uniform. Her caution was warranted. Other POWs had encountered angry mobs while being transported, and as the bombing of Germany's cities intensified, there were reports of civilians assaulting and in some cases killing prisoners.

The trip to Berlin was fitful. A train in front of Gertie's was bombed, forcing those behind to reroute. Hours were spent waiting on the line. On either side of the tracks, destroyed railway cars littered the ground like broken toys. From the Lichterfelde neighborhood into the center, Berlin's classic five-story apartment buildings stood off the tracks like an honor guard of ruin, the roofs and floors having collapsed to the foundations, the windows agape. "There is block after block where man-made fire has swept the life from every building, leaving nothing but the raw, scorched walls," one witness wrote.

Gertie arrived in central Berlin at 3:00 p.m. Clutching her Red Cross box and shoulder bag, she was pushed out of the station by her guards through dense crowds of soldiers and civilian passengers—people scrambling madly for seats on the chronically overcrowded trains. Away from the bustle of the station, the center of the capital of what was once imagined to be the thousand-year Reich was a "dead city." The buildings were broken. The streets were all but empty. Rubble blocked sidewalks and spilled into the streets. Few buses or streetcars ran, and there were almost no private cars. The gaunt pedestrians, Gertie thought, wore "masks of defeat and apathy."

Beattie said the despair he saw in the demeanor of Berliners reminded him of the "faces of refugee columns fleeing down the roads of Poland and France in blind terror of the Nazi *panzers* . . . I can't hold down my satisfaction at a debt repaid in full."

Gertie walked through the streets with her guards to 8 Prinz-Albrecht-Strasse—Gestapo headquarters. The high stone entryway was as forbidding as ever. Swastika flags and busts of Hitler decorated the central passageway of the building, the former School of Industrial Arts and Crafts. But the large windows were covered with cardboard, and inside it was dark and frigid, drafts gusting around Gertie's ankles. Parts of the staff and their files had been evacuated that August as the bombing of the center of Berlin intensified. The imposing marble lobby no longer reeked of fear and malevolence but was redolent of the coming defeat, even though the remaining party officials continued to "strut around with the old pomposity."

For close to three hours, Gertie sat bored in a hallway, snacking on her Red Cross treats as her escorts sought guidance on what to do with her; it apparently was hard to find someone to make a decision. Eventually, two women from the Kripo, the criminal police, emerged as her new custodians, and Gertie followed them outside to a limousine with a soldier at the steering wheel. The car passed by the Brandenburg Gate and crossed through the Tiergarten before heading for Berlin's southwest suburbs.

As darkness fell, they drove through iron gates onto a graveled driveway leading to a large house with a manicured lawn stretching down to a lake. Gold lettering over the main entrance designated it as the headquarters of the Internationale Kriminalpolizeiliche Kommission—the forerunner of Interpol. The Nazis had taken over the Vienna-based organization after the *Anschluss* with Austria and moved it to Berlin, where senior Nazi security officials—Reinhard Heydrich, Arthur Nebe, and Ernst Kaltenbrunner—served in succession as president. In his role as head of the Reich Security Main Office, Kaltenbrunner—a zealous loyalist and boyhood friend of Adolf Eichmann's, a key implementer of the Final Solution—also issued directives on the treatment of captured prisoners, mostly fliers picked up by police after bailing out of their planes. If they put up resistance or wore civilian clothes under their uniforms, he instructed, they were to be shot immediately. It was Kaltenbrunner who ordered the execution of the OSS and British officers and the AP reporter Morton, who were captured behind the lines in Slovakia in December 1944.

The International Criminal Police Commission essentially ceased to exist as a functioning organization during the war, though it still managed to publish its journal, *Internationale Kriminalpolizei*, which now churned out "articles on racial inferiority and crime, praiseworthy reviews of books on racial laws, and reports concerning preventive arrest."

The commission's headquarters on Little Wannsee Street was to be Gertie's place of detention in Berlin.

The custodian of the house, not hiding her scorn, escorted the American prisoner, followed by the two female policewomen, to a second-floor bedroom. Gertie noted the abundant vases of flowers, fine furnishings, and plush carpets. Her room, with an en suite bathroom, was open and cheerful with large French windows and two beds. She was silently admiring her surroundings when she realized, to her dismay, that her guards—introduced as Frau Krautheim and Frau Sebastian—would be staying in the room with her.

A male officer came by as they were settling in.

"You are comfortable here, are you not, Mrs. Legendre?" he asked in English.

"Yes, this is quite comfortable, thank you," Gertie replied. "But when do I leave for Sweden?"

The officer paused before replying, "You are comfortable, why should you worry?" He turned and left.

Gertie asked her guards about Sweden, one of whom laughed and turned out the light as she settled into the second bed. The other woman took the couch.

Gertie—described by one senior Foreign Ministry official as a "little problem child"—appears to have been brought to the commission headquarters as a kind of adjunct prisoner to the nearby Stalag III-D camp in Berlin's Zehlendorf neighborhood. Beattie, the American correspondent who was held at the camp, described one section of it—Kommando 806—as a place for "odd lots whom nobody knows quite how to handle, or individuals being kept handy to Berlin at the disposition of one Nazi agency or another, possibly because they might prove useful to the German cause." Beattie's fellow prisoners included Italian military priests, South African officers, about a dozen Russians, and a few Frenchmen. Beattie and Gertie shared the same Foreign Ministry official who had watch over their cases for that agency. The official seemed confident that Gertie would be transferred to Switzerland, a fate Beattie was also hoping for as a noncombatant. The Gestapo, despite memos stating it would soon turn Gertie over to the ministry, was in no hurry to arrange her transfer and eventual release.

The day after her arrival in Berlin, Gertie was questioned by Kurt Lischka, an SS lieutenant colonel and Gestapo department head, and Major Wilhelm Clemens, who headed the section under

Lischka that dealt with counterespionage against the United States and Britain, including efforts to "turn" captured enemy agents. The two men—both in their thirties, younger than the century and steeped in its blood—had long careers in the Nazi security services.

Lischka had joined the SS in 1933. His focus, according to one biography, "was 'the Jewish Question,' in which he had specialized since 1938 when he took over . . . (Jewish Affairs) in the Gestapo." At the end of 1938, he had been appointed head of the Reich Center for Jewish Emigration in Berlin. He went on to head the German police and intelligence apparatus in occupied Paris in 1943, where he was responsible for the deportation of eighty thousand French Jews to Auschwitz.

"His face was perpetually set with hard, cruel lines," said Gertie, "and I hated him from the moment we met."

Clemens had previously headed the intelligence arm of the SS in Prague. Gertie found him quiet-spoken, kindly, and polite but "insistent with his questioning, which seemed interminable."

In this first interrogation, Gertie again recounted how she was captured at Wallendorf and described her clerical work for the U.S. government. Her lies flowed easily because she had created a whole imaginary life around her job as the embassy file clerk who had unfortunately stumbled into enemy hands. "I now began to think that what I had been saying was really true," she felt. Clemens, however, emerged from the encounter insisting that Papurt and Jennings were intelligence officers and suspicious that Gertie might be as well. Lischka was upset that Gertie assumed she would be exchanged and wanted to know who at the Foreign Ministry or elsewhere had discussed the matter with her or made such a promise.

A second interrogation by Clemens was organized several days later as an informal tea party, and the major was joined by two Gestapo interpreters, Werner Müller and Ursula Zieschang. Müller, thirty-three, who had worked in the hotel industry, including in England, before the war, spoke fluent English, French, and Italian and had worked for a Wehrmacht counter-Resistance unit in France before he was transferred to the Gestapo in 1944. One of the "best linguists" at the Reich Security Main Office, he would also act as the interpreter at the interrogation of the OSS and British officers and Morton while they were held at the Mauthausen concentration camp.

Zieschang, twenty-five, joined the Gestapo in January 1943 after graduating from translator school in Leipzig. She had been based in Trebnitz, just south of Leipzig, since the evacuation of her offices on Prinz-Albrecht-Strasse in August 1944. In late October, she received orders to travel to Berlin for a "special operation"—to act as the "companion" of an important American woman being held in the city.

Müller was briefed by Clemens to keep the second questioning as informal and relaxed as possible, but to touch on a specific list of subjects: Gertie's contacts with VIPs, living conditions in Britain, the effects of the buzz bombs, and American attitudes toward the Soviets.

Gertie discussed Patton, Ambassador Winant, the Duke of Windsor, Marian Hall, Marie-Pierre Koenig, and the U.S. secretary of the navy, her friend James Forrestal, but in "pleasant generalities," according to Müller. Gertie told her hosts that the German fear of the Bolsheviks was "an anxiety psychosis" and the United States would be able to handle the Soviets after the war. On the prospect of an Allied victory, Gertie expressed "great optimism" and said Patton had told her that he would be in Berlin within eleven days of crossing the Rhine. And Gertie dismissed the damage caused by the V-1 and V-2 weapons in London as "unimportant." When she was asked what the reaction would be to the aerial bombing of New York, Müller said that Gertie replied that "she wished it would be attempted. The effect would be to wake up Americans to the gravity of the war; at present they were too easygoing."

For all her loquaciousness—and occasional heedlessness—over the course of the two-and-a-half-hour discussion, Gertie drew the line on some subjects. When Clemens pressed her on the military situation in Luxembourg near the front, Gertie "refused flatly to say anything," according to Zieschang, who also noted that when she later asked for Gertie's help to properly describe a piece of Allied military equipment in a translation she was working on, Gertie angrily dismissed the request as inappropriate.

Zieschang typed up Clemens's reports on Gertie, which were sent to Himmler, after being reviewed by Lischka, Kaltenbrunner, and Heinrich Müller, the head of the Gestapo. Clemens ultimately concluded in his reports that Gertie had little intelligence of value to offer and came to believe—not entirely inaccurately—that her low-ranking position in London was probably just a rich lady's excuse to be abroad during wartime.

Himmler's interest in Gertie likely stemmed from the possibility of using her as an intermediary with some of her influential friends such as Patton and Winant. To the war's end, Himmler made "a series of attempts, albeit hesitatingly and indecisively to the last, to come to a political agreement to end the war," according to one of his biographers. And he harbored some illusion that Germany could forge a separate peace with the Western powers, to the exclusion of the Soviet Union. This Nazi fantasy held that the United States and Britain would tire of heavy casualties as they pushed into Germany and awoke to the danger of the Bolshevik hordes in the east.

Himmler had also shown a willingness to negotiate the release of Jews and some prominent French prisoners in exchange for cash and war matériel, possibly as the preamble to wider diplomatic negotiations. He allowed 318 Jews to leave Germany for Switzerland in October 1944 and continued to negotiate the release of more with Swiss and Swedish intermediaries. "In a grotesque irony, Himmler had convinced himself that the key to the Reich's salvation lay with the people which for three years he had been annihilating as its greatest enemy, the Jews," the historian Peter Black wrote. Himmler indulged "in the illusion that once a good business relationship had been established between the SS and World Jewry, the latter would exercise its legendary influence to induce the Allies to open peace negotiations." The negotiations were also a self-deluding effort to

Gertie (*left*) was born Gertrude Sanford in Aiken, South
Carolina, on March 29, 1902. She is pictured here with her older
siblings: Jane, who went on to marry an Italian diplomat, and
Stephen, better known as Laddie, who became an international
polo player.

Gertie (*left*), wearing a cowboy hat and holding a rifle, in the
Teton Range in Wyoming in the summer of 1920 with a friend
and a cowboy guide. She shot her first elk on the trip, sparking a
lifelong passion for hunting.

RIGHT: Gertie (*second from right*), smoking a pipe, with (*from left*) T. D. Carter, an assistant curator of mammals at the American Museum of Natural History; Morris Legendre, Gertie's future brother-in-law; and Sidney Legendre, her future husband, during the 1928–29 Abyssinia expedition

LEFT: Gertie holding the head of a lion, with an African guide to her left, during a 1927–28 East Africa expedition. She continued to hunt so she could showcase her trophies at institutions such as the American Museum of Natural History in New York.

BOTTOM: The nyala diorama in the Akeley Hall of African Mammals at the American Museum of Natural History was created from the specimens Gertie, Sidney, and Morris hunted in Abyssinia in 1928 and 1929.

MOUNTAIN NYALA
GIFT OF
GERTRUDE SANFORD   SIDNEY J. LEGENDRE   JOHN MORRIS LEGENDRE

Gertie and Sidney were married on September 17, 1929, at Manhattan's St. James' Episcopal Church. A reception for several hundred followed at the family's Seventy-Second Street mansion. The newlyweds spent their wedding night at the Waldorf.

In 1930, Gertie and Sidney purchased a house and plantation called Medway near Charleston, South Carolina. They refurbished the dilapidated house and eventually acquired more than seven thousand surrounding acres.

Gertie in 1933, reclining in an armchair at Medway

Gertie and Sidney in 1935 at Medway with their daughter Landine, who was born in 1933

Sidney at Medway in 1935, the family dog at his feet

Sidney reads a newspaper on the street in this undated photograph.

Gertie, here smoking a cigarette, preferred hunting over debutante balls.

Gertie, Sidney, and their dog in a convertible in an undated photograph

Sidney (*right*) and Morris Legendre received commissions in the navy reserve after the attack on Pearl Harbor.

Gertie at her desk in the London branch of the Office of Strategic Services (OSS) in 1943

TOP: Gertie enjoyed a hectic social life when time allowed; here she sits on a couch with friends at a party at her London home in 1944.

LEFT: General William Donovan, head of the OSS (*left*), and United States ambassador John Gilbert Winant at Gertie's home in London in 1944

BOTTOM: Bob Jennings fixing a tire in northern France, as he and Gertie drive toward Luxembourg in September 1944

Life magazine photographer Margaret Bourke-White in front of the Flying Fortress bomber from which she had photographed an attack on Tunis in 1943. She was "the first woman ever to fly with a U.S. combat crew over enemy soil," *Life* noted.

Maxwell Jerome Papurt, an OSS officer, served in U.S. Army intelligence in Naples (where he fell in love with Bourke-White) and transferred to the OSS before D-day. He was based in Luxembourg City when he met Gertie and Jennings.

Doyle Dickson, a young private attached to the OSS, was the driver when Gertie, Papurt, and Jennings went to Wallendorf. He is seen here in an undated photograph.

Gertie was questioned at Diez Castle in 1944. Located on the Lahn River northwest of Frankfurt, it was used by the German military as an interrogation center for prisoners of special interest who had been captured on the western front.

Wilhelm Gosewisch, Gertie's chief interrogator at Diez Castle, immigrated to the United States in 1921 and returned to Germany in 1934.

Edward W. Beattie Jr., a United Press correspondent who was captured in France in 1944, was also questioned at Diez Castle before he was transferred to Berlin.

35.. Marian,   October 12th:

You see how my innocent little trip to Luxemburg has ended up! -
I am behind a double row of iron bars in a 13C. Prison, eating black bread and potato soup, with plenty of time to catch up on my sleep, no alcohol or fattening foods to spoil the healthy regime, and I shall come out a new woman - (some day.) -
I escaped death by a miracle so have much to be thankful for - Two of the party were badly wounded, but Jennings and I came through unhurt despite the barrage of machine gun fire that riddled the jeep and missed my nose by inches -
I appear to be the only woman to come through the fighting line and be deposited in a Stalag with 80 American P.W.'s, and it seems to be a problem to know what to do with one -
I am really quite weary of repeating over & over again my history of army file clerk job at the Embassy, and Red Cross work in Paris, as I have been questioned so many times about it, but considering I have little else to do but answer questions or dream of home - it does not really matter -
Old B.o.g. will be by soon and change the picture -

The first page of the letter Gertie was allowed to write to her friend Marian Hall while she was held at Diez Castle. Although she also wrote to her husband, he never received those letters.

Gertie's Supreme Headquarters Allied Expeditionary Force permit, which was issued to her in August 1944, before her transfer from London to Paris

A charcoal drawing of Gertie made by Toni May, one of her guards, while she was held captive in Flamersheim, southwest of Bonn

Gertie leaning against a post at the villa in the Wannsee section of Berlin, where she was held in November and December 1944

Policewoman Ursula Sebastian (*left*) and interpreter Ursula Zieschang at the villa in Berlin

Marie-Agnès Cailliau, General Charles de Gaulle's sister, and her husband, Alfred, after their liberation at Castle Itter in Austria, in May 1945. Marie-Agnès and Gertie were imprisoned together at a hotel on the Rhine in early 1945.

Hans H. Grieme and his wife, Nena, housed Gertie at their home in Kronberg, just outside Frankfurt, in March 1945.

The Griemes' home in Kronberg

The railyards at the border crossing between Constance, Germany, and Kreuzlingen, Switzerland, where Gertie made her escape in March 1945. The crossing was used only for the special rail transfer of prisoners and others and was not a regular border post.

Gertie in Kreuzlingen, Switzerland, after her escape from Germany

Gertie's sister, Jane (*left*), and her husband, Mario Pansa, an Italian diplomat who was close to Italian dictator Benito Mussolini, in an undated photograph

A painting of Sidney Legendre by the British artist Simon Elwes that hung at Medway

A painting of Gertie by the Irish artist William Orpen that hung at Medway

Gertie, on a visit to Islay, Scotland, in 1993, when she was ninety-one

burnish his credentials for a role in postwar Germany and an attempt to distance himself from the regime's crimes.

In a world where this kind of fevered thinking was possible, Gertie was another potential stratagem, and one that carried fewer internal political risks than his dealings with the Swiss and Swedes. Besides Himmler, a series of senior Nazi figures—including Goebbels and Kaltenbrunner—had contemplated some kind of peace accord with either the Anglo-Americans or the Soviets, in order to divide the Allies, but all faced the same insurmountable hurdle. Hitler was completely opposed to negotiations. If Germany—and he—were to be defeated, then Germany, in his mind, did not deserve to exist.

So while much of the suspicion that Gertie was a spy was lifting—with the Foreign Ministry concluding that her "capture was a mistake with no sinister tinge about it"—there was still interest in learning if she could be used to support German war aims or provide insight into the enemy. An official from the Propaganda Ministry along with his wife, who spoke excellent English, questioned Gertie about the attitudes of Americans to the war and asserted that undisciplined U.S. soldiers would surely tire of the fighting—a perennial and wishful Nazi trope. Gertie was roused to inform him that the war would be very short and the outcome certain. "There's no question about it," she said, smiling.

The man, nonplussed, asked Gertie if she would like to write a note to Patton.

"Of course, but how do I know it will be delivered?" Gertie asked.

"There are ways," came the reply.

"Dear General Patton," Gertie immediately wrote on a piece of proffered notepaper. "I am waiting like Lili Marlene at the barracks gate for Old Blood and Guts to come and get me. Gertrude Legendre."

The official took the note, folded it carefully, and left; it would not make for good copy.

A succession of Gestapo and other officials came by to speak to her, some simply curious to see an American woman in uniform. "I feel like a rare animal in a zoo," she shouted at one visitor. "Couldn't I charge admission for your people to come and look at me."

At another point, it was suggested that Gertie might get to meet Hitler. It was unclear to her what was meant by the offer, or even if it was real, but she said she wasn't interested, infuriating her hosts, who railed at her for her impertinence. Later, she wondered if she hadn't been too hasty in her refusal. "It might have been interesting to have a close look at the tyrant," she mused.

At the lakeside villa, Gertie was mostly surrounded by true believers who had absorbed (or at least appeared to have) the relentlessly promulgated Nazi line that German retreats on both fronts were temporary setbacks. Beattie also said the people he encountered in Berlin "live[d] in a strange world of fears and fantastic hopes." The Russians, they believed, had stalled out on the Reich's eastern border, while the Allies, should they attempt to cross the Rhine, would be wading into a bloodbath—reminiscent of World War I's Verdun or the Somme—as they encountered Germany's stoutest defenses.

"They were convinced of an ultimate German victory, even if it took two years to win it," Gertie noted. "Only in Berlin did I find such confidence and assurance. Elsewhere, soldiers and civilians alike put up a token show of diluted patriotism, but they were like small boys whistling in the dark to keep up their courage."

On her second night at the house, when the air raid sirens began to howl, Gertie and the others rushed to a bunker in the garden, about forty feet from the building. They went down a narrow passage paneled with pine to a stuffy underground room. Gertie thought it was a death trap and that the villa's cellar would have been much safer. She came to dread the time spent in the shelter—during the day when the American bombers came, at night when the British struck. Gertie had a fear of being enclosed underground. She could tolerate a small cell—or a night in a hunting blind—if there was a window to allow in daylight or see the stars, but she found the claustrophobia of bomb shelters unbearable.

Sitting in the semidarkness, she could feel the concussion from the bombs exploding in the city. After raids, the garden was littered with slivers of silver tinfoil, dropped by the Allied planes as they approached Berlin to confuse German radar systems. One day, Gertie saw "two of our planes destroyed" and "nose dive to earth in black smoke," though some of the crew appeared to escape as two parachutes were visible in the sky. For the most part, southwestern Berlin was not a target of the Allied attacks, but there was still visible damage from errant bombs—some destroyed villas, broken roof tile and shards of glass in the gutters, and big craters in the woods.

On December 5, the city witnessed a massive daytime raid by the U.S. Army Air Forces, with the distant murmur of up to five hundred B-17 Flying Fortresses and B-24 Liberators, accompanied by groups of fighters, becoming a wall of noise as the planes approached. "All traffic had stopped, even to the subways, and the whole city was under cover," Beattie wrote. "As the bombs struck in thick swarms, the ground even here on the southern edge of the city shook and shuddered. In the northern distance, we could see the great columns of smoke and dust billow up and then stretch out eastward in a heavy pall over the whole city."

There were, he noted, no German planes in the sky to defend Berlin.

Several weeks after Gertie arrived in Berlin, on December 16, 1944, the Germans launched a surprise attack in the Ardennes and quickly overran weakly defended American lines, seizing thousands of prisoners and, for a brief period, looking as if they had the Allies on the run. But the Wehrmacht, even though it had shifted some of its best divisions and equipment to support the offensive, no longer had sufficient military and industrial strength to defeat the Allies, though it did inflict a serious bloodying. Each side suffered tens of thousands of casualties.

The attack, and its early success, was a matter of jubilation at the villa. One of the staff told Gertie that the Wehrmacht was on a straight path back to Paris. Gertie, yielding no ground, said she still fully expected to be greeted by Patton in Berlin. And indeed the Battle of the Bulge—so-called for the protrusion of territory the Germans temporarily held—was Hitler's last throw of the dice on the western front. Begining in early January, it was apparent to the more clear-eyed Nazis that from now on there was only defense.

Occasionally, the most senior Nazi officials, including Kaltenbrunner—"a tall man, slightly stooped with an unpleasant face"—came to the villa, but Gertie had no interaction with them. When Heinrich Müller, the head of the Gestapo, visited the house, she asked to speak to him to plead her case for release but was not allowed near him. (Kaltenbrunner, following his trial at Nuremberg, was executed by hanging by the Allies on October 16, 1946; Müller vanished at the end of the war but is believed to have committed suicide a few hundred yards from Hitler's bunker, though a body has never been found.)

Gertie's world mostly centered on the bedroom and an office–cum–sitting room across the hall that was decorated with a terracotta bust of Hitler, which she found "revolting," and a propaganda painting of a heavily pregnant young German woman. At night, when no guests were present, she was sometimes allowed to sit downstairs with one of the staff and listen to music on the radio.

Gertie gradually developed a friendship with Zieschang, the young interpreter, who brought her English books to read and walked with her in the garden. There were weeping willow trees around the house, including one at the edge of Little Wannsee Lake, and just beyond it a wooden dock jutting out into the water. Directly across the lake from the International Criminal Police Commission building was the boathouse of a rowing club.

The policewomen didn't share Gertie's enthusiasm for exercise, so she and Zieschang were left alone on the grounds of the villa;

when an official from the Foreign Ministry visited, he gave permission for Gertie to walk, with her female guards, in the surrounding neighborhood. "It was an odd feeling, walking undetected as an American along streets filled with Germans," Gertie noted. In her raincoat, she "looked like the other untidy civilians." The ability to walk outside the wire was a privilege accorded to other POWs; American and British soldiers who had been interned for a long period were allowed such supervised walks at some camps. Beattie strolled in nearby Zehlendorf, recording his observations in his journal, which he published after the war as *Diary of a Kriegie*. ("Kriegie" was the English abbreviation of the German word for prisoner of war, *Kriegsgefangener*.)

The Germans, remarkably, allowed prisoners to keep diaries, though they were subject to examination and confiscation. Gertie was careful to write nothing that would lead to the seizure of her journal. But in recording the day's activities, she was also creating prompts to recall what was not included. Beattie, another avid diary writer, included as many "hints" as possible about the incidents or thoughts he couldn't explicitly record. "The job was made the easier," he noted, "by the fact that a prisoner's existence is so dull that even minor events take on tremendous importance at the time and impress themselves deeply on the mind."

Gertie and Zieschang talked endlessly, and the interpreter, who had never been out of Germany and had been weaned on Nazi propaganda, seemed bewildered and upset by some of what she learned from their conversations. When Gertie told her that most of the Jews in Germany had been murdered by the Nazis, Zieschang cried, "No. That cannot be! They have only been deported"—a measure of either how sheltered she was or her willful ignorance, because Germany was "awash with rumors about the mass killing of Jews in the east." Moreover, Zieschang had spent the previous two years in the employ of the Gestapo.

Some Germans believed the bombing of their cities was vengeance for the pogroms against the Jews, especially the events of November 9, 1938—*Kristallnacht*—when anti-Semitic violence broke out across the Reich. Some of the Nazi structures built on the scorched ruins of Jewish life were now emblematic of the Reich's destruction. "In Wetzlar, Braunschweig, Solingen, Frankfurt am Main, Berlin, Siegen, Cologne, Emden and Hamburg, massive concrete bunkers had been erected on vacant sites where synagogues had stood until November 1938. In Cologne and Aachen, people connected the burnt synagogues with the churches destroyed in the air raids, evoking a sense of divine retribution," according to the historian Nicholas Stargardt. "As a clerical informer summarized such views for the local Gestapo: 'Yes, it's deserved . . . everything avenges itself on earth.'"

Zieschang was equally incredulous that the Nazis used slave labor, even though most of the work around the villa was performed by two Russian women who had no coats or stockings but were required to shovel snow, feed the rabbits and chickens kept on the grounds, and work in the kitchen. "But the wages are high," Zieschang protested when Gertie told her millions of people were being "driven like beasts" and that Germany would pay for its crimes.

Zieschang translated the newspapers every day and listened to Gertie's assessment of the war's actual progress, despite the "strategic retreats" and "stout resistance" of Germany's defenders cited in Nazi propaganda. Zieschang even risked her life on one or two occasions to let Gertie listen to the BBC, standing guard as Gertie glued her ear to the radio set.

While she was sent into the Wannsee house to interpret for Gertie and report on her, Zieschang developed "sincere affection" for Gertie, according to OSS officials who questioned the German woman after the war—so much so she seemed to them reluctant to say anything that might cause Gertie trouble.

Zieschang brought shoe polish, sewing thread, and face cream to the villa, as well as bottles of beer to supplement Gertie's diet. At the villa, Gertie typically had coffee, bread, and jam for breakfast; soup and potatoes and occasionally lung or liver for lunch; and potatoes, cabbage, semolina pudding, and cheese or pumpernickel for dinner. Compared with the rations of ordinary Berliners, it was a daily feast and was designed to impress on Gertie that the food situation in Germany was fine, according to Zieschang. Gertie also got a pack of cigarettes each week. "Awful," she declared, but she smoked them nonetheless.

Gertie was shedding pounds and none too happy with her appearance. "My hair, with little natural curl, hung much too long and gave my face an even thinner aspect, pointing up the hollows in my cheeks and the blanched skin. I looked much worse than I felt. I felt fine. I liked the idea of being thin," though she noted that her "unpressed skirt was too large around the waist" and "baggy in the seat." She used her pocket comb and Revlon lipstick to do what she could and employed her small pocketknife to both trim her nails and spread jam.

When her underwear had fallen to shreds, Müller, the Gestapo interpreter, was ordered to get her a new set. The orange-colored items he returned with, including stockings that seemed designed for a "muscular trapeze artist," led Gertie to observe that as a personal shopper the official was "something less than a novice."

14

Cologne

Christmas arrived bitterly cold under clear skies and a pale sun. Gertie was allowed a hot bath—her first non-sponge cleaning since the shower fiasco in Wittlich shortly after her capture. It felt like a luxury, and Gertie was serenely content when she emerged from the water. Zieschang and Sebastian, the more pleasant of the two policewomen, took Gertie on a walk across the frozen lake past the holiday skaters to the pine forest on the opposite shore. The snow there was soft and untouched.

"All about us was unfenced space," Gertie recalled. "I exulted in the feeling of freedom."

Gertie and her minders made Christmas cards for one another, drawing and coloring in the days leading up to the holiday. Zieschang also wrote a fairy tale about a little girl called Gertie whose "magic boots" took her to a strange land where she was imprisoned first in a castle and then in a big house: "Everywhere there was busy life going on, but she was secluded, all she could do was sit there and wait for her old friend who was full of blood and guts, that he might come to her rescue. But he could not come as the strange country was surrounded by a strong wall and he had to fight fiercely and tried in vain to break through."

That night, wearing a beard of white cotton, Gertie played Santa Claus, filling a rucksack with potatoes wrapped in homemade tinsel—the silver tinfoil dropped by the American bombers. The others shared wine and champagne, chocolate and cookies—war loot that was given to the villa's German staff as gifts. Gertie also got some presents from her minders—writing paper, a candle, face cream, stockings, a pencil and eraser, and—her favorite—a flask of vodka. It was a choice bounty compared with the Christmas of ordinary Berliners, who were subsisting on meager rations and trading in gallows humor—"Be practical, give a coffin."

The festivities couldn't prevent a feeling of gloom settling over Gertie. For weeks, all her inquiries about Sweden had been dismissed with a curt "no news."

"Your side has not yet asked for you," one official said.

"They probably don't even know I'm alive," Gertie protested.

She was allowed to write a cable to the U.S. ambassador in London, but never knew if it was sent.

Her mind inevitably drifted to Sidney, her girls, and the plantation in South Carolina. Sidney wrote to her on Christmas Day, telling her—in a letter she never received—"about the only consolation that I can give you is that you can be fairly certain that this will probably be the worst Christmas that you will ever spend."

Gertie's children passed Christmas in New York with their nanny and maid. They trimmed the tree on Christmas Eve and the following morning opened their stockings before breakfast, but the main presents had to wait until the meal was over. "It smacks of Miss Evans and is unmitigated cruelty," Sidney wrote in another undelivered letter to Gertie, referring to the children's governess.

Back in Hawaii following his leave on the mainland, Sidney said he dreamed of Gertie, seeing her on the horizon, coming into sight, coming toward him. "I could see your smile, your brown eyes and the little curls on your forehead," he wrote. "This letter brings you all my love and I can only hope that before very long they will exchange you."

Gertie's journey through Hitler's collapsing Reich was far from over. The custodian of the house, who made no secret of her dislike for Gertie and had some influence with Kaltenbrunner, wanted the American woman, her guards, and her interpreter out of the villa. Clemens, the Gestapo officer, proposed in a memo that Gertie be transferred back to the Allies but after she had been indoctrinated with the idea "that German defeat was impossible." The proposal never reached Himmler, because Müller, the Gestapo chief, refused to endorse it and believed there was some possibility she was a spy. Moreover, Gertie, who was told by Zieschang of the plan to brainwash her, said she would never agree to be anyone's stooge—"even to save her life."

Clemens next proposed that Gertie be sent to the Liebenau women's and children's internment camp near Lake Constance. Before the war, the camp had been a facility for people with mental disabilities and was run by Catholic nuns. It was now used to house American and British female civilians and their children who were in Germany when war broke out or had been detained when the Germans overran the Low Countries and France. Treatment of the prisoners at the facility was relatively good, with adequate food and medical care.

Gertie, however, was told that she was being transferred to a concentration camp in Czechoslovakia, leading to hours of panic. The prospect of being imprisoned in one of the Nazis' notorious death camps, some of whose horrors had already been chronicled in the press before Gertie's capture, was a moment of genuine and abject fear for her in an experience that for the most part she treated as another escapade. "My anxiety rose to fever proportions," she said of the thought of the "cold and starvation or worse" if she was sent to a camp. But even when that threat eased, she still didn't know her next destination, so her sense of dread during her final hours in Berlin never fully abated.

The proposal to take Gertie to Liebenau was rejected by Himmler. The *Reichsführer-SS* had other plans for her. December 28 was her last day in Berlin.

After leaving the villa, where Zieschang and other staff lined up to wave good-bye, Gertie was briefly taken back to Gestapo head-quarters on Prinz-Albrecht-Strasse. "Town flat. Awful mess," she observed as she passed back through the center of the city. She spent several hours in an office while a parade of officials glowered at her. She was driven from there to another packed train station, where soldiers were carrying their backpacks, guns, gas masks, and blanket rolls to the various platforms.

The Gestapo agent who was escorting her, joined by the police-woman Sebastian, cleared a path through the crowd, which had surged toward the doors when the train—destination Cologne—first arrived. The station was full of shoving, shouting crowds desper-ate to get out of the doomed city. The agent, wearing a black coat and black fedora, merely announced himself, and people who had just been jostling for position in a scrum around the door meekly stood aside. With a word to the conductress, the official also secured a large first-class cabin, forcing about a dozen occupants out into the corridor. The carriage was left with numerous empty seats, and some of the displaced visibly seethed at their high-handed master but kept their counsel. The Gestapo agent "was all-powerful in gain-ing anything he wished by merely whispering the magic word of who he was," Gertie observed.

The following morning, all passengers were forced onto the platform in Solingen, north of Cologne, because a train just ahead had been destroyed by fighter planes and it blocked the tracks. The Gestapo agent commandeered places in a passing army truck, and Gertie and the policewoman clambered into the rear, where they joined eight shivering, silent soldiers. "I was never colder in my life," said Gertie, who sat on a wooden bench under a canvas top as they drove first to Düsseldorf. "Our feet and hands were near to freezing."

At a café in the city, they secured a surprisingly good meal of hot soup, ham, boiled potatoes, and cabbage. Despite the heat in the café, Gertie was told to keep her coat buttoned so she would not be recognized as the enemy. The Americans, the Gestapo agent told her, are "gangsters" and a "bunch of murderers," and he insisted that German soldiers hated the United States with a homicidal intensity.

Nazi propagandists portrayed enemy fliers as murderers, and Goebbels, in articles in 1944, said they should be killed like "mad dogs" when they bailed out of their stricken planes and were captured. There was also a desire to frighten German soldiers who were considering desertion by implying that they might face the same treatment from the Allies. As Hitler explained, "If I make it clear that I show no consideration for prisoners, but that I treat enemy prisoners without any consideration for their rights, regardless of reprisals, then quite a few [Germans] will think twice before they desert." There were numerous atrocities against Allied prisoners—as they were captured, in the camps, and, especially, when the Germans were in retreat and moving POWs with them—but summary execution was never adopted as policy, in part because the regular German army, concerned about its own men, resisted any such move.

On the road to Cologne, the truck twice pulled over and sheltered under trees as U.S. fighter planes raked the road. When they reached the Rhine just outside the city, the truck dropped Gertie and her escorts off to walk the rest of the way. They crossed the Hohenzollern Bridge in a snowstorm, the city's famous cathedral rising blackened in front of them. Its twin spires were all the more spectral because so much of the rest of Cologne was flattened. "Nothing left," Gertie thought.

The city on the Rhine had been bombed more than 260 times; the cathedral by the shining curve of the river made Cologne easy to find for navigators. In 1942, it had been subjected to the first "thousand-bomber" raid by the Allies, and the Swiss consul described civilian morale "as well below zero." A year later, over three consecutive nights of bombing, more tonnage fell on Cologne than all previous bombings combined. Whole sections of the city burned and collapsed. Clouds of phosphorus hung in the air from the incendiary bombs. Nearly six thousand people were killed.

One former aircraft gunner told the German writer W. G. Sebald that he "could still see the burning city of Cologne even when they were on their way out again over the Dutch coast; it was a fiery speck in the darkness, like the tail of a motionless comet."

Gertie's hair was white with snowflakes as she and her guards picked their way through the ruins. It seemed as if no one lived above-ground. Eventually, they descended into a fetid underground passageway lined with women, children, and babies huddling listlessly together—"the plight of the doomed," Gertie thought. The Gestapo agent took her to a room where police officers were eating soup and bread. As they entered, an old man who tried to slip in with them had the door slammed in his face. "It's all gone," one of the police-men screamed. Gertie was given soup and coffee and then taken to an empty section of the cellar complex where a radio was broadcast-ing William Joyce, the American collaborator better known as Lord Haw-Haw—no doubt for her benefit.

Gertie had thought Cologne was her destination, but the stop was just to obtain new transport. An hour later she was on the move again—and freezing again—this time in the back of a convertible that took her out of the city. Through a heavy mist, she began to see the night sky shimmering pink in the distance. Ahead was Bonn, and it was burning.

The city had been hit by a heavy incendiary attack that afternoon, and whole sections were still ablaze. Driving through the streets, Gertie's escorts stared ahead fixedly as the car skirted around burn-ing rubble and blackened craters. Occasionally, she could hear the crash of a falling building. Residents were hauling furniture out of homes near the fire line, while women carried and dragged children as they rushed to safety. What struck Gertie most was the strange quiet in the cauldron; people rushed about, but whatever noise they made was enveloped by the roar of the flames. The driver was forced to make numerous detours, sometimes stopping to remove debris from the street. But just beyond the worst of the fires, he hit an object in the street, and the front axle was damaged. The car was immobilized, but another vehicle was quickly commandeered and the journey continued, out of Bonn, along the Rhine, in silence.

At 2:00 a.m., the car passed by a series of machine-gun posts and entered a yard surrounded by a ten-foot-high barbed-wire fence. Gertie trudged through the snow toward a large building perched on the Rhine embankment. She found herself in the lobby of an aging hotel with soldiers behind the reception desk. "I was completely befuddled," Gertie said. She was escorted to a dark room on the third floor and told to report downstairs for breakfast at 9:00 a.m.

"Are there other Americans here?" she asked. "Am I alone? Where am I?"

"I don't know" was the only answer the policewoman Sebastian could give her.

Gertie watched from her window as the Gestapo agent and Sebastian left. "Wish to God I knew where I was," Gertie said to herself. "So much mystery."

She was happy to be near the front, however. "Better chance for liberation," she decided.

The room was sparsely furnished, but the bed was comfortable and warm and Gertie was soon asleep. She woke in time to meet her 9:00 a.m. summons and walked downstairs unescorted, passing soldiers posted on every floor. As she reached the lobby, she followed the buzz of multiple conversations to a large salon where about 130 men—and 1 woman—milled about.

A hush fell over the room. A man rose to meet her. "*Madame, bienvenue à Godesberg,*" he said. "I am General Germain. Allow me to introduce you to my compatriots."

Gertie wasn't wearing the magic boots of Zieschang's Christmas fairy tale, but she had crossed into a strange world within Hitler's realm.

Bad Godesberg

The crowd of Frenchmen and one Frenchwoman were called "special and honored" prisoners of the SS. The place was the Rheinhotel Dreesen, one of Hitler's favorite places to stay before the war. And Gertie had entered a parallel Nazi detention system whose relative privileges stood in stark contrast to the horrors and barbarism of the death camps.

The Nazis created a network of castles, hotels, private villas, and purposely built houses inside concentration camps to detain mostly high-ranking aristocratic, political, diplomatic, or military figures from the occupied countries. King Leopold III of Belgium, for instance, was held under house arrest at his royal castle of Laeken before he was transferred to a castle in Hirschstein in eastern Germany in June 1944, and from there, near the end of the war, to a villa on Lake Wolfgang in Austria.

There had been a small number of "special and honored" prisoners before the war—mostly at the Sachsenhausen concentration camp in Oranienburg, just north of Berlin, where prominent detainees, including the former Austrian chancellor Kurt Schuschnigg, were held in comfortable quarters apart from other prisoners; Schuschnigg's wife and daughter came to live with him and were allowed to come and go from the camp as they pleased. A castle in Itter, Austria—converted into a hotel and then a prison—held the former French prime ministers Édouard Daladier and Paul Reynaud along with some other French luminaries.

"Special prisoners were prisoners that for reasons of state were to be kept separately in or near the camp [and] were not supposed to mingle with other prisoners, or whose imprisonment was to be kept secret," said Rudolf Höss, the notorious commander at Auschwitz. "Before the war, they were few; during the war, the number increased considerably."

Eventually, the system would house hundreds of prisoners: members of several European royal families; German dissidents whom Hitler or Himmler didn't wish to be killed, at least not immediately; senior political officials from erstwhile allies, including Italy and the Baltics; the large group of French nationals now surrounding Gertie—and Gertie herself.

"Mrs. Legendre was not treated as a prisoner of war but as a special prisoner," according to Zieschang.

Most of the French gentlemen greeting Gertie were retired generals and colonels who had been arrested in the run-up to D-day or shortly thereafter and taken to Germany, ostensibly to prevent their recall into government or military service following liberation. Some had been summoned for routine questioning and had shown up voluntarily, not imagining that the Nazis would have much interest in retired officers. But they were wanted as bargaining chips in any future negotiations with the Allies, and their detention was also a kind of implicit threat that German prisoners of war, about to be captured in large numbers, should be well treated or else these elderly French citizens could suffer more.

Gertie was initially swamped by dozens of people wishing to shake her hand and ask her about the state of France, especially Paris. "Had much damage been done to the city?" "Was the Metro running?" "Was there enough food?" The prisoners were starved for information, and Gertie became aware that they had received no letters from home. Their only news was German.

Interrupting the crush of questions, a young boy stepped into the room and rang a small bell: breakfast was served. The Rhein-hotel Dreesen was still a hotel with its own civilian staff all within the accoutrements of a military prison camp. The Nazis' code name for this special camp for French VIPs was *Winzerstube*—the "wine-maker's lounge."

The Frenchwoman at the center table in the dining room—her tangle of gray hair resistant to her efforts to pin and bun it—appearing gaunt but still exuding a composed authority was Marie-Agnès Cail-liau de Gaulle, the older sister of General Charles de Gaulle, leader of the Free French. Gertie was seated next to her. She would come to know Cailliau well within this cloistered community and found her kind but deeply despondent over the fate of her husband, impris-oned at the Buchenwald death camp.

She was endowed with some of the copious haughtiness of her distinguished sibling. "At times we could distract her with questions about her famous brother. She would become proud as she extolled 'Mon Frere Charles' as the saviour of France, and would forget for a moment that the soup had no seasoning," Gertie recalled.

Cailliau was also bemused by Gertie, who struck her as out-rageously American in her casual approach to life and her gender. "She was a smart and friendly woman, but her hair was very short, she wore men's pants, and the fact that she smoked a pipe did not make her very feminine and astonished my comrades," the French-woman observed.

After the fall of France, Cailliau and her husband, Alfred, had lived outside St.-Étienne, part of Vichy France, the southern part of the country not occupied by the Nazis and governed by a collaboration-ist regime led by Marshal Philippe Pétain. The Cailliaus, fervent if quiet supporters of de Gaulle and the Resistance, had moved there from their home in Le Havre, on the coast of Normandy, to try to live beyond the scrutiny of the Nazis. Three of their sons had joined the Free French in either England or North Africa, while another, having escaped from a POW camp in Germany, was part of the Resistance. A fifth son—twenty-four-year-old Charles—was killed in combat fighting the Nazis in 1940. A sixth son, the youngest, lived with his parents.

In April 1943, on a visit to Normandy, Alfred and Marie-Agnès were arrested at the home of a cousin and transferred to separate wings of Fresnes Prison, a facility south of Paris where the Gestapo interrogated and brutalized captured members of the Resistance. The Cailliaus, because of Marie-Agnès's lineage and their minimal intelligence value, were not tortured, but the poor diet and crowded cells took a toll on the couple; she was fifty-three, her husband sixty-six, when they were arrested. For Alfred, Fresnes was prelude to the nightmare of Buchenwald, the concentration camp outside Weimar in central Germany. In January 1944, Marie-Agnès heard through the prison grapevine that her husband had been taken to Germany. She did not know that he had been stripped naked and put in a cattle car in bitter cold for the three-day trip.

The Nazis had different plans for Madame Cailliau. In July 1944, as the Allies broke out of Normandy and threatened Paris, the Gestapo began to summarily execute prisoners at Fresnes. But Marie-Agnès was a potentially valuable chit. She was taken under armed guard to the Gare de l'Est in Paris and placed in a reserved compartment on a train bound for Germany. "I was sad to leave France," she recalled, "while everything announced the imminent deliverance of Paris."

Cailliau arrived at the Rheinhotel Dreesen to find it already packed with retired French officers—forty-two generals and seventy-five colonels—and a smattering of other nationalities, including a former Lithuanian diplomat and a Montenegrin prince. Their political leanings ran the spectrum from supporters of the Vichy regime to de Gaulle's Free French, but ideological differences were kept in check within the cocoon of the hotel, and General Maxime Germain's authority as the senior officer was respected by all, as was the social preeminence of Cailliau.

There were also two German prisoners: an industrialist who claimed to have been a friend of Hitler's at one time but had fallen out with the dictator, and his invalid sister who spent most of her time in her room watched by a German nurse. The industrialist, a large, bald man, wrote almost daily letters of complaint to the führer, as well as "I told you so" notes about the disastrous progress of the war. "We called him 'Le Mammouth,' after the lumbering prehistoric creature he resembled," Gertie said, "and suspected that he was in reality a stooge planted by the Germans in our company for the purpose of picking up odd scraps of information."

After breakfast, General Germain gave a speech thanking the United States for the liberation of France and noting that an American in uniform "in their midst was a symbol of brotherhood and hope." Gertie spoke briefly to say how happy she was to be among them.

The Rheinhotel Dreesen, which opened in 1894, was a distinguished if faded Art Nouveau structure with a five-story central building and two wings, all painted white, under steep roofs. On the north side of the hotel was a small garden by the Rhine where the prisoners could exercise.

The hotel dining room with its walls of glass offered a panoramic view of the Rhine and the shrinking number of barges that plied its waters—their few captains avoiding the large chunks of floating ice while watching the skies for the Allied planes that routinely attacked river traffic.

Hitler had stayed at the hotel many times in what became known as the *Führersuite,* located on the first floor with a bedroom behind bulletproof glass, a reception area, and working rooms. Along with Goebbels, he had planned the 1934 purge of Nazi leaders, known as the Night of the Long Knives, at the hotel. And in September 1938, he met Neville Chamberlain, the British prime minister, there, one of a series of meetings that led up to the Munich agreement and the

Nazi seizure of the Sudetenland from Czechoslovakia. Chamberlain, staying at the Hotel Petersberg, in Königswinter on the other bank of the Rhine, took a ferry across the river to his meetings with Hitler. The banks of the river were crowded with journalists and spectators, and one British official said the spectacle reminded him of the Oxford-Cambridge boat race on the Thames.

The Nazis had first used a section of the Rheinhotel to house South American diplomats until they were repatriated in early 1944. That April, the SS turned the whole hotel into a detention center—technically an adjunct to the Buchenwald concentration camp—while paying the hotel's owner 15 reichsmarks per prisoner per day. The contract even specified "afternoon coffee" for the VIP detainees.

The grounds were secured with watchtowers, machine-gun emplacements, barbed wire, and a detachment of sixty SS troops. The hotel owner was provided with ration cards that allowed him to buy meat, potatoes, fresh vegetables, bread, margarine, marmalade, cheese, and canned fish—in far greater quantities than the per-person ration of ordinary Germans. Gertie immediately noticed there was abundant bread and sometimes two or three servings of soup. There was even ice cream for dessert. The Nazis weighed the prisoners three times a month, presumably to pass along the statistics to the Red Cross, and on those days there were unlimited helpings of bean soup. "It's amazing how good the food is considering how really hard it must be to secure," Gertie observed. "I am continually surprised that the menus keep their usual quality despite their lack of seasoning and repetition."

On top of that, each prisoner got forty-nine cigarettes, sixteen cigars, or seventy grams of pipe tobacco a week. Beer was available for purchase, and Sekt or cherry brandy was served on special occasions, as it was on New Year's Eve, when the dinner menu consisted of cold fish, hot consommé, braised beef, green string beans, asparagus, roasted potatoes, and rich pudding with fruit sauce. The meal was followed by a radio speech from Goebbels at 9:00 p.m. and one from Hitler at midnight, both of which were interpreted for the prisoners. "Hitler's speech chiefly concerned their spirit of continuing the war to the end and never capitulating," Gertie recorded. The SS guards welcomed 1945 with gunfire. Gertie, sipping vodka in her room, wondered where her family was and how Sidney was ringing in the New Year.

Her husband was in Hawaii and, to his immense frustration, knew nothing of her whereabouts or health. The OSS, equally ignorant, was unable to help. American diplomatic inquiries about Gertie, and suggestions that the two sides exchange female prisoners, had been rebuffed by the Germans, who claimed, implausibly, they couldn't locate her.

For months, Sidney had been writing every week to Gertie in the care of the International Committee of the Red Cross but had never received a reply. Finally, in January, he learned about and read Gertie's letter to Marian Hall. "Isn't this a grand, cheerful letter!" Hall told Sidney when she forwarded it.

Sidney wrote to Gertie immediately, drawing on the details she had provided of her incarceration in hopes of cheering up his wife. "Were the lice in your hair as big as the ones we pulled out in Iran?" he asked. "Also I should think that sleeping on straw must have brought back the memories of those days when you use to curl up on a rock and tell me that you never had been so comfortable in your life. Worst of all however I think was the solitary confinement because you could not give anyone hell."

But a week later, in another letter, he was unable to joke and expressed his frustration at her continued detention. "The war seems to be moving so quickly that I am hoping the Germans will release rather than move you from camp to camp," he wrote, "because I cannot possibly see what earthly use you are to them or what purpose is being served by detaining a woman."

In this strange dialogue of unread letters, Gertie assured Sidney in a letter written on the same day, "Maybe this restrained life of inactivity under armed guard is good for my soul—for it is decidedly a novel experience for any independent spirit."

Gertie quickly realized that the Rheinhotel had taken on the complexion of an old people's home—lots of distracting daily activities and outbursts of pique over petty issues. "The old timers were extremely possessive of their comforts. Each has his favorite chair and considered it his private property," and feelings ran high if someone else dared to sit where he or she should not. Gertie was offered an armchair, and it became, by default, hers and no one else would use it.

Germain at one point had to address the geriatric warring over issues of property and said that people could not lay claim to things when not in the room. Dining was another major source of grumbling. "Trivial unimportant food items become a no. 1 major problem," Gertie noted. "The toast is not toasted, the coffee is lukewarm. Insufficient potatoes . . . While everyone, including C, are stuffing themselves."

Days at the Rheinhotel began with prayers before breakfast, organized by Cailliau, an ardent Catholic. On Sundays, a French priest, who was arrested because he was a retired reservist, said Mass in the dining room. Gertie, never very religious and in any case not Catholic, didn't attend but sometimes went to an improvised Protestant service in a cold upstairs bedroom. The group of five non-Catholics said the Lord's Prayer and read from the Bible before returning to the salon—which, in contrast, was insufferably hot from the steam heat kept at a constant eighty-five degrees.

"One old gentleman with faltering step had the self-appointed duty of keeping the windows sealed and would hop, fuming, like an arthritic bird for the casements when he detected the slightest whiff of fresh air."

When the furnaces stopped working, the room was heated by a woodstove, and the old men gathered around it, "huddled, shivering and complaining, like baby chicks about a brooder." Apart from the daily chatter, the room was also cacophonous with coughing, sneezing, and nose blowing. The Germans organized periodic visits to a doctor and dentist in the town of Bad Godesberg.

A hot-water bottle was placed in every bed at night to mitigate the hotel's temperamental heating system; it switched off completely when spring rains caused the Rhine to flood its banks and flow onto the hotel grounds and into the cellar, dousing the furnaces.

Most daylight hours were spent in the large rectangular salon, under its high ceilings and huge crystal chandeliers, with games of chess, bridge, and Chinese checkers taking place in different parts of the room. There were lessons in German, Russian, and Spanish, and Gertie was appointed professor of English, teaching her class after breakfast from 9:30 to 10:30. *Uncle Tom's Cabin, Adventures in the South Seas,* and *Three Men in a Boat* were her study texts because they were the only available books in English. At first, she had two students, but the class grew to nine. "Not only did I enjoy teaching, but I found the hours slipped by with greater ease," Gertie recalled. In turn, a general helped her with her French pronunciation.

There were classes on higher mathematics and specially organized lectures on topics such as "the atom" and "hunting with a dog." The group even produced a magazine of poetry and drawings. In one piece of doggerel called "Godesberg," Gertie described life at the hotel. It read, in part,

> *Every morning sharp at nine*
> *We watch the ice float down the Rhine*
> *A twinkling bell means Come and get it!*
> *That ersatz coffee—you'll regret it!*
>
> *The microbes float through clouds of smoke*
> *We breathe, we sneeze, we laugh and choke*
> *The sick with fever and the grip*
> *To the doctor make a trip*
>
> *The view from here is a sensation*
> *We all agree a revelation*

We see the smoke of our front line
We see the bombs drop up the Rhine . . .

The cannons shelling of each town
And watch the flares as they drop above
The war comes nearer in each day
We've front row seats to watch the play.

Twice a day, at 3:00 p.m. and 10:00 p.m., scratchy newscasts from Berlin were piped into the room and were interpreted by Paul Dungler, one of the youngest prisoners and described by Gertie as "our German scholar." Gertie learned that he had an OSS connection and had been sent into Vichy by American operatives based in Algiers, but Dungler had been betrayed by a comrade who "turned him over to the Germans only with the stipulation that he would be treated civilly."

Dungler, a royalist and driving force in the non-Gaullist Resistance in Alsace-Lorraine, was in fact closely tied to the leadership of the Vichy regime and had been sent to Algiers in 1943 to forge some kind of rapprochement with their nemeses, de Gaulle and Henri Giraud, then the commander of French forces in North Africa. The offer was rejected, but Dungler, in January 1944, was parachuted back into Vichy by the OSS to make contact with anti-Hitler elements of German military intelligence as part of what one historian of the agency called a "fantastic scheme" to divide the Nazis. After an expected assassination of Hitler, Dungler would facilitate communications to allow dissident elements in the German military to negotiate with the OSS and end hostilities in North Africa. Instead, the Frenchman was arrested, but his old Vichy connections might have saved him from a fate far worse than Bad Godesberg.

A map of the front, with pins denoting the various forces, hung on one of the walls and "raised great clouds of debate" among the retired officers who interpreted German propaganda to decipher the real progress of the war. Official communiqués used "expressions like *'Abriegelung des Angriffs'*—sealing off the attack . . . to gloss over serious enemy penetrations by pretending they have been halted." No one believed these bulletins—not the French generals or those guarding them. The noise of battle from the approaching front told them all otherwise.

Gertie spent much of her time with Jean Couiteas de Faucamberge, a former French tennis champion who consistently beat her at deck tennis in the hotel garden, where they played even with snow on the ground. "Brilliant and fluent, he combined wit with intelligence to keep me amused," Gertie recalled. She heard that he was arrested on the Riviera as a member of the Resistance but escaped execution by mesmerizing the German officer in charge of his case; he was said to have hypnotic powers. Gertie found him a brilliant conversationalist who could range over subjects as diverse as enology, Egyptian astrologers, yoga, and modern warfare.

Couiteas de Faucamberge also had an endless array of card tricks and, with limited success, tried to teach Gertie how to play contract bridge. She finally bested him when she bet she could balance a glass of water on her forehead while lying flat on her back and stand up without spilling a drop or touching her hands to the floor or the glass. It was a trick she had learned as a child and still managed to pull off to the delight of the French crowd. Several of the generals got drenched trying to replicate Gertie's feat, which left her as chuffed as the Riviera waterskiing triumph in her evening dress had.

There were frequent visits to the hotel cellar during air raids. *"Keller, Keller!"* the Germans shouted when the planes were already bombing nearby targets because the advance warning system no longer functioned. Two kerosene lanterns provided the only lighting, the air was foul, and Gertie hated the place, preferring to hide in her bedroom rather than go down.

She sometimes used these attacks to hang back and steal some of the hotel's limited hot water, because there was a monthly rotation for baths. "Without a twinge of conscience, I hopped into many a tub not meant for me and thus increased my baths far above my legal quota. If I ever was under suspicion of foul play, no word or look betrayed it," she confessed. "I felt classed with all the other wily women of the ages, but unashamed—I was keeping cleaner than the others."

Cigarettes were the coin of the realm, traded for food, warmer clothes, and toiletries, even though the tobacco was "ineffably poor" because it was "adulterated with all kinds of trash." In the hotel's strange economics, four caramels would buy eight cigarettes, two spoonfuls of soap powder was worth five cigarettes, and one cigarette would buy a pail of hot water from one of the hotel maids on days when the furnace was out. Prince Michael of Montenegro, a chain-smoker, had traded away almost everything but his dressing gown to keep himself in tobacco. Gertie, when her ration had expired, would sometimes smoke tobacco scraped from cigarette butts in her German-issued pipe—a lust for nicotine that raised Madame Cailliau's disapproving eyebrows.

When the cellar was flooded, the prisoners stayed in the garden during air raids. They could watch fighter planes diving toward their targets—the railway station at Godesberg or a coal barge on the river. Once they witnessed a dogfight between one German and two British planes, and bullets from the engagement rained down on the Rheinhotel grounds. Sometimes on the horizon Gertie saw the vapor trail of rockets—V-2s, she believed, directed at London. "The feeling of being on the front line . . . adds a certain zest to our incarceration," Gertie decided, as well as the "hope of deliverance."

The routine was rarely broken, but one afternoon, following her French lesson, Gertie was astonished to find Gosewisch in the hotel lobby.

"What in the world are you doing here?" she asked, rushing over to greet her former interrogator.

"Thought I'd drop in . . . to check up."

The German major's real business was checking on his potentially valuable American ally as the course of the war became ever clearer.

Gertie asked about Jennings.

"He's alright," Gosewisch told her.

"And the major?"

"Dead," he replied, explaining that an Allied attack had hit the hospital where Papurt was being treated.

"How dreadful!"

The brief visit—Gosewisch was brusquely ordered to leave by the SS colonel in charge at the hotel—left her dispirited. "There were no assurances of early release and I began to share the feeling of helplessness, the submission to the inevitable, which characterized the defeated old Frenchmen about me."

Königswinter

Gertie's despondency didn't last long. By early February 1945, the prisoners began to hear the persistent boom of American guns. On February 9, Gertie wrote in her diary, "The cannons sound closer, the bombings are more frequent and the news on the west front is improving. The 3rd Army appears to be on the move. The Russians have crossed the Oder and are only 45 kil. from Berlin."

The Allied push toward the Rhine across a broad front from Nijmegen in the north to near the Swiss border in the south had begun in earnest. It was the U.S. First Army, under General Courtney Hodges, that was driving toward the river between Cologne and Koblenz, including Bad Godesberg, with Patton's Third Army operating to the south, with Frankfurt in its distant sights. The city of Düren, among the first in Hodges's path, was described by an American engineer, when it was overrun, as "the most totally destroyed city I have ever seen." Almost no building among the city's nine thousand structures was left intact under the relentless barrage of tank and howitzer shells. The horizon burned, and the Americans, with bulldozers clearing their path, advanced through the stench of death. From the air, fighter-bombers "harried the fleeing enemy in what one pilot called a 'rat hunt: You beat the ground. You flushed the vermin.'"

The Germans referred to these fliers as *"Terror Flieger."*

On February 21, Gertie recorded that the guns resounded all

day and a bombing raid on the town of Bad Godesberg blew out all the windows on the west side of the hotel. Despite the increasing danger of a strike on the hotel itself, Gertie was gripped by "a feeling of suspense and excitement."

On the last day of February, the SS commander at the hotel ordered a retreat across the Rhine. That night, Herr Dreesen, the owner of the hotel, gave everyone a bottle of local wine at dinner and wept as he bade his guests farewell. (American troops when they finally reached the hotel found a huge wine cellar.) "With the wine we drank toast after toast to victory and liberation," Gertie said. "Some dared to discuss the possibility of escape or hiding until allied soldiers appeared. But the wild plans were only flights of fancy. We were placed under even more strict surveillance."

The following morning, the prisoners were divided into two groups: those who would be able to walk up the steep incline to the Hotel Petersberg, their destination across the river in Königswinter, which stood on a rise about a thousand feet above the Rhine, and those who would have to be bused. Gertie, despite the jumpy soldiers and nervous prisoners, was "enchanted with the idea of a full morning's exercise." Before leaving, she asked Dreesen's nephew, who spoke a little English, to tell Patton's troops that she had been held at the hotel and where she was being taken. As Gertie drove down to the ferry, she could see the consternation on the faces of the town's residents. The departing soldiers and prisoners did not bode well for those left behind.

On the other side of the river, Gertie bounded up a switchbacking mountain road, which rose through heavy forest, to the hotel. She was eventually ordered to slow down and wait for those struggling up behind her. When she reached the hotel, she could see the roof of the Rheinhotel and hear the roar of cannons pressing in on the besieged town. "If only," she thought, "the Americans would hurry!" But Königswinter, too, was a temporary stop.

. . .

The Petersberg Hotel, shuttered since 1939, was not prepared for guests and was without heat, water, and light. Gertie was assigned to a once luxurious room overlooking the river, though the cold forced her to sleep fully clothed and with her coat on. That night she watched the artillery fire flash like lightning and "signal flares hung in the sky like Japanese lanterns." But conditions at the hotel were miserable. Water was brought in by the pail but was not potable, the toilets didn't flush, and no one could bathe properly. The prisoners, already dirty, became even more disheveled.

The amount of food fell sharply; ginger biscuits replaced bread. A small ration of cider or white wine was issued to compensate for the lack of drinking water. Gertie used the wine to wash her teeth and cleaned her face with cold cream.

The Germans had finally agreed to Cailliau's repeated pleas that her husband be transferred from Buchenwald, and he joined the evacuees at the hotel. "The man was like a walking cadaver," Gertie noted; he had lost so much weight that his wife at first had difficulty recognizing him.

He provided the group with its first hard knowledge of the depravity at Buchenwald, describing the hundreds who died or were murdered every day, their bodies dumped in pits, doused with gasoline, and burned. "We were told of prisoners, too weak to stand, being clubbed to death and thrown into the pits, in some instances before they were actually dead," Gertie said. "The stories of M. Cailliau underscored the patent savagery we knew the Nazis employed in their treatment of the lesser orders of their prisoners. Now that the Germans were at bay, we were not a little alarmed that it might extend . . . to those of us who were considered special prisoners." It was a legitimate fear. As the regime collapsed, it began to execute some of this category of prisoner, particularly prominent Germans involved in anti-Hitler plots who had been kept alive with a view to using them for show trials or other propaganda purposes after the war was won. In April 1945, Admiral Wilhelm Canaris and the theologian Dietrich Bonhoeffer were both hanged at the Flossenbürg concentration camp, while Georg Elser, who had tried to kill Hitler in 1939, was shot at Dachau, where he had been kept in special accommodations pending his public prosecution. "But such killings were merely the tip of the iceberg," the historian Ian Kershaw noted. "With the regime lurching almost visibly out of control, prisoners, whether in concentration camps or in state penitentiaries, lived or died at the whim of their guards or jailers. Violence towards prisoners, already escalating wildly, now became ubiquitous."

On March 4, about eighty of the French officers were taken away. Rumor had it they were going to Bavaria, but no one at the hotel was certain of their fate. Their departure deepened the anxiety of those left behind.

By March 6, the gunfire was heavy and close. Ferries and row-boats shuttled back and forth across the Rhine as people fled the advancing Allies. Word reached the hotel that Cologne, the fourth-largest city in the Reich, had been breached and was about to fall. VII Corps had pushed into the almost empty city, reduced to 10,000 residents from its normal population of 770,000. "Sherman gunners systematically burned out upper floors with white phosphorous while GI infantrymen grenaded the cellars," the historian Rick Atkinson wrote. They often found themselves fighting pensioners, because the main German forces had already left, blowing up the Hohenzollern Bridge, which Gertie had crossed in snowfall months earlier.

On the night of the seventh, the thunderous assault on Bonn, its center just five miles up the river, caused the windows of the hotel to rattle continuously. "The wind that brought the exhilarating sound to me was chilling, but I did not mind it so intense was my excitement," Gertie said. She could hear American tanks rumbling on the other side of the river; she sometimes thought she heard the shouts of American voices. Tracer fire snapped across the river in both directions. There were German machine-gun nests in the forest around the hotel. To the northeast, the town of Siegburg was on fire after coming under assault with incendiaries. Gertie could hear the whoosh of buildings crumpling in sheets of flame. The artillery fire was relentless. Cracks appeared in the hotel walls, and plaster fell from the ceilings. Glass was strewn all over the floor as window after window blew out with a loud crack.

"The effect from our lofty perch was like that of witnessing a pageant of destruction," Gertie said. "It was a wildly exciting experience and I was thrilled as I have never been before."

It was already clear the Germans planned to retreat again. They had begun packing up equipment that afternoon. And as the evening wore on, they moved about the hotel in a state of panic. At seven the following morning, Gertie, having finally gone to bed, was awoken by a soldier flinging open her door.

"*Funf minute!*" he shouted. "*Schnell! Schnell!*

"*Sie sind die letzte . . . verstanden!*" he shouted at Gertie. "You are the last one . . . understand!"

She rushed down to the lobby and stuffed some gingersnaps in her pocket. Outside, a column of the remaining prisoners had been formed to march down the mountain. This time there would be no buses, and some of the French officers were forced to abandon their suitcases. Gertie carried just a small rucksack with a few essentials, including a pint of white wine and her trusty tin hat. She had left a straw bag behind to lighten her load on the forced march.

The column struggled down the mountain in a cold sleet, flanked on either side by German soldiers and detouring around bomb craters, before they eventually reached a main road. There they joined a procession of fleeing civilians—some pushing carts or baby carriages, others on bikes and horse-drawn wagons or jammed into trucks. Some vehicles were abandoned in ditches. Mixed in among the stream of humanity were other prisoners, Russians and Poles, being driven along roughly by soldiers. Camouflaged tanks and military trucks added to the caravan.

Some of the French prisoners were struggling, but Madame Cailliau, Gertie noticed, "was swinging along remarkably well" in the rain. There were occasional breaks to rest, smoke, and munch on the gingersnaps.

By noon, they had reached the village of Oberpleis, where they were taken to the railway station and piled into empty freight carriages so they could shelter and rest. Several hours later, three men, whose smug authority marked them as Gestapo, approached the carriages and scanned the prisoners. One of them nodded at Gertie.

"*Kommen Sie,*" he said.

Gertie said good-bye to her French comrades; she had a list of their names prepared by Prince Michael stitched into the lining of her coat. Her plan was to turn it over to the Allies if she was freed first. She dreaded being separated, believing that she was safer in the company of these "Internés d'Honneur." But protest was futile.

Gertie was deposited in the rear seat of a car and found the straw bag she had discarded at the hotel; clearly, the Germans had already planned her separation from the French group before she left Königswinter.

The SS colonel who had commanded the guard force at the Rheinhotel came over to say good-bye.

"You understand where you are going, do you not?" he said in English.

"No, I haven't the least idea," Gertie replied.

"You will be sent to your people; then you will return to us again," he said.

He offered her a cigarette, turned, and left. The driver started the car and pulled away.

Gertie couldn't decipher what the colonel had meant. Was she going home? Why would she come back?

She thought of *Alice's Adventures in Wonderland,* her favorite storybook, and said to herself, "My, I wonder what in the world is going to happen next?"

Kronberg

A couple of weeks later, Gertie was back in a familiar if wildly improbable stance deep inside Nazi Germany—sitting in a deck chair, the afternoon sun on her face, with a loaded .22 rifle across her knees.

She was scanning the sky for a hawk, which had attacked and killed two chickens at an estate near the town of Kronberg, a rich suburb of Frankfurt. Gertie's German hosts wanted someone to kill the bird of prey. And who better than the American hunter? She had taken yet another strange detour on her journey across the Reich and become a houseguest at the country home of a German industrialist.

After leaving the railway station at Oberpleis, the car carrying Gertie wound through a series of back roads before taking a major highway back toward Limburg an der Lahn and Diez. Progress was slow because the road was pockmarked with craters, some of them wide and deep. Three men in civilian clothes accompanied Gertie. The one in the front passenger seat watched for the approaching dots of Allied planes, and the driver sometimes pulled over to find cover until the threat of strafing had passed. No one spoke to her.

Limburg had been badly damaged since Gertie last passed through on her way to Diez Castle, and the town was reduced to what she described as a series of "scarecrow houses." The car continued south for another thirty miles before eventually pulling over by a large wrought-iron gate in Kronberg. Inside, a large modern home, camouflaged with green paint, sat at the base of a wooded hill with the rolling countryside of the Rhine-Main plain stretching out before its windows and terrace.

One of Gertie's escorts went inside, and ten minutes later a young woman, her coat draped casually over her shoulders, emerged from the house.

"I am Mrs. Grieme," she said in English. "You will stay here with us. We are very glad to have you." Gertie followed her into a comfortable, well-furnished home as one of the men took up guard at the front door. Nena Grieme was warm but appeared unsettled, and it seemed clear to Gertie that her host had taken in this woman in an American uniform only at the insistence of the Gestapo and had not had much time to prepare.

"Would you like a bath?" Grieme asked.

"More than anything else in the world!" Gertie replied, her wide-eyed enthusiasm drawing a smile from the young German woman.

Grieme led her to a bathroom with a large tub and a glass-doored shower, cakes of soap, and piles of towels, and Gertie tingled with excitement. "I soaked, scrubbed and luxuriated in the bath. I lathered myself repeatedly. I washed my hair over and over again, thoroughly for the first time since my capture. Refreshed, I put on my clean change of orange Gestapo underwear and washed out the set I had been wearing."

Gertie emerged to a cup of real, not ersatz, tea.

"This is serving [as] a prisoner de luxe, in the most unconventional and perfect way," she thought.

Gertie was in the residence of Hans H. Grieme, a former executive with IG Farben, the massive chemical conglomerate that was a major contributor to the German war effort. He told Gertie he owned a machine tools factory in nearby Frankfurt.

Grieme arrived home from the city that evening and immediately complained about the guard at the front door, deeming his presence an insult to the dignity of his household. After a loud argument with Gertie's escorts and an equally tense phone call with persons unknown, the guard departed.

Gertie was left with the impression that Grieme, forty-four, soft-featured and sporting thick spectacles, was "a man of unusual influence, for nowhere else in Germany had I seen or heard another person speak up" to Nazi officials in that manner.

He asked Gertie for a promise that she would not try to escape and told her she was his guest until arrangements could be made to send her across the front lines. "My heart leaped at this information," Gertie recalled. "I assured him that I would attempt nothing rash."

The lines were moving closer by the day. At that moment, some American forces had already formed a bridgehead on the eastern bank of the Rhine at Remagen, between Bonn and Koblenz, and U.S. and British forces were staging to cross or push toward the river up and down hundreds of miles of front. "The inner door to Germany," as one Wehrmacht general called it, had opened. And it was Patton's divisions that were staring down Frankfurt, a city that the general called "another brick and stone wilderness" because of the bombing campaign.

Gertie's hosts lived in a twilight world of afternoon walks, evening cocktails, and dinner conversation laced with the dread of approaching ruin. The skies above them buzzed with American aircraft, and the air reverberated with the bombing of nearby cities, including Mainz, Wiesbaden, and Frankfurt, each tremor a harbinger of defeat. Yet, with a kind of equanimity bestowed by the certainty of their fate, the Griemes carefully packed their fine china for safekeeping, drank the best of their champagne, practiced their anti-Nazi lines, and waited, one day falling into the next, like a terminal patient conscious of every breath. "They are punch drunk, waiting to die, about to go down for the last time," Gertie observed.

On that first night, after a glass of French cognac, followed by a mouthwatering dinner of fresh eggs and canned tomatoes, Gertie went to bed and, bereft of the anxiety troubling the Griemes, fell into a deep sleep.

The following morning, a beautiful spring day, Gertie circled the property. The structure, with its sharp lines, flat roof, and terraces, reminded her of "a modern country house in California." The view was spectacular, but the pastoral setting was an illusion. The afternoon brought a series of air raids, and Gertie saw a squadron of B-26 Marauders just overhead before retreating to the house cellar, which was packed with frightened women and children; the Grieme house already held eighteen evacuees from Frankfurt. Grieme, who still commuted in and out of the city, reported later that night that his factory had just been destroyed in a bombing raid.

Gertie settled into a sojourn of killing time and waiting for release while exploring the surrounding countryside with her new companions. Hans Grieme took her on a walk to Königstein im Taunus to get some milk. Her raincoat covered her uniform, and she drew no attention. The village of stone houses and narrow cobbled streets seemed physically untouched by the war, but there were signs warning residents not to provide shelter to deserting soldiers— an increasing problem on both fronts, but especially in the east; Martin Bormann, Hitler's private secretary, estimated that 600,000 soldiers were avoiding combat. "Men who take themselves from the front are not deserving of bread from the homeland," said Himmler, in an appeal to the German people in late January 1945, saying that "shirkers," "cowards," and "weaklings" must be returned to the battlefield. A few days later, he ordered deserters shot "on the spot."

Gertie was impressed that the shops were still honoring ration cards, even though the "American Army at this time was not more than 25 kilometers distant." Mrs. Grieme had been provided with a ration card for Gertie; food was scarce and the family relied on preserved vegetables and fruits from the previous summer to supplement their food allowance.

· · ·

Grieme, relaxing in her presence, began to tell Gertie of his antipathy for the Nazi regime, emphasizing that he was not a party member and only wore a party pin on his lapel when at work; members were obliged to wear it at all times.

"When Hitler came to power . . . we were quite sure he symbolized the hope of the German nation, but now . . . ," Grieme said, trailing off. "But you see he went too far. Before the German people realized it they had an absolute dictator on their hands whose capricious word became the supreme law."

Though she found him "intelligent, worldly, open-minded," Gertie regarded his professed antifascism as a little too expedient. She was grateful for the hospitality of the Griemes, but the evidence of their proximity to the Nazis was everywhere, from his business position and well-appointed home to the Russian girl, a forced laborer, tending the house and garden.

"I thought to myself how easy it was for him to plead his case, in the shadow of doom for the structure he had somehow fitted into by reason of force or convenience," she recalled. The Griemes' wealthy friends, industrialists and bankers sheltering in the countryside as well, also voiced their hostility toward the regime—"no doubt, for my special benefit," Gertie concluded.

As Martha Gellhorn wrote in *Collier's* magazine on May 26, 1945, in a report from defeated Germany, "No one is a Nazi. No one ever was. There may have been some Nazis in the next village, and, as a matter of fact, in that town about twenty kilometers away it was a veritable hotbed of Nazidom . . . We have been waiting for the Americans. You came to befriend us. The Nazis are *Schweinhunde*."

"They knew they were losing," Gertie said, and she was left to wonder if their warmth toward her was sincere or if they expected reciprocity should they soon become prisoners.

Grieme was terrified not by the approaching Americans but by the possibility of the Soviet Union dominating a defeated Germany. It was a fear that the Nazis exploited endlessly to keep their people fighting. To stiffen resistance, for instance, Goebbels fabricated U.S.

propaganda leaflets that he then had dropped on German cities promising all manner of revenge by the Americans, including the forced transfer of all German POWs to the Soviet Union regardless of where they were captured. It was part of a pervasive campaign and had some success, because Grieme, who had picked up some leaflets, believed they were produced by Americans. Beattie noted that German steadfastness "sprang from the devouring fear of 'Bolshevism,' the mass hypnosis with the impending Communist chaos, which the Nazis have managed to invoke."

Grieme argued repeatedly to Gertie that the United States was not fully aware of the Soviet danger. In stressing the matter so emphatically, he might have been following instructions to make a significant impression on Gertie before her repatriation. The OSS learned from the interrogation of one of Gertie's interpreters of such a plan. "Prior to exchange she was to receive a suitable anti-Bolshevist indoctrination under the auspices of the Frankfurt Gestapo," the interpreter Werner Müller told his American interrogators in April 1945. And to some extent Gertie's jailors were successful. She wrote a series of memos for Donovan on conditions in Germany, noting in one the deep fear of Soviet domination.

"The hand that fed the German people would be the one to rule them," Grieme warned.

"America must keep a political hand in our business. It is absolutely necessary," he insisted. "My people cannot control themselves. That has been proven. Left to their own devices, immediately twenty-five or more parties will spring up. That was the situation when Hitler came in. I know my people. They have one inherent weakness: they must be given orders . . . They must learn democracy and your people must stay to teach it."

A German man who occupied a room over the Griemes' garage invited Gertie to walk through the Opel estate, a nearby nature preserve with wild elk owned by the family of the German car manufacturer. The two-hour trek was refreshing but exhausting, and Gertie realized how much of her old vigor had dissipated; she had lost twenty pounds while in captivity.

On another walk, the bombing of Wiesbaden was audible, and Gertie was once again struck by the weirdness of her situation—tromping through beautiful German countryside while just a short distance away German towns and cities were being obliterated by her countrymen. On the way back, looping through Königstein, she passed a medical facility with young amputees out in the courtyard, some of them no more than sixteen, moving about awkwardly as they learned how to use their crutches. On another afternoon, she visited a family farm where she was treated to a thirty-minute impromptu concert. The German farmer's son played piano, accompanied by a Frenchman, a forced laborer, on violin. It was momentarily transporting and deeply peculiar. Everywhere people were looking for ways of escape.

Other days Gertie sat in a chaise longue on the terrace, sunbathing—"delicious"—and rereading *Gone with the Wind*. "Love it," she raved.

The Griemes socialized frequently with friends in and around the town and took Gertie with them—a strange American exhibit in their collapsing world. On one evening, five people, including Gertie, were standing in the corner of a large room, sipping Rhine wine mixed with champagne, mint, and ice, when bombs struck. "The flash which preceded the sound of the explosion lit up the room; then came the reverberations. The walls seemed to sway slightly."

A wall of fire erupted near the house, and black clouds of smoke plunged through its blazing hue. The Germans stood in silence, momentarily frozen with shock, but when the threat of conflagration seemed to subside, they quickly resumed drinking and later produced a gala meal. Gertie wondered about their ability to continue the dinner party. "Were they heartless . . . or did they have the stoutest of hearts?" she asked herself. "Then I remembered we had acted much the same way in London."

Nonetheless, she decided, "It was a queer feeling being an American in enemy country and being entertained."

As she tried to kill the chicken-marauding hawk for Grieme, she asked him if he could contact Gosewisch, saying that she was due some Red Cross boxes. Two days later, the lieutenant and his commanding officer at Diez, Colonel Willibald Köstner, showed up—presenting Gertie with three food boxes, a pair of silk stockings, and a bunch of violets and white snowdrops. "I was delighted with their loot," said Gertie, the incongruity of the flowers and stockings notwithstanding. If nothing else, she was back to smoking Camels and Chesterfields. "So good!" she exclaimed.

Gosewisch and Köstner also carried with them the illusion of a deal with the advancing Americans—with Gertie, in their minds, exploiting her contacts and acting as some kind of intermediary with officers like Patton while they facilitated communication with the German military command. "If only your side wanted to talk, wanted to stop this useless killing right now . . . it could be done with the stroke of a pen," Gosewisch asserted.

Gertie listened politely but didn't have the heart to tell them that their proposal would have no more impact on Patton or any other U.S. general than the "chirping of sparrows to warring eagles."

Roosevelt had announced the policy of unconditional surrender at the Casablanca Conference with Churchill in January 1943 and would brook no dilution of the demand as the war progressed. He believed that abject defeat was the only outcome for a country that had "been engaged in a lawless conspiracy against the decencies of man." The Nazis exploited Roosevelt's position, telling their people it meant "slavery, castration, the end of Germany as a nation," and subjugation, in particular to the Russians. There was no alternative, according to the Goebbels propaganda machine, but to fight to the death. Whether the Allied policy had the effect of prolonging the war, and whether elements of the German high command, or even the Nazi Party, might have sued for peace sooner without it, were the subjects of debate during and after the war. But it was a fantastical notion that a couple of Wehrmacht officers and an American civilian, the tiniest of dots in the continent-wide enterprise around them, could silence the guns. Gertie, unlike her delusional interlocutors, recognized the desperation and folly of the request, but she happily played along with the notion of being a courier, hoping it would speed her release.

Constance

On the evening of March 21, Grieme fetched his best bottles of extra-dry Moët & Chandon champagne from the cellar. Gertie's departure was imminent, and they drank to it.

At 6:00 p.m. the following day, the car to take her away arrived. A Gestapo official from Frankfurt—introduced as Mr. Gay, no first name—who spoke English with a British accent, said he had orders to get her across the German-Swiss border. Nena Grieme prepared a food box with a flask of cognac. Gertie wrote a note for the Griemes to hand to U.S. troops:

To Whom It May Concern:
As an American prisoner of war who has been kindly
treated in this house by Dr. and Mrs. Grieme, I ask that
in return for their hospitality they be given full consideration and a minimum of trouble by representatives of the
American Army. I ask that this note be delivered to Colonel
Charles Codman, Aide-de-Camp to General Patton, or to
the General himself.

—Gertrude S. Legendre, WAC, Simulated Rank, 1st Lt.

They drove first to Frankfurt, which was even more of a waste-land than the city Gertie had seen in late October on her way to

Berlin. "A few facades, like the false fronts of a movie set, stood along our way."

As they continued south in the pitch black, the thunder of warfare was almost continuous. Before she left Kronberg, Grieme had told her that American troops were already in Mainz and Bingen, just to the west. Heavy vehicles clogged the roads, some stuck in mud, which occasionally forced the car to detour around them, with Gay picking out the way with a hooded flashlight. In heavy rain, they passed through endless crowds of fleeing civilians who rapped on the car and begged for help. Their "faces drifted by the window like phantoms."

"I tried to close my eyes to the misery all about me," Gertie recalled. "Old women and children, even tiny tots, struggled along the swamped road carrying bundles and boxes."

Gertie thought the night and its endless cavalcade of shattered humanity would never end. "I was cold and cramped and my heart ached," she said. In the gray mist of dawn, they entered the city of Ulm on the river Danube, now a shattered ghost town because the Allies had targeted some of its factories and destroyed most of its housing stock in the process. Gay directed the driver through the ruined streets and had him stop in front of a stone building with a balcony. "This is my house," he said, before he climbed out and entered. He returned smiling to say his wife and mother were safe. The journey continued south to the Untersee, part of Lake Constance, where they took a ferry to Constance. They arrived in the German city right on the Swiss border on the morning of March 23, 1945.

Gertie immediately remarked on how intact Constance looked. Geography had helped preserve it. Allied bombers could not distinguish Constance from the adjoining Swiss settlements, and the city, which didn't observe a blackout so its lights would blend with those of Switzerland, had been largely untouched by the air campaign.

After leaving the ferry, they drove to a government building in the center of town where Gay—Gertie described him as secretary of the SS office in Frankfurt—went in to finalize her passage across the border. The crossing at Constance had been used repeatedly for prisoner of war exchanges, including the repatriation of seriously wounded soldiers and the transfer of noncombatants.

An hour passed and Gay did not reemerge. When he did reappear, he looked dejected. He stood before the car and spread his arms.

"They will not permit you to leave Germany," he said. "They say you are an American prisoner in uniform, and there is no reason why you can be allowed to cross the border."

"You have my orders, haven't you?" Gertie pleaded, her voice breaking in distress.

"Verbal orders," Gay said. "No doubt written ones will arrive from Berlin someday." Gertie was unsure who had approved her transfer to Switzerland, though Gay's involvement and his reference to Berlin indicated that someone in the Nazi security agencies had sanctioned it. But his arrival in Constance without documents also suggests that the plan to get Gertie out of the country was at least partially improvised and that Gay might have overestimated what he could achieve merely because of his status as an SS official.

"Won't the officials in the Custom House take your word for it? Ask them, beg them!" Gertie implored.

"No," Gay said. "Their word is final. I can do nothing."

They drove to a boardinghouse, where Gertie, inconsolable, collapsed into an armchair.

Gay stood before her, brooding. "I have pledged my word to get you over the Swiss border," he said, though he never said to whom he had given his word—Grieme, Gosewisch, Clemens, or someone more senior.

"What can I do then?" Gertie asked. "I won't go back to Germany. You certainly wouldn't make me do that." She momentarily forgot she was still in Nazi Germany—an unbombed corner, but still Germany.

"There is only one thing to do," Gay said. "You will have to escape."

. . .

The evening train from Singen, just twenty miles to the north, arrived in Constance, unloaded its passengers, and continued into Kreuzlingen, just over the line in Switzerland, according to Gay. The cities of Constance and Kreuzlingen bordered each other, linked by railroad tracks, just west of Lake Constance. Gay said his plan was to get Gertie on the train after the passengers were off and have her hide until it reached Switzerland.

Gertie was suddenly excited.

"And I must get on the train after the others get off," she repeated. "I must hide until it crosses the border."

"Precisely," Gay said. "As soon as you are safely in Switzerland, ask the first person you see to direct you to the nearest phone. Call up the American legation."

He made it seem comically easy to depart the Reich.

Gay returned the cash that had been taken from Gertie after she was captured, which confirmed to her that she had been brought to the border under official purview, though one insufficient to get an exit visa. As darkness fell, Gertie and Gay walked to the train station and on to the far end of the platform. Gertie's coat was again buttoned tight to cover her uniform. She also wore a beret given to her by one of the French generals and carried a rucksack and leather shoulder bag. She was uncommonly nervous.

Within minutes they were joined by a man, never introduced by name to Gertie but obviously part of the plot. Tall and wearing a light overcoat, he spoke rapidly in German to Gay, who interpreted for Gertie. The man said that when she reached Switzerland, Gertie had to say she had been helped by French workers who had arranged rides on trucks that moved her from town to town and that she had been put on the train at Singen, not Constance. Under no circumstances, he said, should she mention that she was helped by Germans. Unspoken was that she could use the same tale if captured on the German side of the frontier. The fiction of French assistance seems to have been a hastily constructed cover to protect Gay and his accomplice. By that moment in late March 1945, there was surely enough general chaos for them to dodge responsibility until the final collapse.

The train was late and the three paced nervously. Ten minutes later, Gay raised his finger and said the train was crossing the nearby Rhine bridge several hundred yards away. Gertie soon saw the round glow of a single light on the lead locomotive.

"Now we go," said Gay as he and the other man walked away down the platform. "Good luck."

Gertie was on her own.

The train rolled past her and ground to a stop. Immediately passengers began to disembark. Gertie blended into the exiting crowd but then turned around as if she had forgotten something and slipped into an empty car. She moved to the center of the carriage and sat in the aisle between the seats, in darkness. She was breathing heavily, sweating, fearful. The minutes passed. Would the train never start?

As she waited in the shadows, she saw a conductor in the next car swinging a lantern and inspecting the seats. She ran hunched through the carriage, slipped into a toilet, and latched the door. She could hear the man approach. He moved on without trying to unlock the door and look inside. "The sound of moving feet almost made me gasp with relief," Gertie said. A second individual passed through, but he also didn't inspect the toilet.

With a whistle from the lead engine, the train began to move. "I think for the first time in my life I was genuinely scared," Gertie recalled.

If the security checks for a train about to leave Nazi Germany seemed extraordinarily lax, they were. The train was not crossing the border. Gay's information was inaccurate.

A few minutes later—what seemed an eternity to Gertie—she heard the brakes being applied. She counted to sixty, opened the toilet door with what sounded to her like a "terrific scraping sound," and crept to the carriage exit. She was uncertain if the conductor or guards were still on the train. The door to leave the train "groaned hideously" as she opened it; every noise was accentuated, sounding to Gertie like an alarm to summon the authorities.

Taking in her surroundings as she peered out from the carriage door, she realized to her horror that the frontier gates were still about a hundred yards up the line, bathed in harsh spotlight. The crossing itself was little more than a four-foot-high gate, a marker sandwiched between two tracks. It still looked formidable to Gertie.

"I was in a tough spot, and knew it," Gertie recalled.

She dropped onto the tracks and began walking in the shadow of freight cars. But when she reached the end of the train, there was still open railyard up to the frontier. As she prepared to dash, she was startled by Gay, who had crept up on her; he had not left but continued to monitor her progress. "He told me to run as fast as I can to the white rails," Gertie recalled. He grabbed Gertie and shoved her forward, almost causing her to fall. She was now out in the open, in a stumbling run, visible in the shroud of light along the frontier. A whistle sounded. It was followed by a shout of "Halt!" Adrenaline surging, Gertie tried to run faster. She could hear chasing footsteps behind her. A German border guard kept shouting at her to stop. *"Ich werde schiessen,"* he shouted, "I'll shoot." He was running beside her. She felt the muzzle of his gun prodding her in the shoulder and then the ribs. The border was just yards ahead. A Swiss guard leaned on the barrier and watched the foot chase.

"Identité?" he shouted.

"American passport," Gertie screamed.

"Lift the gate," Gertie panted to herself. "Oh please God . . . lift the gate." For some reason, the German border guard, still yelling angrily, didn't shoot; "maybe it has been a long time since he killed someone and he did not have the heart to shoot a woman." Or was the guard, too, in on the scheme of Gay and his mysterious colleague? Gertie would never know.

As she threw herself at the gate, it opened, and the Swiss guard pulled her across. Her entry time was recorded as 9:30 p.m. The German stood on the other side, still shrieking at her. It didn't matter.

Gertie was in Switzerland.

Bern

Gertie was soon back in jail, behind a heavy metal door, in a cramped cell with barred windows above her reach. But it was a Swiss and auspiciously neutral cell; her incarceration, she knew, was a temporary detour—a night's sleep at most. "This time . . . jail is not so bad," she wrote in her diary. "Tomorrow may mean liberation."

After falling across the border, Gertie had been brought to a guardhouse where she recovered on a wooden bench with a cigarette, dragging heavily on it as her head rested against the wall. A couple of Swiss guards stood over her, speaking German but smiling and shaking their heads, as if to say, Gertie thought, "Mad fools, these Americans."

She was brought to a room where an officer spoke to her in French and asked how she had reached the border. She repeated the story prepared with Gay about receiving the assistance of French workers and getting on the train in Singen. He didn't challenge her description of events.

"May I telephone the American legation at Bern?" Gertie asked.

"No, not until the district governor sees you in the morning," the officer said, referring to the local official called the *Bezirksstatthalter*.

This first interview over, she was escorted through the streets of Kreuzlingen, the Swiss town she had entered, until they reached the local jail. Her passport was examined and her bag searched before she was directed up a steep flight of stairs to her cell. She kept her toothbrush and was given a basin and a jug of cold water.

After nearly twenty-eight hours on the road, she slept without interruption until 7:30 a.m., when a female guard brought her a café au lait and two thick slices of black bread. She could hear church bells and singing birds.

"I lay there for a long while, thinking how wonderful it was to be alive."

The guard fetched a copy of Balzac's *César Birotteau* from Gertie's rucksack, and she read the novel until the district governor, Otto Raggenbass, arrived. He was accompanied by his wife, who spoke English, and they explained that there were various bureaucratic requirements to be met before Gertie could be handed over to U.S. diplomats in Bern. Already, Raggenbass said, the Germans had filed a formal protest and were demanding Gertie's return, insisting that the Swiss should only have allowed her entry as part of a formal prisoner exchange. The German position was a show of indignation; all sides understood the Swiss would not return an American to the Nazis.

The Raggenbasses invited Gertie to be a guest at their home until her situation had been resolved. She was given a hot shower before she left the station, and as she dried herself, she was already making plans to buy new shoes as well as underwear to replace her Gestapo-issued garments.

"I was almost giddy and felt like skipping as I walked through the prison door into the sunshine," she recalled.

Word quickly reached Bern, Paris, London, and Washington of the escape of an American woman in uniform into Switzerland, and the first OSS cables indicated it was probably Gertie, though they noted that positive identification had yet to be established.

The story also broke quickly in the press. A Reuters report out of Zurich noted that "the first American woman to be captured on the Western Front last night fled from captivity in Germany across the Swiss border."

The story added, "Today she said that she wished to return to the front as soon as possible." Gertie never spoke to a reporter, and the information was no doubt provided to Reuters by the Swiss, but her wish, if she ever actually expressed it, was preposterous, given that she should never have been near the front in the first place.

Sidney was elated. On March 24, the day Gertie left the Swiss jail, Washington HQ cabled the OSS office in Honolulu to instruct officials there to tell Gertie's husband the news but insisted that he be warned not to discuss the matter with anyone—a position that Sidney found mystifying because the story was already on the news wires. "I told the man it was in the papers in New York but he just shook his head and looked mysterious," Sidney told Gertie in a letter.

"If you are out I think it is the most wonderful thing in the world and cannot wait to hear the story of what happened to you and how you have been treated," Sidney wrote. "It must be absolutely amazing . . . You have seen a side that not many men and practically no women have experienced and must be as full of adventures as a pot full of water. No doubt you are thin but I know you are in the best of spirits because that is the one thing that never leaves you."

He later told her that the only thing that made him worry a little about her health was the news that a German soldier had poked her with a pistol as she fled. "In the old days," Sidney said, "you would have given him hell and rapped him on the head with it."

Gertie was soon enjoying herself in Kreuzlingen. On March 25, a Sunday, she biked with Risa Raggenbass to a nearby castle and had a fish dinner by the lake. "Charming day," she noted in her diary.

"I felt at last I was again a free citizen. The sensation was like walking on air."

Her U.S. uniform, which she now wore openly, turned Swiss heads, and she felt like a minor celebrity. "Everyone was staring at me as it was an extraordinary thing to see an American in uniform in the town." On Monday, she had a checkup with a local doctor and went shopping, buying a pair of square-toed oxfords, new underwear, silk stockings, fresh handkerchiefs, a new toothbrush and toothpaste, a Dunhill lighter, and several packs of Swiss cigarettes. "I reveled in the variety of my loot." Photographed by her hosts, Gertie looked thin, her hair a little lifeless, even as she summoned a smile for the camera. The uniform she had worn for six months looked remarkably good—a testament to the care she had taken to keep it clean and presentable.

At the Raggenbass apartment, Gertie took a phone call from a U.S. legation official in Bern who warned her not to talk to anyone about her experiences. (The United States would not establish a full embassy in Switzerland until 1953.) Already, a *Life* magazine reporter had managed to contact her through the Raggenbasses, but she declined to be interviewed.

Her story was drawing some skepticism from the Swiss. In a report on the incident, Raggenbass wrote, "The fact that this woman dressed in US uniform with luggage could move from Kronberg to Konstanz unchallenged, and observations during her border crossing, suggest that her escape was organized and monitored by German officials."

Raggenbass told Gertie he knew she had been escorted to the border by a German. "I flushed a little and then laughed with him as he raised a glass to toast my health and speedy return to my family." He said that his intelligence suggested that Gay would not be punished, because the German did have orders to get her across the border. Raggenbass maintained close relations with the German authorities, including the Gestapo, in Constance, and he acted as an intermediary with advancing French forces the following month, leading to the peaceful surrender of the city. Constance would eventually name a street after him, but his hostile attitude to Jewish refugees during the war would lead to charges that he was an anti-Semite.

Gertie would never learn what decisions lay behind her release—who specifically had ordered it and why. Discussion at the Gestapo of sending her back after she had been indoctrinated about the Soviet threat suggests there was a plan, albeit one that was absurdly futile. Gertie was never going to move the needle on U.S. policy toward the Soviet Union. But by March 1945, some Nazis dwelled in their own phantasmagoria—that they somehow could make common cause with the Americans to avoid total defeat.

On March 27, Risa Raggenbass accompanied Gertie on the train to Bern, the Swiss capital, about 115 miles to the southwest. They spent most of the trip in the dining car as Gertie, making up for the deprivations of prison life, gorged herself.

Security remained a live issue for the OSS because Jennings was still in a prison camp and they had no word on Dickson's fate. A cable from London warned, "Vitally important Gertrude connection this organization be treated on most secret basis. Two other lives still involved and foresee possibility of great danger if there is general relaxation of security in this respect now that she has escaped."

Bern was a city crawling with spies, and the OSS wanted no one to learn Gertie's true employer. All negotiations with the Swiss were handled by the military attaché at the U.S. legation. "Every security measure taken," the Bern branch of the OSS assured Washington and London.

Once she was safely in American hands, Gertie was greeted by Tracy Barnes, an OSS officer and old friend. "Tracy!" she exclaimed when she saw him. "I don't believe it."

Gertie was quietly whisked to the home of Allen Dulles, the future CIA director, who ran OSS operations in Switzerland. He lived in the ground-floor apartment of a large gray sandstone building on a street with old paving stones. The terraced garden behind the house looked out on the river Aare. Gertie was delivered to the study, and a snack of tea with thin watercress sandwiches and chocolate sponge cakes was served.

"Ah, this is too good to be true," she cried, immediately digging in and eating without restraint.

Dulles entered. "Surely this can't be our Gertrude Legendre

returned from the beyond," he said, shaking her hand warmly. The two hadn't met before.

"Surely, I have much to thank you for in getting me safely out of Germany," Gertie began.

"No," Dulles said. "The OSS did not dare touch you, nor did the American embassy. You were 'too hot.' We could not acknowledge you, or have anything to do with you whatsoever."

Dulles said any effort to use OSS channels to contact her might have endangered networks inside Germany as well as the safety of those captured with her. "We could not risk having it known by anyone that you had any connection with our work," he said. "It was too dangerous for you and for the others."

He looked at her closely. "I am surprised you are here at all," he said. "I can hardly believe it."

Others at the OSS were more than disbelieving; they were highly doubtful of Gertie and her story. In a cable marked "top secret" from London to Washington, one official asked whether Gertie was released as part of an exchange or as the result of some kind of diplomatic pressure.

"This important from CE [counterespionage] standpoint in determining her future treatment and disposition," the official wrote. "If she was not subject of exchange or agreed release her story to me would indicate she may possibly be at least unconscious DA [double agent] rpt. DA. I am not satisfied with her story and think she has not told the truth. I also feel that she had been sold a bill of goods and should not be permitted to peddle it in the United States."

That suspicion didn't persist, but it did reflect some of the lingering anger within the organization toward Gertie and Jennings. Upon Jennings's release, Donovan would want him immediately sent to the brig. Others prevailed on him to issue a reprimand and dismiss the navy commander from the OSS instead. Nothing so severe was contemplated for Gertie, but a lot of agency officials were still smarting over her caper, the intelligence gathering it had risked, Papurt's death, and the overall embarrassment to the OSS, especially with the British.

"I think Gertrude was rather contrite," Dulles wrote in a memo to Donovan. "She made no effort to make excuses for her escapade. I did not comment on this one way or another as I had no facts on the background of the case, and it was not my job to take her to task. She obeyed instructions explicitly while she was with us, and impressed me as being a person of a good deal of resourcefulness."

That night Gertie, Dulles, and Barnes ate a fine French meal prepared by the spymaster's staff. "An equal pleasure was that of being served by perfectly trained and friendly French servants," Gertie observed, settling back nicely into her life of expected privilege.

She recounted her story in detail after dinner as Dulles's secretary recorded it. When she reached the part about the Rheinhotel, she cut open the sleeve lining of her raincoat with a pocketknife to retrieve the list of French officers at the hotel that Prince Michael had prepared. With a flourish, she handed it to Dulles, proud of her tradecraft. Dulles scanned the names and asked her if she had read an accompanying note in German.

Gertie's ears burned as the clearly entertained Dulles translated:

For the information of Mrs. Legendre.

So that you may not have a bad impression of the Kreuzlingen police and of the Swiss border control we wish to inform you that we found the attached list of addresses at the time of your arrest by the Kreuzlingen police. As we ascertained that it was only a charitable service for the benefit of prisoners we put the document back in its hiding place. Have a good trip and greet America for us.

Kreuzlingen. 24 March 1945. Der Bezirksstatthalter, Raggenbass

Dulles forwarded it to Donovan as an "amusing sidelight" and sent Raggenbass and his wife flowers and a bottle of champagne.

In his report to the director, Dulles said he judged from the good treatment they had received that the story Gertie and Jennings fed to the Nazis had been believed. He noted Gertie's report of Papurt's death and said that the driver—Dickson—was "presumed safe."

Stripped by Dulles of all her personal papers, including the diary she had kept during her detention, Gertie was driven to Lyon on March 28 and put on the Paris express train. She carried official army orders to maintain her cover. Dulles, following a stern admonition from Washington, cautioned her to talk to no one. "Avoid newspaper reporters above all," he said. "No one must know of your return."

Sidney was eager to learn of her plans. "What do you intend to do now?" he wrote. "Do you think you will stay with the children in New York a while and rest or are you going to be off again on another tour of duty for your organization?"

The children weren't at the front of Gertie's mind; nor was duty. She wanted to hang out in Paris, where she celebrated her forty-third birthday on March 29 with Marian Hall and other friends. She asked the OSS Paris branch for permission to stay in the city despite her orders to return to the United States. "We have seen Gertrude and she is in excellent health," the Paris office cabled Washington. "She personally feels it much better for her to cool off here for 10 days rather than come immediately to States. She will not come near this office, maintains the same cover she had throughout, that is [as a] member of the American embassy, London, and will make no public statements. She urgently requests you reconsider your former cable. Please advise."

Gertie also suggested that rather than return to the United States she and an OSS officer might drive back to the Frankfurt area, now overrun by American forces, to try to find Jennings, the Griemes, and Gosewisch.

Donovan's response was immediate. "This is a very serious matter," he said in a rocket back to Paris. "She will not remain there but will be returned to Washington by first available means."

Gertie was put on a military transport flying to the United States via Iceland on April 2, Easter Monday. "One of those awful flights where you lie on the floor with the GIs who were going home."

"Hated to leave Paris," she complained.

Gertie returned to New York City, where a governess, Miss Evans, who was called Mamie, and a maid, Rose, had been raising her children. "One afternoon, long red fingernails tap-tap-tapped against the frosty glass of our front door," Bokara, the younger daughter, then four, recalled. "Mamie opened the door to a strange woman with dark hair and small brown eyes, dressed in a black suit. I ran to hide but Mamie caught my arm.

"Say hello to your mother, Bo," she said. "She's home from the war."

Brandenburg

At 4:00 a.m. on January 12, 1945, the Soviet Union launched its final push into the Reich. Hitler's forces were vastly outnumbered—in infantry, tanks, guns, and airpower—and the offensive was devastatingly swift. By the following month, the Wehrmacht had ceded large tracts of East Prussia, East Brandenburg, and Silesia, a key industrial sector for the Nazi war machine, and major cities, including Königsberg and Breslau, were besieged. Hitler's command center near Rastenburg in East Prussia, called the Wolf's Lair, was overrun. Auschwitz was liberated on January 27, laying bare the depravity of the regime.

The scale and success of the Soviet onslaught was not immediately apparent to many in Berlin. "We know no more about [the offensive] than the bare fact," Beattie noted in his diary on January 13, "but think it's significant that the High Command speaks of 'heavy defensive fighting' everywhere and makes no claim to have halted the drive." Over a week later, Beattie observed that "the public is interpreting the news at its worst, and for the first time I can see real signs of panic in the people outside the camp."

German civilians by the tens of thousands were fleeing west—better to face frostbite and starvation than the advancing Soviet troops whose thirst for vengeance, in the form of summary execution and rape, was living up to Goebbels's propaganda and accelerating the stampede. As refugees poured into Berlin, initially sheltering from the frigid cold in train stations and makeshift shelters, the Nazis began to convert what had been camps for prisoners and forced laborers into centers to house the displaced. Prisoners like Beattie had to leave the capital to make room. He was transferred on January 25 to Stalag III-A, a POW camp in the market town of Luckenwalde, about sixty miles south of Berlin.

At Anhalter station, as he departed, he witnessed the chaos of a city in its death throes. The train station was full of refugees from the east "screaming, shoving, and crowding their way to the emergency soup kitchens, to the toilets, to the waiting rooms and above all to the trains that might carry them farther away from the Russians."

The German civilians on the train out of the city seethed with anger, disillusionment, and fear. The average German, Beattie concluded, "hates Hitler and condemns him bitterly, not because Hitler plunged Europe into chaos, not because he trampled over a dozen 'inferior' nations or because he ordered the mass destruction of millions of human beings, but purely and simply because Hitler, who told the average German he was of *Herrenvolk* and gave him the dream of world domination, had failed to bring it about."

The camp at Luckenwalde held seventeen thousand men, including more than six thousand Americans, their numbers swollen by POWs transported to the facility from the east, many force-marched there. The prisoners endured "mediaeval conditions of filth," and the camp's few medics were overwhelmed by rampant dysentery, pneumonia, frostbite, and depression, all compounded by malnutrition. Thousands of Russians were buried in mass graves on the camp's perimeter, the victims of typhus and willful brutality. Frantic prisoners, acutely aware of how close the Red Army was, prayed for liberation before they too were killed by disease, starvation, or Nazi zealots.

One measure of the increasing desperation of the regime was an attempt to distribute pamphlets soliciting fighters from among the POWs at Luckenwalde. "Soldiers of the British Commonwealth!

Soldiers of the United States of America!" the missive began, before declaring that a final conflict with the Russians was also "the decisive battle for England, the United States and the maintenance of western civilization . . . Are you for the culture of the West or the barbaric asiatic East?"

It asked the POWs "as white men to other white men" to volunteer to fight with the Nazis in return for repatriation via Switzerland when the offensive was won. There were no takers.

The Wehrmacht was being decimated by the Russian advance; losses on the eastern front in the first two months of 1945 numbered 450,000. Regular forces were being supplemented with the poorly equipped and untrained older men of the Volkssturm, a recently formed national militia, and the boys of the Hitler Youth movement for the final defense of Berlin. Hitler would not contemplate surrender or even the possibility, however remote, of a negotiated end to the war. On February 4, 1945, the Big Three—Roosevelt, Churchill, and Stalin—gathered at Yalta for several days of meetings and reaffirmed the policy of unconditional surrender. Germany would be divided, the Nazi Party would be abolished, and its leadership would be prosecuted for war crimes. "I've always said there can be no question of capitulation," Hitler said in response to the announcement.

The Anglo-American bombing campaign intensified. Just before Yalta, on February 3, Berlin was struck by fifteen hundred American planes that dropped more than twenty-two hundred tons of bombs, the heaviest raid of the war on the capital. In the government district, the Reich Chancellery, Gestapo headquarters, and the Foreign Ministry were hit. Nearly three thousand people were killed; Allied planners had hoped for thousands more dead.

The firebombing of Dresden, killing twenty-five thousand, occurred on February 13 and 14. Separately, Operation Clarion targeted small-town Germany that month to remind its burghers they were not immune to the destruction. Goebbels wanted to kill thousands of Allied prisoners of war in retaliation for the relentless aerial bombardment.

Among those prisoners was Doyle Dickson, still recovering from his wounds. Like Papurt, the other casualty of Gertie's joyride to Wallendorf, Dickson first was taken to the POW hospital at Limburg but was subsequently moved east to Stalag III-B. That was a camp for enlisted men in Fürstenberg, about seventy-five miles east of Berlin on the Oder River. It was a vast facility that held over twenty thousand Russians, French, Serbs, and other nationalities, including nearly five thousand Americans captured in North Africa or on the western front.

The camp was evacuated on January 31, 1945, as the Red Army closed in, and most of the prisoners were moved to Luckenwalde, where Beattie was being held. Dickson, however, was housed some distance away, in a makeshift hospital in the city of Brandenburg, just west of Berlin. The Germans were using the facility to treat wounded POWs, and it was staffed mostly with American, Yugoslav, and French POWs who were either doctors or medics.

On March 31, the hospital was struck by bombs in an Allied air attack on Brandenburg. Dickson was among eighteen American prisoners killed. He had just turned twenty-one that January.

By the second week of March, the photographer Margaret Bourke-White was up in one of the twin spires of Cologne Cathedral looking down on the ruined city and across the Rhine to its eastern bank, still held by German forces. The iron arches of the Hohenzollern Bridge lay crumpled in the water beneath her. On the door of the cathedral, a sign read, "YOU ARE NOW IN COLOGNE, COMPLIMENTS 1st Bn. 36th Armd. Inf. Reg., Texas Spearhead."

The *Life* magazine journalist was back at the center of the action. After she did penance in Italy, where she again demonstrated her skill and grit, the army lifted its ban on her covering the invasion of Germany, though not without some caveats. "Never let that woman out of your sight," the commanding officer of the division she was assigned to warned her minder, a young rifleman. She was traveling with part of Patton's Third Army, and Bourke-White photographed the general at his headquarters. "Don't show my jowls," Patton shouted. "Stop taking pictures of my teeth." Bourke-White did make sure to show the newly acquired third star on Patton's steel helmet as the general looked away to the left, his preferred profile.

Patton sent his forces across the Rhine at Oppenheim, south of Mainz, on March 22, stealing a march on British field marshal Bernard Montgomery as the main American and British thrusts began the following day. "I want the world to know that Third Army made it before Monty starts across," said Patton, who took a symbolic piss from a pontoon bridge as he traversed the river and then picked up some souvenir dirt on the far side "in emulation of William the Conqueror."

The Allies—ninety divisions facing what was in effect two dozen German divisions—now began to sprint across Germany. The fighting was still intense, with more than ten thousand U.S. soldiers killed in action in April 1945, a monthly total higher than in June 1944 after the D-day landing. But the outcome was certain. "We correspondents were hard-pressed to keep up with the march of events," Bourke-White recalled. "No time to think about it or interpret it. Just rush to photograph it; write it; cable it."

When she entered Frankfurt, she had to drive carefully to avoid the "mangled remains of the dead on the street." She observed German women emerging from their cellars, picking magnolias and lilacs from among the city ruins. "It was a sense of return to life that had impelled them to fill their arms with all the pink and purple boughs they could carry."

The Griemes, too, survived to see the blooms of spring. They managed to hand Gertie's note to Patton's troops and, in turn, sent a message to their former guest via the American soldiers who had overrun their town. The message was passed to a *Chicago Sun* reporter who wrote a story about Gertie and the Germans. "We hope you arrived in Switzerland all right and are well," the Griemes wrote in early April. "The Cherry trees are blossoming here now and Spring has come in full. How about spending Easter here in the 'House under the Trees'?"

A week later, Bourke-White entered Buchenwald, the concentration camp whose main entrance displayed the words *"Recht oder Unrecht, mein Vaterland"*—"Right or Wrong, My Fatherland." Bourke-White suddenly wished that the bright April sun would melt away so that she wouldn't have to confront the horror before her. She photographed the skeletal figures staring back at her with little or no reaction amid the sickening charnel: the heaped corpses; the lines of hooks on the walls where prisoners were garroted and hung; the block for gruesome medical experiments; the dissecting room where gloves for the commander's wife were fashioned from human skin; the ovens to dispose of the dead. "Using the camera was almost a relief; it interposed a slight barrier between myself and the white horror in front of me," Bourke-White wrote in her book on Germany, *"Dear Fatherland, Rest Quietly,"* which was published in 1946. Its dedication read, "For M.J.P. who died too soon."

Buchenwald was the first major concentration camp liberated by American troops, and Patton, enraged, ordered one thousand citizens of nearby Weimar to be brought to the facility to bear witness, and his GIs, equally disgusted, forced twice that number to walk through the camp. Bourke-White captured them covering their noses and mouths from the stench, turning their faces away as they passed the stacks of corpses.

"We didn't know. We didn't know," the Germans insisted, forming what Bourke-White said was the beginning of "a national chant."

"You did know," the camp survivors replied.

Jennings was among the first American POWs to be liberated. After the last of his interrogations, he had been transferred to a prisoner of war camp at Wetzlar, about thirty miles northeast of Diez Castle. He survived a long bout of pneumonia that winter as well as the bombing of the hospital where he was being treated. While he was ill, his weight fell to 105 pounds. When he recovered, Jennings served as camp librarian and executive officer to the senior American officer at the facility.

On the morning of March 27, 1945, the camp's guard force abandoned their posts, taking eighty-three prisoners and leaving behind the sick and wounded with a handful of officers, including Jennings. Later that morning some German troops who had been fighting in the vicinity retreated into the camp and surrendered to the remaining prisoners. Sporadic, heavy fighting continued into the night, but the following morning an American officer drove a jeep into the camp. The gates were already open and the watchtowers were manned by U.S. troops.

By April 3, Jennings was at OSS headquarters in Paris. Donovan, still furious about the Wallendorf incident, ordered him immediately returned to the navy and recommended that he be held in the brig until disciplined. "His actions exposed OSS to great criticism and discredit and gravely reflects on his suitability to continue holding a Naval commission," Donovan wrote. Jennings was formally reprimanded by the OSS, but it was not included in his navy record. He returned to the United States, where he was honorably discharged.

Jennings and Gertie met for lunch at the River Club in Manhattan in early May 1945 to reminisce but then fell out of touch. "I guess we both got away awfully lucky," Gertie concluded.

The war ended badly for Gosewisch; his mother was killed, shot through the head and back, in early April 1945, and the family home in Eitzendorf, near Bremen, was destroyed. Gosewisch was captured by Americans who were curious about his background in the United States. An FBI report from an agent accompanying troops in the field noted that he "acted as an interrogator in a case of considerable importance," referring to Gertie, but said "there is presently no reason to believe that Subject played the role of an espionage agent while located in the U.S." American officials didn't deem him important enough to hold, and he was released in early June, returning to his destitute wife and two children.

On the morning of April 21, the day after Hitler's birthday, when Soviet guns first began to shell Berlin, German guards abandoned the Luckenwalde camp, leaving the prisoners to manage themselves. The following morning a small Russian armored car pulled in, sparking raucous celebrations. The driver was mobbed, kissed, and tossed repeatedly in the air to shouts of "U-rah! U-rah!" from his compatriots. To the immense frustration of many of the prisoners, however, it took another two weeks before the various militaries began to organize their evacuation. There were still large pockets of German forces in the region, and the POWs were forced to sit on their hands as the Russians conducted mop-up operations—"free men unable to taste freedom," Beattie lamented.

At dawn on May 4, Beattie was driven out of the camp by two American reporters, one from his own service, United Press, and the other from *The Baltimore News-Post*. They crossed into a U.S.-controlled zone near Wittenberg and within minutes, as Beattie recorded with glee, were eating a breakfast of grapefruit juice, pancakes, bacon, and real coffee from a GI chuck wagon. Three hours later Beattie was on a military shuttle plane that touched down in Weimar, Nuremberg, and Regensburg before finally heading for Paris.

By evening, he was drinking champagne cocktails with friends. He had burned his lice-ridden uniform, taken a long bath, and eaten "three good American meals" over the course of the day. "My hotel bed," Beattie noted, "has a thick soft mattress, and sheets."

Madame Cailliau's liberation and return to France took longer and involved one of the last and more unusual engagements of the war, a battle that saw U.S. and regular German soldiers together fight troops from the Waffen-SS, the military arm of Himmler's organization.

Hours after Gertie's departure to Kronberg and the Griemes' house, Cailliau and her husband were also separated from the group of French officers, along with the German prisoner who claimed to have been Hitler's friend and the man's invalid sister. Under guard, they traveled slowly by train, truck, and foot into southern Germany.

On April 13, they arrived in Munich, where the two Germans were released. The Cailliaus, escorted by four soldiers, continued on to the village of Itter, about sixty miles south of Munich, just over the border in Austria.

Dominating the village was a thirteenth-century castle that had been a hotel before the war but was seized by the SS and turned into another facility for French VIP prisoners. It was designated a satellite facility of the Dachau concentration camp, just outside Munich, and drew its guard force as well as forced laborers from there.

The castle sits at a height of 7,500 feet, and it was a tough hike up. The Cailliaus were exhausted when they finally crossed the bridge to the gatehouse entrance on April 15. They were almost denied admission by an SS lieutenant who at first refused to accept the transfer of more prisoners into his custody. Madame Cailliau said they looked like "vagabonds." The name de Gaulle, however, quickly opened the prison gates.

The wall above the castle's entryway had been inscribed with a famous line from Dante's *Divine Comedy:* "Abandon hope, all ye who enter here." It was a salutary warning. The SS captain and commander at Schloss Itter was Sebastian Wimmer, a thuggish former police officer from Bavaria who joined the SS in 1935 and went on in 1939 to operate behind the German lines in Poland as part of a unit killing Jews, Polish nationalists, Catholic clergy, and other resisters. He also served at the Majdanek concentration camp in Poland before he transferred to Dachau and from there to Itter in 1943.

The Cailliaus found an astonishing who's who of French politics at the castle: the three-time former French premier Édouard

Daladier—Chamberlain's co-signer at Munich—and the man who replaced Daladier as premier, Paul Reynaud. They despised each other with a spitting vehemence. Also present and unhappy to share the same prison were General Maurice Gamelin, the French army chief when war broke out, and the man who preceded and succeeded him in that position, General Maxime Weygand.

Gamelin, a Daladier appointment, was fired by Reynaud on May 18, 1940—eight days after the German blitzkrieg began to overrun French forces. Reynaud replaced Gamelin with Weygand, a decision he later regretted after the general joined the government of Philippe Pétain and sued for peace rather than keep fighting. "Traitor, collaborator!" Reynaud greeted Weygand when he saw him at the castle.

The Itter group also included some former members of the Vichy government—François de La Rocque and Jean Borotra—as well as their ideological opposites, the French trade unionists Léon Jouhaux and Augusta Bruchlen.

Unlike at the Rheinhotel Dreesen, where political differences were stifled for the overall comity of the group, the castle at Itter was a nest of open enmities. Fourteen prisoners in all with the arrival of the Cailliaus, the French VIPs "could not possibly have been more politically diverse, more determinedly irascible, or more obstinately quarrelsome," as the historian Stephen Harding put it.

They were in the end forced to cooperate with one another to ensure their collective survival. On April 30, 1945—the day Hitler committed suicide in Berlin—Eduard Weiter, the commandant of Dachau, arrived at the castle. He had ordered the execution of two thousand prisoners before fleeing the death camp, and the prisoners at Itter became aware of the atrocity when he drunkenly boasted of it to Wimmer. They began to fear for their own lives. Weiter's plan, however, was to emulate his führer; he did so with a shot to the heart that failed to kill him. He finished himself off with another shot to the head.

The castle's guard force fled on the morning of May 4, and the French armed themselves with weapons the Germans left behind.

The nearest Allied troops were still more than a dozen miles away, and Waffen-SS units were in the immediate vicinity—troops who might seize the castle as a last redoubt and execute its French occupants.

Two of the castle's forced laborers—a Yugoslav named Zvonimir Čučković and a Czech cook named Andreas Krobot—volunteered to go out and alert any American forces they could find to the castle's stranded prisoners. Čučković eluded the Waffen-SS units and found his way to U.S. forces in Innsbruck. Krobot was also fortunate and stumbled into Wehrmacht soldiers who were intent on surrendering to the Americans. Their commander accompanied Krobot to the U.S. lines.

Instead of detaining the Germans, U.S. forces pressed them back into action, and a small joint U.S.-German group of troops fought their way into the castle. "The arrival of the eagerly anticipated rescue force left Castle Itter's French 'guests' decidedly unimpressed," wrote Harding, especially at the sight of armed Germans.

The French and their unlikely allies were soon fighting together, however, as Waffen-SS troops attacked the castle. They kept them at bay until a second group of American soldiers, drawn by Čučković's pleas, arrived and the SS troops were scattered. It was among the last skirmishes of the war and the first combat in which U.S. and German soldiers fought together.

The French were taken to U.S. headquarters in Innsbruck and within days were back in Paris. Separately, the other French prisoners who had been held at Bad Godesberg were also liberated from various locations in southern Germany.

"It was intoxicating to feel free," Madame Cailliau said.

On May 7, 1945, General Alfred Jodl, operations chief for the Wehrmacht high command, and Admiral Hans-Georg von Friedeburg signed the surrender papers at Allied headquarters in Reims, France.

"Do you understand the terms of the document of surrender you have just signed?" Eisenhower asked.

"*Ja. Ja,*" the two general officers replied.

A short time later, the supreme commander dictated a message to his troops: "The mission of this Allied force was fulfilled at 0241, local time, May 7, 1945, Eisenhower."

Across the Continent, twenty-five thousand GIs lay in unmarked or unregistered graves, Doyle Dickson among them. After the March 31 attack on Brandenburg, a group of French POWs was commandeered to bury the dead in a graveyard. In an effort to help with future identification, each grave was marked by a wooden stake with a metal plate with a name and number that was supposed to match a number on the coffin below.

The Dickson family had first been informed of Doyle's capture on October 27, 1944, and the news was received "in good spirit by his mother and father," the OSS noted in a report. On July 19, 1945, the family's spirits soared. A captain in the OSS told Dickson's mother, Amy, that Doyle had been released from a POW camp and would be coming home soon. For Dickson's parents, the notification—coming two months after the end of the war, when they had had no word from Doyle—must have come as an enormous relief.

How the military made such an egregious error is unclear. Nine months later, after finally having been informed that her son was dead, Amy Dickson wrote to Major General Edward F. Witsell, the adjutant general, or chief administrative officer, in the military, to demand an explanation. She told him that given the confusion surrounding her son's circumstances—his body still had not been located—she could not, despite the death notice, entirely give up the hope that he might be alive.

"I cannot understand why I was told [about his release]. Cannot see any reason for it," Amy Dickson wrote on March 18, 1946. "If the Captain was mistaken why does he not acknowledge it but since he has not I cannot seem to give up all hope that my son will return yet."

Amy Dickson went on to ask, "Where is my son buried and may I visit the grave?"

She wouldn't get an answer for three more years.

A French doctor who was present during the bombing eventually told the American Graves Registration Service approximately where the U.S. servicemen in Brandenburg were buried, but the city was in the Soviet sector, and as tensions between the occupying powers grew, U.S. officials found access "extremely limited," according to military documents. The Graves Registration Service had no specific information on which servicemen might be buried there except that there were eighteen Americans interred in the city.

On May 1, 1946, Witsell, the adjutant general, wrote back to Amy Dickson. "Your desire for further details concerning the death of your son is most understandable and I sincerely regret that nothing can be added to the information furnished in previous correspondence," he said. "The official report of death was based on information discovered in captured enemy records and on statements obtained from liberated prisoners of war who were imprisoned in the same camp with your son."

A few weeks later Witsell's office told her, "You may be assured that the American Graves Registration Service is endeavoring to locate the graves of our deceased military personnel. This practice will continue until every means of locating the graves has been exhausted."

U.S. military officials continued to press for access to Brandenburg and in the summer of 1947 found the remains of thirteen GIs from among the eighteen believed buried in the city. (The remaining five were found by a French team in September.) On one grave, the name on the metal plate was "Dickson," but there were no other tags or identification with the remains.

The eighteen bodies were transferred to the Ardennes American Cemetery in Belgium, where the body suspected to be Dickson was held as "X-4222" pending positive identification. When the military eventually compared Dickson's dental records with those of X-4222, there was no match, however, forcing officials at the cemetery to examine the records of all eighteen men transferred from Germany.

The Dickson dental chart was then found to be in "exact agreement" with the body buried as Private First Class Niles C. Ballard, a West Virginian who had been serving as a medic in the 168th Infantry Regiment, 34th Infantry Division. (Ballard was subsequently identified as the body designated X-4222.) The mistake was made because Ballard's driver's license had somehow ended up in Dickson's clothing when the bodies were first disinterred in Brandenburg.

In November 1949, the military wrote to Dickson's parents to let them know that they had finally identified the remains of their son. "I regret that it was not possible to furnish you with this information sooner, however, I feel sure that you realize the necessity of first completing the investigation. Remains have been casketed and are being held in above-ground storage pending instructions from the next of kin."

The Dicksons decided to repatriate Doyle's body rather than have him buried at the U.S. military cemetery in Belgium. His casket left the port of Bremerhaven on May 26, 1950. He was buried on July 26, 1950, at the Fort Rosecrans National Cemetery by the Pacific Ocean in San Diego.

Papurt was buried in the Lorraine American Military Cemetery and Memorial in the French town of Saint-Avold, just eighty miles south of Wallendorf.

Papurt's brother, Sol, wrote to Gertie after the war to learn what he could about Jerry's fate. Gertie drafted a reply but it's unclear if she sent it as the OSS, which she informed about the communication, said it was better that the agency respond to the Papurt family.

Gertie's draft letter recapped the events of September 26, 1944, and the wounding of Papurt but without—perhaps kindly—ever admitting there was no purpose to the trip to Wallendorf beyond sightseeing.

"Major Papurt was great company," Gertie wrote. "He had lots of courage and guts and, although I only met him for the first time on our trip to Wallendorf, I shall keep a happy souvenir of a cheerful personality who was calm and humorous in an emergency."

Gertie apparently never learned of Dickson's death and didn't have to reckon with her role in the decisions that led to it. The harrowing memory of the trembling, wounded young man—whose name, she believed, was Dick—faded into idealization. In her memoir she wrote, "It is the picture of Dick I choose to keep in mind when reflecting on the general character of the American GI in the war just passed: boyish, uninhibited, courageous, resourceful, nonwhimpering and with spirit unbroken."

Epilogue

Back in New York City that summer of 1945, Gertie was quickly unhappy—at Sidney's continued posting in Hawaii as the war in the Pacific ground on; at the seeming obliviousness of her compatriots to the hardships of conflict; and at the demands of her children, who, once they had their mother back, wanted her undivided attention. "To try and interest myself in Peter Rabbit . . . nearly kills me," she complained.

"N.Y.C. is a terrible comedown," she told Sidney. "Everyone fat, bored, overfed, sodden with liquor [and] stupid." Gertie, despite her disdain, feasted just as avidly on the bounty of the home front, telling Sidney she had put on five pounds and would soon turn into a blimp. "The food is all too astounding for words and I haven't stopped drinking milk and orange juice for a minute—to say nothing of ice cream—soft shell crabs, asparagus and soft boiled eggs."

She was also discovering, to her dismay, that there was little interest in her time as a prisoner. As Nazi Germany surrendered, the demand for war stories flagged, and Gertie's approaches to magazine editors were discouraging. "It's too late . . . now I am told."

Nor beyond the first stories of her escape had there been much interest in the press in following up on her story, and she suspected OSS-imposed censorship. The press had been "completely throttled," she told Sidney. "Not a mention of my name in any papers so far." The *New York World-Telegram* noted on April 12 that details of her experiences must remain secret "for the duration" but that she had "never looked more attractive than when glimpsed yesterday" in Manhattan.

Gertie was also frustrated that the OSS was not returning her papers, including her POW diary, and insisting that in any story or book she might write, she could not identify the spy organization, a restriction that would drain much of the drama from her account. "The whole thing as you may guess is under such an absurd cloud of secrecy that I hardly know my own name," she told Sidney, adding in a later letter, "I think it would make a great seller if it is ever allowed to be released."

Gertie, unlike Jennings, left the OSS on good terms. Donovan wrote to tell her, "You have made a real contribution to this organization and I will always remember the enthusiastic interest and intelligent effort you gave to all the duties you were called upon to perform. Most of all, I am glad your understanding is so clear on what could have been a very tragic experience." But Donovan's indulgence didn't negate an OSS conclusion that "the return of these documents to the owner at the present time might prove a source of embarrassment to the Agency and constitute a definite threat to its security."

It would be months before she finally got her papers back, and when she published a memoir in 1947—the poorly titled *The Sands Ceased to Run*—it drew little attention from a public that was too busy catching up on lost time to dwell on yesterday's derring-do.

Gertie stayed in touch with many of the people she encountered in Germany, sending letters, cash, food packages, or other gifts in the first years after the war to Gosewisch, Sebastian, Zieschang, and the Griemes. She also established a foundation to help European cities recover. Its first project was the adoption of Flers de l'Orne in Normandy by the city of Charleston. More than three hundred European cities were adopted by American counterparts as the program was picked up by other municipalities.

She also helped Gosewisch move back to the United States. Trading on his language skills, Gosewisch had been hired after the war as a liaison between British military headquarters and the new German authorities in the city of Hannover. He and his family lived on a farm outside the city and began planning their return to New York. Gosewisch's son was the first to go, facing no barriers because he, like his younger sister, was a U.S. citizen, having been born in Brooklyn.

It took much longer for Gosewisch and his wife to get visas. "How often did I wish together with my wife that I would have never left the States," he told Gertie in a 1946 letter, before asking her to write a letter of recommendation to the U.S. consul in Bremen, which she did.

In his visa application, Gosewisch asserted that his membership in the Nazi Party and other Nazi organizations was "involuntary"—a falsehood—and he held "no rank and was not an officer" in them, so he argued he was entitled to an exemption under U.S. immigration law that would allow him to enter the United States. His visa was granted.

Gosewisch returned to the United States in September 1951, his passage paid for by Gertie. He eventually settled in Columbia, South Carolina, working for a soft drink company. He and his wife became U.S. citizens in 1958, when Gosewisch changed his first name from Wilhelm to William and his wife changed hers from Henrietta to Rita.

He and Gertie occasionally saw each other—polite but fleeting encounters. "Every Christmas he sends me roses and once in a while we lunch and reminisce," Gertie said.

Witnessing Gertie's discontent after returning home, Sidney reminded her she couldn't always live her life at top speed and that her sense of deflation was not unlike the letdowns she had felt when an expedition was over. "We would revel in the luxuries of hot baths and soft beds for a few days and then there would be a strange yearning for sunrises and sunsets. For the cold winds that sweep over one's sleeping bag and whip your cheeks in the morning," he recalled, with a nostalgia that was more Gertie's than his.

Sidney also cautioned that the war against Japan could continue for a long time yet and they would not be quickly reunited. Gertie immediately began to agitate for a move to Hawaii, contacting James Forrestal, her friend who was secretary of the navy, and her contacts at the American Red Cross to find some way out to her husband. But she met the same bureaucratic roadblocks as in 1942 and 1943. The navy would in no circumstance allow the wives of officers to join their husbands on the islands.

Gertie's old suspicions about Sidney's faithfulness returned with a jolt when she discovered from a mutual friend that her husband had opened a dress store with a woman named Gerry in Hawaii. "You have told me nothing about it yourself . . . and I am wondering why the secret from me?" she asked in a letter. "Is it because of your partnership with Gerry that I trust is only a business one—or what?

"From people returning from the island I hear you run a restaurant and a bar also," she added. "You must have quite a setup out there and be busy as a bird dog."

Gertie's feelings of rejection flooded back with the knowledge that Sidney had what appeared to be a secret life, and the discovery prompted a rare instance of anguished introspection in a letter to her husband:

Our life apart is not something either of us will be able to share or understand. We have lived it alone, each separately. We have each had different thoughts, reactions poles apart. We may take up the threads as in the past but the gap between whether for better or for worse will never be known or felt or understood by the other . . .

Maybe to you the time meant freedom. I think it has and it has probably been just what you needed and wanted. To me it has meant courage for I have been lonely in spite of my active full exciting life. I have kept at the highest sort of pitch of activity which has nothing to do with one's inside. Physically busy, mentally occupied but utterly alone. Maybe everyone is really alone all the time as it's hard to ever feel how the other feels, but there is something that makes living worthwhile if you have another person to think of, make them happy and love. As I read this over I doubt if you can follow what I mean as I find it confusing to try and explain and feel I have expressed it very badly. The children don't fill my gap, never have and never will. They are awfully sweet but I can't be satisfied with that.

Although Gertie might not have secured passage to Hawaii, her lobbying seems to have obtained a consolation, albeit a temporary one: a summer assignment to the Advanced Naval Intelligence School in Manhattan for Sidney. And by the time he returned to U.S. Pacific Command in August, Gertie was reassured of his commitment to her.

"How I loved being with you again, what heaven it was to be beside you, to look at you, to feel you—no one on earth Darling has such sweetness—such thoughtfulness, and such charm. I just love you so because I love everything about you," she wrote to him on August 8. "I appreciate your patience with my lousy jealous streak that crops up and eats my heart out—I'll be damned if I'm not going to get the better of it and control it somehow . . .

"Above everything on this earth I want you to go on loving me— it's all that counts, and I know I must conquer jealousy to keep it."

A week later, Japan surrendered, but it would be early October before Sidney was finally discharged from the military. He was awarded the Bronze Star Medal for meritorious service.

That winter the couple were back at Medway, their spread outside Charleston.

"The plantation is something," Sidney wrote to his brother in December, "it is just about three times as much work as the Navy, and never stops."

. . .

On March 8, 1948, Sidney died of a heart attack. He was only forty-four. He was buried at Medway, on a hillock by the lake in front of the house. The Medway staff, led by the head carpenter, who was a Baptist minister, sang "Give Me That Old Time Religion." When the service was over, Gertie was handed a shotgun, which she raised and fired over the grave.

Death seemed to stalk Gertie's family. Her sister Jane's husband, the Italian diplomat Mario Pansa, drowned in July 1946 while swimming at Torre Astura, south of Rome. The couple had emerged unscathed from the war, though not without facing some danger. Pansa was forced into hiding before the Americans reached Rome so he would not be killed by more extreme fascists. He and the Italian foreign minister had been attempting to broker a peace with the Allies.

Morris Legendre and his wife were killed in a plane crash in the Gulf of Mexico in February 1953. Their bodies were never recovered. Two other Legendre brothers also died young.

Gertie never got over the loss of her husband. She died at Medway on March 8, 2000—exactly fifty-two years after Sidney. She was ninety-seven. Gertie had suffered a series of small strokes over the preceding two years but never lost her lust for the life well lived. On her last birthday, her daughter, arriving from California, found her laid up with a "sickly, airless smell of rubbing alcohol and unwashed skin in the room" but still worrying about what Pucci pants or shirt to wear with what suede shoes to her party. She was unable to make it down to see her guests but insisted they stay and have fun.

"The power of dying, of waiting to die, for the same moment Daddy had died, was undeniably the fulfillment of a psychic wish on her part," her daughter Bokara wrote in her memoir.

There had been many more expeditions and foreign trips in the decades after Sidney's death—Nepal, Equatorial Guinea, the Galápagos, the Amazon, and New Guinea, among others. Her last major fieldwork was in 1972, a study of the decline of the pygmy gibbon on the Indonesian island of Siberut in the Indian Ocean. "I consider I was fortunate to have been born in 1902," Gertie said, "to have seen it all in B.T. (Before Tourists)."

There was also a second, calamitous marriage in the 1950s that ended in divorce after five years.

Through it all, she remained the matriarch of Medway. One of the doyennes of postwar Charleston, Gertie hosted a famous annual New Year's Eve costume party at the plantation. She was also a committed conservationist who "gave up all development rights for herself and for successive owners" through the donation of perpetual easements at Medway to the Historic Charleston Foundation and to Ducks Unlimited.

"I want Medway to be a place where the beasts can grow old and die," she said. The plantation was sold by her daughter in 2012.

Gertie, finally, became a terrific, beloved grandmother in contrast to her fraught relationships with her two daughters. "She adored her grandchildren," her grandson Sandy said.

In her heart, to the end, there was always only one man—Sidney. Her ashes—held in a silver horse-racing trophy—were poured around the grounds as well as into a grave alongside Sidney's by the lake at Medway. This time it was Sam the butler who fired the shotgun over the grave. A choir sang "I Got Plenty of Nothing" from the Broadway musical *Porgy and Bess* as the funeral ended. Gertie's daughter Bokara said she chose the song as "a sort of joke." Gertie's elder daughter, Landine, declined to attend the funeral, old wounds still open.

Sidney's portrait by the English artist Simon Elwes continued to hang in the dining room at Medway long after his death.

"Every evening, I sit at one end of the dining room table facing his portrait," Gertie recalled later in life. "He stands there in his shooting jacket with a gun over his shoulder, looking cool and detached at the portrait behind me—that of a young, confident woman looking less like me than I remember. Sidney is exactly as he was. I have no memory of his aging. In my mind, I shall always be married to a young and vital man who sees only the youth in me."

Acknowledgments

The generosity of many people helped bring this book to life. I would like first to thank Harlan Greene and the staff of Special Collections, College of Charleston Libraries, and the South Carolina Historical Society, who warmly welcomed me and went above and beyond to help me navigate the papers of Gertie and her family. Just as gracious were Pierre Manigault and Sandy Wood, Gertie's grandchildren, and Sandy's wife, Sally, all of whom encouraged this work and shared their recollections of Gertie. Thanks also to Gertie's secretary, Doris Walters, for her memories.

Archivists are the great allies of writers, and I want to acknowledge the assistance of Abby Houston and Nicole Westerdahl at the Special Collections Research Center, Syracuse University Libraries; Annegret Wilke at the German Foreign Office archives; Kurt Erdmann at the Bundesarchiv, Abteilung Militärarchiv in Freiburg; Tobias Herrmann at the Bundesarchiv in Koblenz; Heinz Fehlauer at the Bundesarchiv in Berlin; Guido Koller at the Swiss Federal Archives; and Pamela Anderson at the National Archives in Kansas City, Missouri.

Susan Strange is a master of the OSS papers at the National Archives in College Park, Maryland, and she found all that that priceless repository of history had to offer on Gertie. I also thank her for introducing me to Douglas Waller, Wild Bill Donovan's biographer, who was kind enough to provide some pointers as I set out to tell this story and read the manuscript in draft. Joe D. Dickson, John Beattie, and Bruce Beattie provided photos of their uncles. Stephanie Phelan gave me permission to use her uncle's poem about food. And Sebastian Pantel at the *Südkurier* in Constance helped me secure a photo of the border crossing.

I am fortunate to have a wonderful group of friends and colleagues who read early drafts, helped with translations, assisted with my research, or just listened to me as I figured stuff out. Thank you to Souad Mekhennet, Patrick Farrelly, Kate O'Callaghan, Ulf and Ingrid Roeller, Boris and Majda Ruge, Steffen Burkhardt, Joby and Maryanne Warrick, Greg Miller, Julie Tate, Steven Rich, Scott Higham, Dan Lamothe, Ian Shapiro, and Jeff Wilklow. Another tip of the hat to Jeremy Crean and Ronan Farrell and Greg and Bill Finn. And thanks to Marc Bryan-Brown for the author photograph.

For more than twenty years, I have worked at *The Washington Post,* where I was given more opportunities than I ever imagined possible. I'm grateful for the paper's leadership: Jeff Bezos, Fred Ryan, Marty Baron, Cameron Barr, Emilio Garcia-Ruiz, and Tracy Grant as well as the national security team and the editors I work most closely with, Steven Ginsberg, Lori Montgomery, Douglas Jehl, Matea Gold, Tiffany Harness, and Andy deGrandpre.

Petra Couvée, my co-author on *The Zhivago Affair,* is a constant source of support and first helped me realize that book writing was possible. My agent, Raphael Sagalyn, is an indefatigable and formidable cornerman. Kristine Puopolo is a dream editor—deft, insightful, and always encouraging. Thanks also to Daniel Meyer at Doubleday and Brandon Coward at ICM/Sagalyn, who make all the logistics seem easy.

My four children, Rachel, Liam, David, and Ria, are a joy and inspiration as they discover and pursue their own passions. My wife, Nora FitzGerald, is the love of my life, my partner in everything, and always my first reader and best critic.

A Note on Sources

Gertrude Legendre wrote a memoir of her wartime service and time as a POW that was published in 1947 as *The Sands Ceased to Run*. It was a valuable roadmap for me. Some of the dialogue in the memoir was reconstructed by Gertie after the fact, though she did have her diary to prompt her memory and she began writing very soon after her release. There are a number of early drafts of the "Sands" memoir, which sometimes include slightly different details about her experience. When I have used these drafts, I have noted so in the endnotes. I also note there some of the small contradictions between her OSS debriefing and her memoir.

Gertie published a second memoir, *The Time of My Life*, in 1987, and it describes her life from her childhood into the 1950s. She was also an inveterate journal keeper on her trips, an avid letter writer, and an enthusiastic photographer. Her voluminous papers, a trove of rich detail, are held at the College of Charleston's Special Collections, and much of that material is available online at the Lowcountry Digital Library. The Legendre Papers at the College of Charleston also includes the letters and writings of other members of her family, including those of her husband, Sidney. I have corrected minor typos in the letters between Gertie and Sidney.

In addition, there are a significant number of documents on Gertrude Legendre in the files of the Office of Strategic Services at the National Archives in College Park, Maryland, including the debriefing by Allen Dulles in Bern shortly after her escape. Gertie also was interviewed for a CIA oral history of the OSS, which is available at the National Archives.

The U.S. military arrested and interrogated two Gestapo interpreters—Werner Müller and Ursula Zieschang—who were present at the questioning of Gertie in Berlin, and the May 1945 OSS reports on their interrogations provide some German perspective on her detention. Zieschang also typed some of the Gestapo reports on Gertie. In addition, she told her American interrogators that she had read Gertie's entire Gestapo file in January 1945. She also kept her shorthand book of all correspondence dictated by the Gestapo officer in charge of Gertie's case and reread it shortly before her arrest. Unfortunately, she destroyed the document as being compromising. But her American interrogators noted that her memory of the Legendre case was fresh and detailed.

I obtained a limited number of files on Gertie from the Political Archive of the German Foreign Ministry in Berlin, which include notes on conversations between the ministry, the Gestapo, and the Wehrmacht on the handling of her case.

Wilhelm Gosewisch's military book, a record of his service, is held at the Bundesarchiv-Militärarchiv in Freiburg, Germany, and the Bundesarchiv in Berlin holds the IG Farben personnel file of H. H. Grieme.

The OSS files at the National Archives contain documents on the three men captured with Gertie: Major Maxwell Jerome Papurt, Lieutenant Commander Robert Jennings, and Private Doyle Dickson. I also obtained the military records of Jennings, Dickson, and Sidney Legendre from the National Archives in Saint Louis. Papurt's file was not available, having been among the records that were destroyed in the 1973 fire that gutted a significant part of the holdings. Some of Papurt's military records are included, however, in his OSS file.

I was able to read Papurt's wartime letters to the photographer Margaret Bourke-White, which are held in the Margaret Bourke-White Papers, Special Collections Research Center, Syracuse University Libraries.

The National Archives in Kansas City contains the immigration files of Wilhelm (later William) Gosewisch and his wife, Henrietta, later Rita.

The wartime diary of the United Press correspondent Edward W. Beattie Jr., published in 1946 as *Diary of a Kriegie,* was invaluable because he was held at the same time and in some of the same places as Gertie.

Notes

ABBREVIATIONS

GL: Gertrude Legendre
LP: Legendre Papers, College of Charleston
MBW: Margaret Bourke-White
MJP: Maxwell Jerome Papurt
NA: National Archives, College Park, Maryland
PAAA: Politisches Archiv des Auswärtigen Amts (Political Archive, Foreign Ministry)
RG226: Record Group 226 is the group number for OSS files at the National Archives
SL: Sidney Legendre

CHAPTER I

3 the rue Cambon side of the Hôtel Ritz: GL, *Sands Ceased to Run*, 25. All quotations and scene details of Gertie's wartime experience, unless otherwise noted, are from this memoir.

3 Göring had taken over the imperial suite: Mazzeo, *Hotel on Place Vendôme*, 18.

3 inventor of such cocktails as the bee's knees: See Meier, *Artistry of Mixing Drinks*.

4 but surreptitiously helped the Resistance: See Mazzeo, *Hotel on Place Vendôme*.

4 "especially potent. It went straight to my head": GL, *Time of My Life*, 58.

4 "couldn't wait to fit my uniform properly": GL to SL, Sept. 21, 1944, LP.

4 "Do you ever cry because you miss me?": GL to SL, June 13, 1943, LP.

6 Gertie cut off the twirl of hair: Autobiographical sketch, box 147, folder 7, LP.

6 "When Gertrude felt strongly about": SL, *Land of the White Parasol*, 3.

6 "I have to leave my personality": Bokara Legendre, *Not What I Expected*, 209.

6 "I look ahead. I always have": GL, *Time of My Life*, xiv.

7 "Life has moved to Normandy": GL to SL, June 29 and August 10, 1944, LP.

7 "Everyone thrust drinks at us": David K. E. Bruce, *OSS Against the Reich*, 171–74.

7 Claude Auzello, the "elegantly unruffled" manager: Mazzeo, *Hotel on Place Vendôme*, 141.

8 Perrier-Jouët champagne: Atkinson, *Guns at Last Light*, 179.

8 "Her obsession was to see the battle": Anne Perin to SL, Nov. 12, 1944, OSS scrapbook, LP.

8 "summers in Biarritz, St. Jean de Luz": GL, *Time of My Life*, 21.

8 "I am getting used to cold baths": GL to SL, Sept. 21, 1944, LP.

9 "I looked around to see": GL, "Sands Ceased to Run," early draft, LP.

9 Gertie knew Patton from London: OSS Oral History, interview with GL, 17, RG263-e84, NA.

9 "It is always fun to meet the guys": GL to SL, Feb. 18, 1944, LP.

9 "bypass and encircle it, then await": Blumenson, *Breakout and Pursuit*, 590.

10 "accumulated a comfortable fortune": Robert Jennings, Military Record, National Archives, St. Louis.

10 He was scheduled to leave for London: Ibid.

10 three correspondents had recently been captured: Beattie, *Diary of a Kriegie*, 97.

11 "The impossible has happened": SL to GL, Sept. 5, 1944, LP.

11 "Watching their lives": Bokara Legendre, *Not What I Expected*, 33.

11 "Just received this minute": GL to SL, Sept. 23, 1944, OSS scrapbook, LP.

CHAPTER 2

12 "We rode along straight roads": GL, "Sands Ceased to Run," early draft, RG226-e190-f771.

14 Papurt spoke German: MJP to Lieutenant Colonel Hinman, May 30, 1942, MJP personnel file, RG226-e224-box 584.

14 "If they gotta, I gotta": MJP to MBW, n.d., MBW Papers, Special Collections Research Center, Syracuse University Libraries.

14 "He was a dead shot with a pistol": MBW, *Purple Heart Valley*, 95.

14 "One soon forgot his ugly face": MBW, *Portrait of Myself*, 309.

14 his wife in Columbus, Ohio: Sorel, *Women Who Wrote the War*, 241.

16 probe the Westwall and be ready: The Wallendorf bridgehead is described in Charles MacDonald's *Siegfried Line Campaign*, 56–65, from which all quotations on the CCR incursion are drawn.

17 Papurt informed his commanding officer: Sept. 29, 1944, Twelfth Army Group Memos, RG226-e190-f772.

17 Papurt, Jennings, and Gertie took off: GL, POW diary, Sept. 27, 1944, entry, transcript, RG226-e190-f772. (The diary is also held at the College of Charleston.)

18 experiencing a frisson of unease: GL, "Sands Ceased to Run," draft, box 135, folder 7, LP.

20 "The hell you have": GL, "Sands Ceased to Run," early draft, 2, LP.

21 "Isn't that a laugh": GL to SL, July 23, 1943. LP.

21 "The Germans continued to give us": Jennings Report on Time as POW, April 4, 1945, RG-226-e99-box14-f5.

21 Gertie pulled a blanket: GL, POW diary, Sept. 27, 1944, transcript, RG226-e190-f772.

21 but now her training flooded back: GL to SL, July 23, 1943, LP.

22 An eternity seemed to pass: Jennings Report on Time as POW.

CHAPTER 3

24 "But it was my elk": GL, *Time of My Life*, 25.

24 "was a real 'let's get cracking'": Bokara Legendre, "Mummy Was a Wild Game Hunter," *The Moth Radio Hour*, Nov. 2, 2001.

25 "In my view, it is most important": Cochran, "Mr. Lincoln's Many-Faceted Minister and Entrepreneur Extraordinary Henry Shelton Sanford," 74.

26 they communicated through notes: Bokara Legendre, *Not What I Expected*, 34.

26 "less companionship" as they got older: GL, *Time of My Life*, 13.

26 estate estimated at $40 million: Robb, *Sanfords of Amsterdam*, 80.

26 "Horses, my mares, my stable": Ibid., 22.

26 "My memories of those early days": GL, *Time of My Life*, 4.

27 "giant French windows with garlands": *New York Times*, Jan. 7, 2001, RE7.

27 the butler placed theater tickets: Bokara Legendre, *Not What I Expected*, 33.

27 on the back of a baby elephant: Beach, *Medway*, 49.

28 "the treasures were piled high": GL, Essay, Egypt and the Nile, 1924, box 129, folder 11, LP.

28 At the port of Mogadishu: All descriptions of the 1927–28 Africa expedition are from Gertie's journal unless otherwise stated. Diary of African Hunting Trip, 1927–1928, box 129, folder 3, LP.

29 "they are called savages": *Brooklyn Eagle*, Aug. 21, 1929.

29 "swarthy, dark-skinned, bandit-looking faces": Persia diary, box 134, folder 5, LP.

CHAPTER 4

31 "no one thought there could be an end to it": GL, *Time of My Life*, 32.

32 "staged, like a still from some adventure film": Ibid., 39.

33 Visiting Oxford, she met two young Americans: SL to GL, June 22, 1943, LP.

34 "masters in the art of living": Tomkins, *Living Well Is the Best Revenge*, 14.

34 "As far as company is concerned": GL, *Time of My Life*, 53.

35 "There was some question": Bokara Legendre, "Mummy Was a Wild Game Hunter."

35 The existence of the animal: Quinn, *Windows on Nature*, 49.

36 "to bring a vision of the world": Ibid., 12.

36 "the gyroscope that kept our tempers": GL, *Time of My Life*, 79.

36 silver mule from the royal stable: Ibid., 58.

37 It was a hard expedition: All descriptions of the 1928–29 Africa expe-

dition are from Gertie's journal unless otherwise stated. GL, Diary of My African Hunting Trip, 1927–1928, box 182, folder 9, LP.

37 "I am looking forward to seeing the specimens": H. E. Anthony to GL, April 25, 1929, Abyssinia Photograph Album, 1929, LP.

37 Morris was the bigger personality: GL to SL, Feb. 17, 1943, LP.

37 "and the thoughtful quality he had": GL, *Time of My Life*, 64.

38 hints in a letter: SL to GL, June 22, 1943, LP.

39 "I must confess that I was rather proud": GL, *Time of My Life*, 67.

CHAPTER 5

40 "Father had very little money in stocks": Beach, *Medway*, 27.

41 "the thrashing of those damn palm trees": Bokara Legendre, *Not What I Expected*, 36.

41 a total of 7,110 acres: Beach, *Medway*, 43.

41 "Virginia has so much to offer": Plantation Diary, 237, LP.

42 "She loved to entertain": Sandy Wood (Gertie's grandson), interview with author, Feb. 18, 2017, Upperville, Va.

42 "Luncheon was laid under the pines": Beach, *Medway*, 93–94.

42 on Gertie's zebra skins: Ibid., 60.

43 Gertie took a "terrific beating": All descriptions of the 1928–29 Indochina expedition are from Gertie's journal unless otherwise stated. Box 130, folders 12–13, LP.

43 "saddles, zinc-lined chop boxes": GL, *Time of My Life*, 81.

44 "seemed equal only to the Ritz": Persia diary, box 134, folder 5, LP.

44 "It was very fortunate": SL, *Land of the White Parasol*, 3.

44 "in the wickedest city in the world": Ibid., 291.

45 inhaled deeply four or five times: Ibid., 294.

48 "I do hope the U.S.": Persia diary, box 134, folder 5, LP.

48 "With German efficiency, we went": Shooting in Hungary Diary, box 133, folder 3, LP.

48 "Larry is sweet. Very nice": GL to SL, Nov. 22, 1942, LP.

49 "I feel the future and the new horizons": GL to SL, June 7, 1943, LP.

CHAPTER 6

50 Sidney was commissioned as a lieutenant: Sidney Legendre, Military Record, National Archives, St. Louis.

50 Hoover told the White House: Waller, *Wild Bill Donovan*, 86.

51 she wrote to F. Trubee Davison: GL to Davison, June 9, 1942, RG226-e92-box16-f261.

51 "I am physically fit": GL résumé, RG226-e92-box16-f261.

52 "I would stick at a job": GL to David Bruce, June 28, 1942, RG226-e92-box16-f261.

52 "He was the most marvelous man": GL, *Time of My Life*, 147.

52 "All around you anti-aircraft guns": Virginia Cowles, *Looking for Trouble* (New York: Harper & Brothers, 1941), 404–5.

52 "intrepid and madcap": Smith, *OSS*, xii.

52 "Woe to the officer": Ibid., 3.

53 Her background security check: OSS investigation report, Aug. 3, 1942, RG226-e92-box16-f261.

53 "instructed him in what to wear": Martin Clark, *Mussolini*, 70.

53 Her salary was $150 a month: GL to SL, Oct. 19, 1942, LP.

54 "Wartime Washington, in the view of those": Brinkley, *Washington Goes to War*, 144.

55 "We get all the crocks": GL to SL, Feb. 6, 1943, LP.

55 sanctioning bizarre schemes: Waller, *Wild Bill Donovan*, 101.

56 "We don't seem to be doing anything": GL to SL, Oct. 19, 1942, LP.

56 "there are so many damn islands": GL to SL, Nov. 20, 1942, LP.

56 "those sinking burning ships": GL to SL, Nov. 8, 1942, LP.

56 "haunted. He could not have been more": SL to GL, Nov. 29, 1943, LP.

56 "I know more about paper clips": SL to GL, Oct. 3, 1942, LP.

57 "zealous, aggressive and unceasing devotion to duty": Sidney Legendre, Military Record, National Archives, St. Louis.

57 nearly $4 a minute: GL to SL, Aug. 25, 1942, LP.

57 "two fried eggs, three pancakes": SL to GL, Sept. 7, 1942, LP.

57 "I sat between Henry Hopkins": GL to SL, Oct. 16, 1942, LP.

58 "Sat beside John D. Rockefeller Jr.": GL to SL, Dec. 13, 1942, LP.

58 "When I hung up the telephone": GL to SL, March 1, 1943, LP.

58 "Many women's husbands will never come back": SL to GL, Jan. 13, 1943, LP.

58 "a life that was almost mythical": SL to GL, Jan. 20, 1943, LP.

58 "You said I did not understand": GL to SL, Oct. 16, 1942, LP.

59 "I am afraid I selfishly hope": GL to SL, Jan. 4, 1943, LP.

59 "Every night I kiss": SL to GL, Nov. 3, 1942, LP.

59 family lore suggests he wasn't: Sandy Wood (Gertie's grandson), interview with author, Feb. 18, 2017, Upperville, Va.

59 "I do all the work": GL to SL, Oct. 19, 1942, LP.

59 "invisible apron strings of an organization": McIntosh, *Sisterhood of Spies*, 11.

59 "has energy and initiative as well": OSS memo, March 20, 1943, RG226-e190-f772A.

60 "entrusted with the responsibility": GL to Alfred Tozzer, Feb. 19, 1943, RG226-e92-box16-f261.

60 "I should also add a doubt": Legendre correspondence, Feb. 19, March 2 and 11, 1943, RG226-e190-f772.

60 "Would like Legendre to handle crèche": OSS memo, June 10, 1943, RG226-e92-box16-f261.

60 "craves affection": SL to GL, Dec. 31, 1942, LP.

60 "I do believe that the lonely hotel life": SL to GL, Jan. 20, 1943, LP.

61 "didn't much like children around": Bokara Legendre, *Not What I Expected*, 40.

61 "worlds to conquer type of thing": GL to SL, May 11, 1943, LP.

CHAPTER 7

62 "NO Portuguese boat has been sunk": GL to SL, Aug. 17, 1943, LP.

62 Gertie's crossing was smooth: GL to SL, Aug. 25, 1943, LP.

63 "certain it is impoverished and a rather unhappy city": SL to GL, Aug. 22, 1943, LP.

64 Her colleagues took to calling her Mussolini: GL to SL, Nov. 19, 1943, LP.

64 "I am about to flounder out": GL to SL, Dec. 4, 1943, LP.

64 carried a blackjack in her purse: GL to SL, Oct. 15, 1943, LP.

64 the OSS provided a list: Waller, *Disciples*, 159.

65 "Mummy was able to have": Bokara Legendre, *Not What I Expected*, 152.

66 "Why don't I go back to Virginia": GL to SL, July 17, 1944, LP.

66 "a choir of 200 Negro soldiers": GL to SL, Sept. 28, 1943, LP.

66 "white women not to go out": Ziegler, *London at War*, 218.

66 "The Colored Troops are much argued about": GL to SL, Nov. 5, 1943, LP.

66 "You can sit in the Ritz": GL to SL, Nov. 27, 1943, LP.

66 "The streets are full of [British] girls": GL to SL, Sept. 30, 1943, LP.

67 "The Russians are going to be the first": GL to SL, Oct. 29, 1943, LP.

67 "It's quite like old times": Ziegler, *London at War*, 269.

67 "I suppose you read in the papers": GL to SL, Jan. 24, 1944, LP.

67 "It is the biggest, bulkiest": GL to SL, April 18, 1944, LP.

68 "all so sad and frightful": GL to SL, Nov. 27, 1943, LP.

68 "Not a soul in the streets": GL to SL, Aug. 10, 1944, LP.

68 She had been practicing her French: GL to SL, Nov. 10 and 14, 1943, LP.

68 "Every big shot I know is over there": GL to SL, Aug. 15, 1944, LP.

69 "The pilotless plane, flying bomb": Orwell, *As I Please*, 177.

69 "One is apt to sleep anywhere": GL to SL, June 29, 1944, LP.

70 "The new development of the Germans": MJP to MBW, June 17, 1944, MBW Papers.

70 "Those Big Shots are all really swell": GL to SL, Aug. 29, 1944, LP.

CHAPTER 8

73 "a nonentity in the huge business of war": Beattie, *Diary of a Kriegie*, 3.

73 slipped Jennings some papers: Robert Jennings Report on Time as POW, April 4, 1945, RG226-e99-box14-f5.

77 "Nearly fried to a crisp": GL, POW Diary, transcript, RG226-e190-f772.

77 "The reaction [to] our terrific might": GL memo, Terror Bombing, RG226-e190-f772.

78 about eight feet by ten: GL statement, Bern, Switzerland, March 28, 1945, RG226-e216-wn27600.

79 American prisoners called "mucker fuck": GL, "Sands Ceased to Run," early draft, 8.

80 "Have no cigarettes, no books": GL, POW diary, Sept. 29, 1944, entry, transcript, RG226-e190-f772.

CHAPTER 9

81 "The party was missing in action": Twelfth Army Group memo, Sept. 29, 1944, RG226-e190-f772.

81 calling Gertie a "loose cannon": McIntosh, *Sisterhood of Spies*, 129.

81 "Her knowledge of these activities": Ibid., 141.

82 "has acquired a tremendous fund": Donovan to McCloy, Nov. 4, 1944, RG226-e190-f772.

82 Donovan personally called Sidney: OSS memo, Jan. 7, 1945, RG226-e190-f772.

82 "Naturally, I had gone over": SL to GL, April 6, 1945, LP.

82 "I'm one of the oldest active jumpers": MJP to MBW, July 13, 1944, MBW Papers.

83 "detection and prevention of the enemy's espionage": SCI, T Force, Report on Missing Personnel, Sept. 29, 1944, RG226-e190-f772.

83 "passes bearing wording of a less": OSS memo, Sept. 19, 1944, RG226-e190-f772.

84 "My general feeling is that": Pearson to Forgan, Oct. 23, 1944, Papurt incident, RG226-e122-box4-f1.

84 under the heading "SCI": The accounts of Gertie, in her Bern statement and memoir, and Jennings, in his statement after being liberated, differ in an important way on what the heading of the Papurt document included. Jennings said it was the letters "SCI" only; Gertie said it was "SCI Agents." If it was the latter, the Germans would surely have seized on the word "agents," and their interrogations would have been much more focused and grueling. The letters "SCI" alone left enough ambiguity for the prisoners to dissemble.

84 One was Lieutenant Pierre Haas: interrogation of Ursula Zieschang, April 26, 1945, RG226-e92-f30126.

85 "told him I was not up": Dulles debrief of GL.

85 "Does not believe me at all": GL, POW Diary, transcript, RG226-e190-f772.

85 "undoubtedly meant 'Supply Corps, Infantry'": Jennings Report on Time as POW, April 4, 1945, RG-226-e99-box14-f5.

87 "Come here, sister, and blow": GL, "Sands Ceased to Run," early draft, 10.

87 ninety-five thousand U.S. servicemen: Foy, *For You the War Is Over,* 13.

87 on the ground in vast tents: Beattie, *Diary of a Kriegie,* 81.

88 "I stood there in the sunshine": GL manuscript on captivity, June 1945, RG226-e190-f771.

88 Of the 5.7 million Red Army soldiers: Burleigh, *Third Reich,* 512–13.

88 "All of these things are partially true": Ibid., 513.

CHAPTER 10

90 "quite well to do": Gosewisch to GL, Aug. 29, 1945, OSS scrap-
    book, LP.

90 offered a number of different explanations: See GL, *Sands Ceased to
    Run;* GL statement in Bern, RG226-e190-f772; Gosewisch postwar
    letters to GL, OSS scrapbook, LP; and Beattie, *Diary of a Kriegie,*
    93–95.

91 joined the Nazi Party, in 1937: Alien case file A8109455 William
    Gosewisch, Record Group 566, Records of the Immigration and
    Naturalization Service, National Archives, Kansas City.

91 about 850,000 Nazi Party members: Gellately, *Backing Hitler,* 16.

91 trained as a military interpreter in Berlin: Wilhelm Gosewisch mili-
    tary file, Bundesarchiv.

93 "New Year's Sonnet": *The Oflag 64 Item,* Jan. 1, 1945, 6. http://www
    .oflag64.us/ewExternalFiles/theitem-01-01-45.pdf.

94 a U.S. military report noted: Foy, *For You the War Is Over,* 57.

94 something "sinister" about their presence at Wallendorf: Beattie,
    Diary of a Kriegie, 99.

94 "A great deal of interest": Report on interrogation of Werner Muel-
    ler, April 25, 1945, SCI, T-Force, RG226-e92-f30126.

95 they were shot without warning: Bard, *Forgotten Victims,* 62.

96 "Mental strain, psychological threats": Foy, *For You the War Is
    Over,* 58.

97 "You probably belong to the FBI": GL, "Sands Ceased to Run,"
    early draft, LP.

97 penetration of Germany by OSS agents: Bruce, *OSS Against the
    Reich,* 182.

97 "Giblin was in a very dangerous business": Robert Jennings Report
    on Time as POW, April 4, 1945, RG226-e99-box14-f5.

CHAPTER 11

99 "Reports concerning [Papurt], though conflicting": OSS report,
    German and Japanese Penetration of OSS in ETO, July 6, 1945,
    RG226-e210-box345-13442.

99 Both Wehrmacht and Foreign Ministry reports: See Interrogation

of Ursula Zieschang, April 26, 1945, RG226-e92-f30126 and PAAA RZ214-100130-199.

99 20 percent of them died: Bard, *Forgotten Prisoners*, 103.

100 "So far as we can learn": Norman Holmes Pearson (acting chief, X-2) to Lieutenant Colonel Russell Forgan, OSS memo, Oct. 23, 1944, Papurt incident, RG226-e122-box4-f1.

100 "German knowledge of OSS was fragmentary": German and Japanese Penetration of OSS.

101 "spent their evenings singing songs": Goldberg, *Margaret Bourke-White*, 277.

101 "From Africa and Italy the word": MJP to MBW, Nov. 19, 1943, MBW Papers.

101 news to his wife: Sorel, *Women Who Wrote the War*, 241.

101 "Don't let your fear spoil": Goldberg, *Margaret Bourke-White*, 277.

101 "I was struck by the polka-dotted effect": MBW, *Portrait of Myself*, 238.

102 "Peggy, you are either the bravest": Goldberg, *Margaret Bourke-White*, 280–81.

102 He told her she had an "adolescent": MJP to MBW, Nov. 19, 1943, MBW Papers.

102 "I'd rather spend two months": MJP to MBW, Dec. 9, 1943, MBW Papers.

103 "a past master of this kind": MBW, *Portrait of Myself*, 310.

103 "I love you. I will marry you": Ibid.

103 He was already up on crutches: GL to MJP's brother, July 30, 1945, LP.

CHAPTER 12

104 "interrogation of Allied POWs": Foy, *For You the War Is Over*, 58.

104 "seeing everything you want": Beattie, *Diary of a Kriegie*, 97.

104 "the hisses and catcalls of the people": United Press report, March 15, 1939, UPI archives.

105 until 2:00 or 3:00 in the morning: GL statement in Bern, RG226-e190-f772.

105 a GI fighting in the Pacific: Wilhelm Gosewisch to GL, August 29, 1946, OSS scrapbook, LP.

105 "I do worry about the distress": Jennings military personal file, National Archives, St. Louis.

106 "You see how my innocent little trip": GL to Marian Hall, Oct. 14, 1944, OSS scrapbook, LP.

106 who the "fair prisoner" was: Beattie, *Diary of a Kriegie,* 95.

106 "Whoever she is, she has given": Ibid.

107 Jennings was taken to an: Robert Jennings Report on Time as POW, April 4, 1945, RG226-e99-box14-f5.

107 "International News Service had the story": OSS memo, Oct. 13, 1944, RG226-e90-box3-f40.

108 "member of New York society circles": OSS dispatch, London to Donovan, Oct. 26, 1944, excerpts from BBC monitoring report, RG226-e90-box3-f40.

108 "they do not regard her as connected": OSS memo, Papurt incident, Oct. 23, 1944.

109 "I do hope you are well": SL to GL, Dec. 7, 1944, LP.

110 authority over all POW affairs: Foy, *For You the War Is Over,* 28.

110 "was interested in Mrs. Legendre": Interrogation of Ursula Zieschang, April 26, 1945, RG226-e92-f30126.

110 "sympathetic treatment" of VIP prisoners of war: Memo on meeting with Obergruppenfuehrer Berger. RZ214-100347-111, PAAA.

110 "explicitly asked for [Gertie]": File note, Oct. 27, 1944, RZ214-100130-200, PAAA.

110 she might in fact be Eisenhower's secretary: Report on the interrogation of Ursula Zieschang, April 26, 1945, SCI, T-Force, RG226-e92-f30126.

110 order came directly from Hitler: Ibid. Zieschang said the order came from Hitler. Zieschang, who worked for the Gestapo and typed some of the reports on Gertie in late 1944, when Gertie was held in Berlin, told her American interrogators that she had read Gertie's entire Gestapo file in January 1945. She also kept her shorthand book of all of the correspondence dictated by the Gestapo officer in charge of Gertie's case and reread it shortly before her arrest in April 1945, when she destroyed the document as being compromising. But her American interrogators noted that her memory of the Legendre case was fresh and detailed.

CHAPTER 13

111 Toward the end of October: Gertie dates her departure from Diez as November 3, but Zieschang's interrogation and documents from the German Foreign Ministry would put her in Berlin on October 28.

111 "that in order to destroy anything": Atkinson, *Guns at Last Light,* 356.

112 "wrecked cities made me realize": Beattie, *Diary of a Kriegie,* 120.

112 "well over one million tons": Atkinson, *Guns at Last Light,* 359.

112 in some cases killing prisoners: Foy, *For You the War Is Over,* 41.

113 "There is block after block": Beattie, *Diary of a Kriegie,* 176.

113 "faces of refugee columns fleeing": Ibid., 103.

113 Parts of the staff and their files: Interrogation of Ursula Zieschang, April 26, 1945, RG226-e92-f30126.

113 "strut around with the old pomposity": Beattie, *Diary of a Kriegie,* 114.

113 two women from the Kripo: Interrogation of Ursula Zieschang, April 26, 1945, RG226-e92-f30126.

114 boyhood friend of Adolf Eichmann's: Wistrich, *Who's Who in Nazi Germany,* 135.

114 they were to be shot immediately: Foy, *For You the War Is Over,* 23.

114 It was Kaltenbrunner who ordered: Bard, *Forgotten Victims,* 62.

114 "articles on racial inferiority": Deflem, "Logic of Nazification," 29.

115 "little problem child": Beattie, *Diary of a Kriegie,* 144.

115 The Gestapo, despite memos stating: Memo, Nov. 7, 1944, RZ214-100130-202, PAAA.

116 "was 'the Jewish Question'": Wistrich, *Who's Who in Nazi Germany,* 157–58.

116 Clemens had previously headed: Michael Wildt, *An Uncompromising Generation: The Nazi Leadership of the Reich Security Main Office* (Madison: University of Wisconsin Press, 2009), 364.

116 Lischka was upset that Gertie: Memo, October 31, 1944, RZ214-100130-201, PAAA.

117 One of the "best linguists": Report on interrogation of Werner Mueller, April 25, 1945, SCI, T-Force, RG226-e92-f30126.

118 "refused flatly to say anything": Report on interrogation of Ursula Zieschang, April 25, 1945, SCI, T-Force, RG226-e92-f30126.

118 "a series of attempts": Longerich, *Heinrich Himmler*, 720.

118 "In a grotesque irony, Himmler": Black, *Ernst Kaltenbrunner*, 227.

119 "capture was a mistake": Beattie, *Diary of a Kriegie*, 144.

120 "live[d] in a strange world": Ibid., 110.

121 "two of our planes destroyed": GL, War Diary, transcript, RG226-e190-f772.

121 big craters in the woods: Beattie, *Diary of a Kriegie*, 115.

121 "All traffic had stopped": Ibid., 169.

123 The ability to walk outside: Foy, *For You the War Is Over*, 95.

123 "awash with rumors about the mass killing": Stargardt, *German War*, 376.

124 "In Wetzlar, Braunschweig, Solingen, Frankfurt am Main": Ibid.

124 Zieschang developed "sincere affection": Major Durand (SCI T-Force) to Chief, X-2, Paris, April 28, 1945, RG226-e92-f30126.

125 "Awful," she declared, but smoked them: GL, POW Diary, transcript, RG226-e190-f772.

CHAPTER 14

126 "Everywhere there was busy life": OSS scrapbook, LP.

127 "Be practical, give a coffin": Beevor, *Berlin*, 1.

127 "about the only consolation that I can give you": SL to GL, Dec. 25, 1944, LP.

127 "It smacks of Miss Evans": SL to GL, Jan. 6, 1945, LP.

128 "even to save her life": Report on interrogation of Ursula Zieschang, April 25, 1945, SCI, T-Force, RG226-e92-f30126.

128 a facility for people with mental disabilities: D'Albert-Lake, *American Heroine in the French Resistance*, 234.

129 "was all-powerful in gaining anything": GL, POW Diary, transcript, RG226-e190-f772.

130 they should be killed like "mad dogs": Foy, *For You the War Is Over*, 24.

130 "If I make it clear": Ibid., 34.

130 "as well below zero": Stargardt, *German War*, 349.

130 "could still see the burning city": Sebald, *On the Nature of Destruction*, 22.

CHAPTER 15

134 "Special prisoners were prisoners": Koop, *In Hitlers Hand*, 8.

134 "Mrs. Legendre was not treated as a prisoner of war": Report on interrogation of Ursula Zieschang, April 25, 1945, SCI, T-Force, RG226-e92-f30126.

135 *Winzerstube*—the "winemaker's lounge": Report on interrogation of Werner Mueller, April 25, 1945, SCI, T-Force, RG226-e92-f30126.

135 "She was a smart and friendly woman": Cailliau de Gaulle, *Souvenirs personnels*, 87.

136 "I was sad to leave France": Ibid., 83.

138 The banks of the river: Reynolds, *Summits*, 56.

138 "afternoon coffee" for the VIP detainees: Koop, *In Hitlers Hand*, 45.

139 knew nothing of her whereabouts: Handwritten notes, OSS memo, London to Washington, April 2, 1945, RG226-e210-wd13271-box330-f13; SL to Red Cross, March 8, 1945, OSS scrapbook, LP.

139 "Isn't this a grand, cheerful letter!": Marian Hall to SL, Dec. 30, 1944, OSS scrapbook, LP.

139 "Were the lice in your hair": SL to GL, Jan. 22, 1945, LP.

139 "The war seems to be moving": SL to GL, Jan. 29, 1945, LP.

140 "Maybe this restrained life of inactivity": GL to SL, Jan. 29, 1945, OSS scrapbook, LP.

141 "Every morning sharp at nine": GL, POW Diary, transcript, RG226-e190-f772.

142 "turned him over to the Germans": GL statement in Bern, RG226-e190-f772.

142 "expressions like *'Abriegelung des Angriffs'*": Beattie, *Diary of a Kriegie*, 94.

CHAPTER 16

146 "the most totally destroyed city": Atkinson, *Guns at Last Light*, 544.

146 these fliers as *"Terror Flieger"*: Foy, *For You the War Is Over*, 23.

149 "But such killings were merely": Kershaw, *End*, 328.

149 "Sherman gunners systematically burned out": Atkinson, *Guns at Last Light*, 546.

CHAPTER 17

153 a former executive with IG Farben: H. H. Grieme file, folder ZA-VI-3472A-01 and 05, Bundesarchiv, Berlin. After the war, when IG Farben was broken up, he got a position with its photographic arm, Agfa, which became an independent company. Grieme never mentioned IG Farben to Gertie, but described himself as a machine tool factory owner.

154 "The inner door to Germany": Atkinson, *Guns at Last Light,* 551.

154 "another brick and stone wilderness": Ibid., 568.

154 "They are punch drunk": GL, Memo, German Ideas on Propaganda, RG226-e190-f772.

155 there were signs warning residents: Ibid.

155 "Men who take themselves from the front": Kershaw, *End,* 218–20.

155 food was scarce and the family: GL, Memo on Food and Clothing, RG226-e190-f772.

156 "intelligent, worldly, open-minded": GL, Memo, List of German Names, RG226-e190-f772.

156 "No one is a Nazi": *Reporting World War II,* 671.

157 transfer of all German POWs: GL, Memo, German Ideas on Propaganda.

157 "sprang from the devouring fear": Beattie, *Diary of a Kriegie,* 200.

157 "Prior to exchange she was": Report on interrogation of Werner Mueller, April 25, 1945, SCI, T-Force, RG226-e92-f30126; OSS memo, April 27, 1945, RG226-e190-f772.

157 She wrote a series of memos: See GL, German Ideas on Propaganda.

159 "So good!" she exclaimed: GL, POW Diary, transcript, RG226-e190-f772.

159 "slavery, castration, the end of Germany": Atkinson, *Guns at Last Light,* 380.

160 hoping it would speed her release: GL statement in Bern, RG226-e190-f772.

CHAPTER 18

166 about a hundred yards up the line: GL statement in Bern, RG226-e190-f772. Gertie offered various lengths in how far she had to run,

but this statement was given shortly after her escape and seems the most reliable estimate.

166 she was startled by Gay: Gertie offers two accounts about who crept up on her on the railroad tracks and told her to run. In her statement to Dulles, made shortly after her escape, she said it was Gay. See GL statement in Bern, RG226-e190-f772. In her memoir *The Sands Ceased to Run*, 231, she said it was the unnamed German who had joined her and Gay on the platform. In her Bern statement, she also said she left Hans Grieme's home with Gay and an SS officer; in the book, it was Gay and a chauffeur. The memoir would suggest the person who suddenly appeared on the Constance platform was a third person, not the driver or the officer she had left Kronberg with.

166 Her entry time was recorded as 9:30 p.m.: E5791-1000-949-230, sub-file 2-4812, Legendre-Sanford, Gertrude, 1902, Swiss Federal Archive.

CHAPTER 19

168 A Reuters report out of Zurich: *New York Times*, March 25, 1945, 8.

169 warned not to discuss the matter: OSS cables on escape, RG226-e90-box 3-f40, RG226-e190-f772.

169 "I told the man it was in the papers": SL to GL, March 27, 1945, LP.

169 "In the old days": SL to GL, April 15, 1945, LP.

169 "Everyone was staring at me": GL manuscript, June 1945, RG226-e190-f771.

170 "The fact that this woman": E5791-1000-949-230, sub-file 2-4812, Legendre-Sanford, Gertrude, 1902, Swiss Federal Archive.

170 Raggenbass told Gertie he knew: GL manuscript, June 1945, RG226-e190-f771.

170 Raggenbass maintained close relations: See "Die Nammen der Strasse," *Südkurier* (Constance), Sept. 25, 2010.

170 he acted as an intermediary: See Raggenbass, *Trotz Stacheldraht*.

170 charges that he was an anti-Semite: See "Nazi-Biografien aus der Region," *Südkurier* (Constance), Feb. 13, 2016.

172 "This important from CE [counterespionage] standpoint": OSS memo, April 2, 1945, RG226-e210-wn13271-box330-f13.

173 "I think Gertrude was rather contrite": Memorandum, 110 (Dulles) to 109 (Donovan), March 29, 1945, RG226-e190-f772.

173 "For the information of Mrs. Legendre": A photograph of the message is included in GL, *Sands Ceased to Run*.

173 flowers and a bottle of champagne: GL, POW Diary, transcript, RG226-e190-f772.

174 celebrated her forty-third birthday: OSS Oral History, Legendre interview, 29, RG263-e84, NA.

174 "We have seen Gertrude": OSS memo, March 30, 1945, RG226-e90-box3-f40.

174 Gertie also suggested that rather than return: GL, June 1945 manuscript, RG226-e190-f771.

174 "This is a very serious matter": Donovan memo, March 30, 1945, RG226-e90-box3-f40.

174 "One of those awful flights": OSS oral history, Legendre interview, 37.

175 "Hated to leave Paris": GL to SL, April 6, 1945, LP.

175 "One afternoon, long red fingernails": Bokara Legendre, *Not What I Expected*, 40.

CHAPTER 20

176 "We know no more about [the offensive]": Beattie, *Diary of a Kriegie*, 191.

176 "the public is interpreting the news": Ibid., 194.

177 "screaming, shoving, and crowding their way": Ibid., 199.

178 "as white men to other white men": Ibid., 218.

178 losses on the eastern front: Kershaw, *End*, 206.

178 "I've always said there can be no question": Ibid., 246.

178 Operation Clarion targeted small-town Germany: Atkinson, *Guns at Last Light*, 535.

179 Among those prisoners was Doyle Dickson: Doyle E. Dickson military file, National Personnel Records Center, National Archives, St. Louis.

179 "YOU ARE NOW IN COLOGNE": MBW, *"Dear Fatherland, Rest Quietly,"* 12.

179 "Never let that woman out": Sorel, *Women Who Wrote the War*, 331.

180 "Don't show my jowls": MBW, *"Dear Fatherland, Rest Quietly,"* 22.

180 "in emulation of William the Conqueror": Atkinson, *Guns at Last Light*, 558.

180 "We correspondents were hard-pressed": MBW, *Portrait of Myself,* 258.

180 "It was a sense of return": MBW, *"Dear Fatherland, Rest Quietly,"* 38.

180 "We hope you arrived in Switzerland": News clipping, April 7, 1945, OSS scrapbook, LP.

181 the dissecting room where gloves: Atkinson, *Guns at Last Light,* 603.

181 "Using the camera was almost": MBW, *"Dear Fatherland, Rest Quietly,"* 73.

181 his weight fell to 105 pounds: GL to SL, May 7, 1945, LP.

182 On the morning of March 27: Jennings Report on Time as POW, April 4, 1945, RG-226-e99-box14-f5.

182 "His actions exposed OSS to great criticism": Memo, Donovan to London, April 5, 1945, RG226-e90-box3-f40.

182 Jennings was formally reprimanded: OSS memo, April 12, 1945, RG226-e90-box3-f40.

182 "I guess we both got away awfully lucky": GL to SL, May 7, 1945, LP.

182 his mother was killed: William Gosewisch to GL, Aug. 29, 1946, OSS scrapbook, LP.

183 "free men unable to taste freedom": Beattie, *Diary of a Kriegie,* 310.

183 "My hotel bed," Beattie noted: Ibid., 312.

184 they looked like "vagabonds": Cailliau de Gaulle, *Souvenirs personnels,* 94.

184 The wall above the castle's entryway: Harding, *Last Battle,* 6.

184 part of a unit killing Jews: Ibid., 19.

185 "Traitor, collaborator!" Reynaud greeted Weygand: Ibid., 54.

185 "could not possibly have been more": Ibid., 62.

186 "It was intoxicating to feel free": Cailliau de Gaulle, *Souvenirs personnels,* 102.

187 *"Ja. Ja,"* the two general officers replied: Atkinson, *Guns at Last Light,* 626.

187 "in good spirit by his mother and father": OSS memo, Oct. 27, 1944, RG226-e90-box 3-f40.

187 "I cannot understand why": Doyle E. Dickson military file, National Personnel Records Center, National Archives, St. Louis. The effort to find and identify Dickson's remains is described in a series of documents in his military file.

189 "Major Papurt was great company": July 23, 1945, RG226-e160a-box 16-f273.

EPILOGUE

191 "To try and interest myself in Peter Rabbit": GL to SL, April 10, 1945, LP.

191 "N.Y.C. is a terrible comedown": GL to SL, April 6, 1945, LP.

191 "The food is all too astounding": GL to SL, April 15, 1945, LP.

191 "It's too late . . . now I am told": GL to SL, May 20, 1945, LP.

192 "The whole thing as you may guess": GL to SL, April 6, 1945, LP.

192 "I think it would make a great seller": GL to SL, May 7, 1945, LP.

192 "You have made a real contribution": Donovan to GL, June 18, 1945, RG226-e190-f772.

192 "the return of these documents": OSS memo, April 13, 1945, RG226-e190-f772.

192 the adoption of Flers de l'Orne: Beach, *Medway*, 61.

193 "no rank and was not an officer": Alien case file A8109455 William Gosewisch, Record Group 566, Records of the Immigration and Naturalization Service, National Archives, Kansas City.

193 "We would revel in the luxuries": SL to GL, April 7, 1945, LP.

194 "Our life apart is not something": GL to SL, May 22, 1945, LP.

195 "How I loved being with you": GL to SL, Aug. 8, 1945, LP.

196 "Give Me That Old Time Religion": Bokara Legendre, *Not What I Expected*, 45.

196 Pansa was forced into hiding: Mario Spezi to Harlan Greene (librarian, College of Charleston), March 21, 2016.

196 "The power of dying, of waiting to die": Bokara Legendre, *Not What I Expected*, 214–15.

197 "I consider I was fortunate": GL, personal essay, March 1987, LP.

197 "gave up all development rights": Beach, *Medway*, 110.

197 "I want Medway to be a place": Ibid., 11.

197 "a sort of joke": Bokara Legendre, *Not What I Expected*, 215.

197 "Every evening, I sit at one end": GL, *Time of My Life*, 77.

Selected Bibliography

Atkinson, Rick. *The Guns at Last Light.* New York: Picador, 2013.

Baker, Richard Brown. *The Year of the Buzz Bomb: A Journal of London, 1944.* New York: Exposition Press, 1952.

Bard, Mitchell G. *Forgotten Victims: The Abandonment of Americans in Hitler's Camps.* Boulder, Colo.: Westview Press, 1994.

Beach, Virginia Christian. *Medway.* Charleston, S.C.: Wyrick, 1999.

Beattie, Edward W., Jr. *Diary of a Kriegie.* New York: Thomas Y. Crowell, 1946.

Beevor, Antony. *Berlin: The Downfall, 1945.* New York: Viking, 2002.

Black, Peter. *Ernst Kaltenbrunner: Ideological Soldier of the Reich.* Princeton, N.J.: Princeton University Press, 1984.

Blumenson, Martin. *Breakout and Pursuit.* Atlanta: Whitman, 2012.

Bourke-White, Margaret. *"Dear Fatherland, Rest Quietly": A Report on the Collapse of Hitler's "Thousand Years."* New York: Simon & Schuster, 1946.

———. *Portrait of Myself.* New York: Simon & Schuster, 1963.

———. *Purple Heart Valley.* New York: Simon & Schuster, 1944.

Brinkley, David. *Washington Goes to War.* New York: Ballantine Books, 1988.

Brown, Anthony Cave. *The Last Hero: Wild Bill Donovan.* New York: Times Books, 1982.

Bull, Bartle. *Safari: A Chronicle of Adventure.* New York: Penguin, 1992.

Burleigh, Michael. *The Third Reich: A New History.* London: Pan Books, 2001.

Cailliau de Gaulle, Marie-Agnès. *Souvenirs personnels.* Paris: Parole et Silence, 2006.

Chalou, George C., ed. *The Secrets War: The Office of Strategic Services in World War II.* Washington, D.C.: National Archives and Records Administration, 1992.

Clark, Martin. *Mussolini.* New York: Routledge, 2014.

Cochran, Gifford A. "Mr. Lincoln's Many-Faceted Minister and Entrepreneur Extraordinary Henry Shelton Sanford." Unpublished manuscript, Legendre Papers, College of Charleston.

Cowden, Robert. "OSS Double-Agent Operations in World War II." *Studies in Intelligence* 58, no. 2 (June 2014): 65–75.

D'Albert-Lake, Virginia. *An American Heroine in the French Resistance: The Diary and Memoir of Virginia D'Albert-Lake.* New York: Fordham University Press, 2006.

Deflem, Mathieu. "The Logic of Nazification: The Case of the International Criminal Police Commission." *International Journal of Comparative Sociology* 43, no. 1 (2002): 21–44.

Dickey, Christopher. "The Socialite Spy Who Played So Dumb She Outsmarted the Nazis." *Daily Beast,* Sept. 25, 2016.

Ford, Corey. *Donovan of OSS.* Boston: Little, Brown, 1970.

Foy, David A. *For You the War Is Over: American Prisoners of War in Nazi Germany.* New York: Stein and Day, 1984.

Fry, Joseph Andrew. "An American Abroad: The Diplomatic Career of Henry Shelton Sanford." Ph.D. diss., University of Virginia, 1974.

Gellately, Robert. *Backing Hitler: Consent and Coercion in Nazi Germany.* Oxford: Oxford University Press, 2001.

Goldberg, Vicki. *Margaret Bourke-White: A Biography.* New York: Harper and Row, 1986.

Grose, Peter. *Gentleman Spy: The Life of Allen Dulles.* Boston: Houghton Mifflin, 1994.

Harding, Stephen. *The Last Battle.* Boston: Da Capo Press, 2013.

Hastings, Max. *Armageddon: The Battle for Germany, 1944–1945.* New York: Knopf, 2004.

Herne, Brian. *White Hunters: The Golden Age of African Safaris.* New York: Henry Holt, 1999.

Kershaw, Ian. *The End: The Defiance and Destruction of Hitler's Germany, 1944–1945.* New York: Penguin Press, 2011.

———. *Hitler: Hubris, 1889–1936.* London: Penguin, 2001.

Koop, Volker. *In Hitlers Hand: Die Sonder- und Ehrenhäftlinge der SS.* Cologne: Böhlau, 2010.

Lankford, Nelson D. *The Last American Aristocrat: The Biography of Ambassador David K. E. Bruce.* New York: Little, Brown, 1996.

———, ed. *OSS Against the Reich: The War Diaries of Colonel David K. E. Bruce*. Kent, Ohio: Kent State University Press, 1991.

Legendre, Bokara. *Not What I Expected*. Bloomington, Ind.: Balbao Press, 2017.

Legendre, Gertrude. *The Sands Ceased to Run*. New York: William-Frederick Press, 1947.

———. *The Time of My Life*. Charleston, S.C.: Wyrick, 1987.

Legendre, Sidney J. *Land of the White Parasol*. New York: Dodd, Mead, 1936.

———. *Okovango Desert River*. Westport, Conn.: Negro Universities Press, 1939.

Longerich, Peter. *Heinrich Himmler*. Oxford: Oxford University Press, 2012.

MacDonald, Charles B. *The Siegfried Line Campaign*. Atlanta: Whitman, 2012.

Marx, Samuel. *Queen of the Ritz*. Indianapolis: Bobbs-Merrill, 1978.

Mazzeo, Tilar J. *The Hotel on Place Vendôme*. New York: HarperCollins, 2014.

McIntosh, Elizabeth P. *Sisterhood of Spies: The Women of the OSS*. Annapolis, Md.: Naval Institute Press, 1998.

Meier, Frank. *The Artistry of Mixing Drinks*. Paris: Fryam Press, 1936.

Molly, Leo T. *Henry Shelton Sanford, 1823–1891: A Biography*. Derby, Conn.: Bacon, 1952.

Orwell, George. *As I Please, 1943–1945*. New York: Harcourt Brace Jovanovich, 1968.

Overy, Richard. *The Bombing War: Europe, 1939–1945*. London: Penguin, 2014.

Owsley, Harriet Chappell. "Henry Shelton Sanford and Federal Surveillance Abroad, 1861–1865." *Mississippi Valley Historical Review* 48, no. 2 (Sept. 1961): 211–28.

Quinn, Stephen Christopher. *Windows on Nature: The Great Habitat Dioramas of the American Museum of Natural History*. New York: Abrams/AMNH, 2006.

Raggenbass, Otto. *Trotz Stacheldraht*. Constance: Südkurier, 1964.

Reporting World War II: Part 2, American Journalism, 1944–1946. New York: Library of America, 1995.

Rexer, Lyle, and Rachel Klein. *American Museum of Natural History:*

125 Years of Expedition and Discovery. New York: Abrams/AMNH, 1995.

Reynolds, David. *Summits: Six Meetings That Shaped the Twentieth Century*. New York: Basic Books, 2007.

Rice, Andrew. "Gertie's Ghost." *New York Times Magazine,* Oct. 14, 2011.

Robb, Alex M. *The Sanfords of Amsterdam*. New York: William-Frederick Press, 1969.

Roosevelt, Kermit. *War Report of the OSS*. New York: Walker, 1976.

Sebald, W. G. *On the Nature of Destruction*. New York: Modern Library Classics, 2004.

Silverman, Jonathan. *For the World to See: The Life of Margaret Bourke-White*. New York: Viking Press, 1983.

Smith, Richard Harris. *OSS: The Secret History of America's First Intelligence Agency*. Guilford, Conn.: Lyons Press, 2005.

Sorel, Nancy Caldwell. *The Women Who Wrote the War*. New York: Arcade, 1999.

Stargardt, Nicholas. *The German War: A Nation Under Arms, 1939–1945*. New York: Basic Books, 2015.

Stevens, William D. *Justifiable Pride: A World War II Memoir*. Lincoln, Neb.: Jemel Books, 1999.

Tomkins, Calvin. *Living Well Is the Best Revenge*. New York: Museum of Modern Art, 2013.

Waller, Douglas. *Disciples: The World War II Mission of the CIA Directors Who Fought for Wild Bill Donovan*. New York: Simon & Schuster, 2015.

———. *Wild Bill Donovan: The Spymaster Who Created the OSS and Modern American Espionage*. New York: Simon & Schuster, 2011.

Winks, Robin W. *Cloak & Gown: Scholars in the Secret War, 1939–1961*. New York: Morrow, 1987.

Wistrich, Robert S. *Who's Who in Nazi Germany*. London: Routledge, 2002.

Ziegler, Philip. *London at War, 1939–1945*. London: Pimlico, 2002.

Index

Abercrombie, David, 37
Academy of Natural Sciences,
    Philadelphia, 42
Addis Ababa, Ethiopia, 4, 30, 36,
    37–38
Alice's Adventures in Wonderland
    (Carroll), 151
Allies
  advance across France, 9, 15
  advance into Germany, 146–47,
    154, 162, 180
  bombing of Germany, 8, 111,
    112, 130–31, 143, 154, 158,
    162, 178
  casualties, 187
  firebombing of Dresden, 178
  German codes broken by, 14–15
  logistics, pursuit of the
    Germans, 17
  Operation Clarion, 178
Alsace-Lorraine Resistance, 142
American Graves Registration
    Service, 188
American Museum of Natural
    History, 35, 36, 37, 42,
    43, 51
Anthony, Harold E., 37
"April in Paris" (song), 71
Arlon, Belgium, 12–13
Atkinson, Rick, 149
Auschwitz, 116, 134, 176
Austria, 48, 184
  Anschluss, 114
  Itter castle as prison, 133–34,
    184–86

Lake Wolfgang, 133
Mauthausen death camp, 95

Bad Godesberg, Germany, 141,
    142, 144, 146, 147, 186
Bad Orb, Germany, Stalag
    IX-B, 99
Ballard, Niles C., 189
Barnes, Tracy, 171, 173
Barry, Ellen, 34
Barry, Philip, 6, 34
Beattie, Edward W., Jr., 10–11,
    104, 107, 111–13, 115, 120,
    157, 176, 177, 179, 183
Berlin, Germany
  Allied bombing of, 120–21,
    178
  Beattie transferred to, 111–13
  bomb damage in, 112–13, 129
  final defense of, 178
  Gertie's detention in, 111–28,
    217n111
  Gestapo headquarters in, 113,
    129
  refugees fleeing and, 176–77
  Soviet shelling of, 183
  Stalag III-D camp, 115
  true believers in, 120
Bern, Switzerland, 170, 171–73
Betts, Thomas J., 84
Bingen, Germany, 162
Black, Peter, 118
Bonhoeffer, Dietrich, 148–49
Bonn, Germany, 87, 131–32, 149,
    154

Bormann, Martin, 155
Borotra, Jean, 185
Bourke-White, Margaret, 14, 83,
    100–103, 179–80
    Dear Fatherland, Rest Quietly,
    181
    Purple Heart Valley, 100
Bradley, Omar, 14
Brandenburg, Germany, 179,
    187–89
Breslau, Germany, 176
Brinkley, David, *Washington Goes
    to War*, 54
Britain, 60, 66
    Battle of, 52
    German bombing of, 67
    Gertie arrives in, 63
    MI6, 82, 84
    See also London
Bruce, Ailsa Mellon, 51
Bruce, David K. E., 7–8, 51,
    64, 97
Bruchlen, Augusta, 185
Bryan, Wright, 10
Buchenwald death camp, 135,
    136, 138, 148, 181

Café Metropole, Hanoi, 43
Cailliau, Alfred, 135–36, 148,
    184–86
Cailliau de Gaulle, Marie-Agnès,
    135–36, 144, 148, 150,
    183–86
Canaris, Wilhelm, 148–49
Carter, T. D., 36, 37, 38, 43, 45
Chamberlain, Neville, 137–38
Charleston, S.C., 197. *See also*
    Medway plantation,
    Charleston, S.C.
Chartres, France, 17
Churchill, Winston, 67, 159, 178
    Ditchley estate, 65
Clemens, Wilhelm, 115–18, 128
Codman, Charles, 161

Cologne, Germany, 129–31, 146
    Allies take, 149, 179
    bomb damage in, 130–31
    Bourke-White in, 179–80
    Gertie arrives in, 130, 131
Compiègne, France, 12
Constance, Germany, 162–64,
    170
Couiteas de Faucamberge, Jean,
    143
Cowles, Virginia, 52
Čučković, Zvonimir, 186
Czechoslovakia, 128, 138

Dachau concentration camp, 149,
    184, 185
Daladier, Édóuard, 134, 184–85
Davison, F. Trubee, 51
Dear Fatherland, Rest Quietly
    (Bourke-White), 181
de Gaulle, Charles, 10, 135, 142
Diaghilev, Serge, 34
Dickson, Amy, 187–88
Dickson, Doyle, 17–20, 72, 73, 75,
    87, 106, 171
    death, 179, 187–89
    Gertie's memory of, 190
    remains and burial of, 188–89
Diez Castle, 88, 89, 104, 152, 181
Djibouti, 36, 37
Donovan, William "Wild Bill,"
    4–5, 51, 52–53, 55, 100, 107
    Dulles memo to, 173
    Gertie and, 57, 60, 70, 81,
    172–74, 192
    Gertie's memos on Germany
    to, 157
    Jennings reprimanded, 182
Dos Passos, John, 34
Dresden, Germany, 178
Ducks Unlimited, 197
Dulles, Allen, 171–73, 221n166
Dungler, Paul, 142
Düren, Germany, 146

Eden, Anthony, 7
Egypt, 28, 33
Eichmann, Adolf, 114
Eisenhower, Dwight D., 5, 6, 9,
    10, 17, 63, 67, 84, 102, 110,
    186–87
Elser, Georg, 149
Elwes, Simon, 197
Ethiopia, 29, 37–38
    See also Addis Ababa, Ethiopia

Fitzgerald, F. Scott, 34
    Tender Is the Night, 34
Fitzgerald, Zelda, 34
Flamersheim, Germany, 78,
    84–87
Flers de l'Orne, France, 192
Flossenbürg concentration camp,
    148–49
Forgan, Russell, 84
Forrestal, James, 50, 117, 194
Fort Rosecrans National
    Cemetery, San Diego, 189
Foxcroft school, Middleburg, Va.,
    23, 41, 42, 54–55
France
    Allied advance in, 69, 83
    American soldiers in, 12
    D-Day landings, Normandy,
        7, 68
    Gertie in the south of, 34–35, 38
    Jews sent to Auschwitz, 116
    liberated, 1944, 13
    Nazi occupation of, 56
    Vichy, 135, 142, 185
    war correspondents captured,
        10–11
    See also Paris
Frankfurt, Germany, 111–12, 153,
    154, 161–62
Free French Forces, 10, 84, 135,
    136
French Resistance, 4, 81, 135–36
Fresnes Prison, France, 136

Friedeburg, Hans-Georg von,
    186–87
Fürstenberg, Germany, 179
    Stalag III-B, 179

Gamelin, Maurice, 185
Gay, Mr., 161–67, 170, 221n166
Gellhorn, Martha, 156
Geneva Convention, 86
Germain, Maxime, 136–37
Germany
    air war above, 77, 87, 144, 154
    Allied advance into, 146–50,
        154, 162, 180
    Allied bombing of, 8, 111, 112,
        120–21, 124, 130–31, 143,
        154, 158, 162, 178
    Allied *Terror Flieger,* 146
    Battle of the Bulge and, 122
    bombing of Britain, 67
    burned synagogues, 124
    capture of war correspondents,
        10–11
    collapsing Reich, 127, 154, 156,
        158, 176
    deserting soldiers, 155
    fabricated U.S. leaflets by,
        156–57
    fear of Soviets, 117, 156–57,
        176–77
    Final Solution and, 114, 123
    firebombing of Dresden, 178
    food shortages, 155
    Kristallnacht, 104, 124
    Nazi Party members, 91
    Nazi propaganda, 129–30
    Nazis disavowed, 156
    Night of the Long Knives, 137
    peace accords and, 119
    retreat of, 75
    Siegfried Line (Westfall), 15, 76
    slave labor used by, 124, 156
    Soviet advance into, 146, 176
    surrender of, 186–87

Germany *(continued)*
  typical Nazi, 78
  U-boats, 62
  U.S.-German soldier alliance,
    186
  V-1 or buzz bombs of, 69
Gestapo, 85, 94, 122
  Berlin headquarters, 113, 129
  execution of prisoners at
    Fresnes, 136
  Gertie in custody of, 110,
    113–20, 129–30, 152, 161,
    216n110
  Gertie's interrogation, 110,
    115–18
  Gertie's release and, 161–66,
    170–71
  Papurt interrogated by, 99
  prisoner interrogation by,
    94–95, 96
Giblin, Walter, 97
Giraud, Henri, 142
Giuseppe Mazzini (ship), 28, 30
Goebbels, Joseph, 100, 104,
    119, 137, 138, 156–57, 159,
    176–79
Göring, Hermann, 3
Gosewisch, Wilhelm, 89–92,
    95–98, 104, 108–10, 144–45,
    159, 174
  fate of, 182–83, 192, 193
Grand Hotel, Paris, 6
Grasshopper planes, 101–2
Great Depression, 40, 45
Grey, Zane, *Sunset Pass,* 92
Grieme, Hans H. and Nena,
    152–57, 161, 162, 174, 180,
    220n153
  fate of, 180–81, 192, 193
  Gertie's note to Patton for, 161,
    180

Haas, Pierre, 84
Hall, Marian, 8, 105–6, 117, 139,
    174

Hanoi, Vietnam, 43
Harding, Stephen, 185
Hayes, Roland, 66
Hearst, Bill, 10
Hearst, William Randolph, 10
Heidelberg, Germany, 48
Hemingway, Ernest, 7–8, 34
Hepburn, Katharine, 6
Heydrich, Reinhard, 94, 114
Himmler, Heinrich, 94, 100, 110,
    118–19, 128, 134, 155, 184
Historic Charleston Foundation,
    197
Hitchcock, Tommy, 68
Hitler, Adolf, 13, 16, 48, 55, 67,
    91, 119, 120, 122, 130,
    132–34, 137–39, 148, 156,
    157, 177–78, 183
  assassination attempted, 100,
    142, 149
  Gertie's fate and, 110, 216n110
  suicide of, 185
  Wolf's Lair headquarters, 100,
    176
Hochschild, Walter, 97
Hodges, Courtney, 146
Holiday (film), 6, 34
Hoover, J. Edgar, 5, 50
Hopkins, Harry, 57
Höss, Rudolf, 134
Hôtel Brasseur, Luxembourg, 13,
    17, 83
Hotel du Cap, Antibes, 34
Hotel Petersberg, Königswinter,
    138, 148
Hôtel Ritz, Paris, 3–4, 7–8, 10

IG Farben, 153, 220n153
Internationale
    Kriminalpolizeiliche
    Kommission, 114–28
International News Service, 10,
    107–8
Italy, 14, 81, 84, 100–102, 134,
    179

Itter, Austria, 184
  castle as prison, 133–34, 184–86

Japan, 10, 43, 49, 50, 56, 194, 195
Jennings, Bob, 10–18, 83, 174
  ambush and capture of, 18–22,
    108
  cover story, 21, 173–74
  fate of, 171, 172, 181–82
  Gertie and, 10, 12–18, 77, 79,
    83, 106, 145, 182
  interrogation, 94, 97, 104, 181
  letters from prison, 105
  OSS reprimand of, 182
  Papurt's document and, 84–85,
    213n84
  places of detention, 72–77, 79,
    84–92, 94, 97, 107, 181–82
Jodl, Alfred, 186–87
Jouhaux, Léon, 185
Joyce, William "Lord Haw-Haw,"
  131

Kaltenbrunner, Ernst, 94, 95, 114,
  118, 119, 122, 128
Kershaw, Ian, 149
Koblenz, Germany, 87, 146, 154
Koenig, Marie-Pierre, 7, 117
Königsberg, Germany, 176
Königstein, Germany, 155, 158
Königswinter, Germany, 138, 147,
  148
Köstner, Willibald, 159
Kreuzlingen, Switzerland, 164,
  167–70, 173
Kripo (German criminal police),
  113–14
Krobot, Andreas, 186
Kronberg, Germany, 152–60, 162

Legendre, Bokara, 11, 42, 54,
  60–61, 127, 175, 197
Legendre, Gertrude "Gertie"
  African safaris, 3, 4, 28–33,
    35–37

anti-Semitism and, 48–49
appearance, 5, 38
background, 23–29
birth of, 26
Bruce as patron for, 51–52, 60
burning of documents, 20, 83
cable to Sidney, from
  Lisbon, 63
character and personality, 5–6,
  8, 23, 24, 33, 43–44, 47–49,
  61, 66–68, 73, 102, 135, 174
children and motherhood, 11,
  42, 54–55, 60–61, 65–66,
  127, 174, 191, 197
contact with wartime friends,
  192
death of, 196
diary of, 174, 192
drinking and smoking, 65, 74,
  87, 127, 135, 139, 144, 158,
  159, 161, 170
freedom in Switzerland, 169–71
funeral and ashes of, 197
as grandmother, 197
honeymoon of, 39
hunting expeditions, 24, 28–33,
  35–37, 42–47
husband Sidney and, 4, 11,
  33–42, 44–49, 51, 54, 56–59,
  61, 65, 66, 67, 68, 69, 109,
  191, 193–95, 197
husband Sidney's death, 196
husband Sidney's portrait,
  197–98
Jennings and, 10, 12–18, 77, 79,
  83, 106, 145, 182
last fieldwork, Siberut, 197
in London, Osterley Park,
  33–34
in London, party for Paris
  liberation, 70–71
Luxembourg City trip, 11,
  12–18, 83
Medway plantation and, 40–42,
  49, 50–51, 66, 195, 197

Legendre, Gertrude "Gertie"
  (continued)
  Middle East trip and Nile
    cruise, 28
  in New York City, 27, 191
  in OSS London, 5, 60, 63–71
  in OSS Paris, 3–4, 6–7, 8
  OSS secrets and, 5, 81–82, 95
  in OSS Washington, 51, 53–61
  Papurt and, 14, 83, 85, 97
  in Paris, postwar, 174
  postwar Charleston and, 197
  postwar discontent, 191, 193–94
  postwar expeditions, 196–97
  postwar foundation established,
    192
  press coverage, 32, 36, 38–39,
    108, 180, 191–92
  prewar political observations,
    48–49
  in prewar Southern France,
    34–35, 38
  The Sands Ceased to Run, 192,
    221n166
  shooting skill and, 23, 152
  trans-Atlantic crossing (1943),
    62–63
  trip to Wallendorf, 17–18
  U.S. return (1945), 174–75
  in WAC uniform, 4, 5
  in the war effort, 8, 50
  wealth and social status, 4, 6,
    23–27, 35–37, 40–42, 51, 57,
    64, 65, 97, 105, 173
  wedding of, 38–39
  on women in uniform, 66
  in Wyoming, 23–24
  —as German prisoner
    air raid and, 77
    Allied advance into Germany
      and, 149–50, 154–55
    ambush and capture of,
      18–22
    in Berlin, at lakeside villa,
      112–28

    Christmas in captivity,
      126–27
    in Cologne, 129–31
    cover story, 21, 76, 106,
      173–74
    daydreaming of, 93
    in Diez Castle, 88–98,
      217n111
    documents of, 78
    ersatz coffee, "mucker fuck,"
      78–79
    escape ideas and, 74
    escape to Switzerland,
      161–66, 170, 220–21n166,
      221n166
    first American woman in
      uniform captured by the
      Nazis, 22, 108
    in Flamersheim, 78–80,
      84–87
    flea infestation, 79
    Geneva Convention and
      prison conditions, 86
    German news of her capture,
      108
    German propaganda and, 119
    German suspicions about, 94
    Gestapo and, 110, 113–14,
      119–20, 129–30, 152,
      216n110
    Gestapo interrogation of, 110,
      115–18
    Gestapo plan for, 151, 157
    Gestapo's intermediary
      request of, 159
    Gosewisch and, 89–92,
      95–98, 104, 108–10, 144–45,
      159, 174
    hides names of captured
      airmen, 79–80
    hides prisoner names, 151,
      173
    at Hotel Petersberg, 147–48
    interpreter Zieschang and,
      122–26, 128–29

Jennings separated from,
  77, 79
Königswinter evacuation,
  150–51
in Kronberg, 152–60
letters sent from prison,
  105–6
letters to Sidney, 139–40
letter to Patton, 119
minders for, 115, 126, 129
mistakes made by, 109
moved deeper into Germany,
  77–78
moved from Diez to Berlin,
  111–12, 217n111
note to Patton for the
  Griemes, 161, 180
Papurt's document and,
  84–85, 213n84
prisoner exchange possibility
  and, 74, 78, 82, 91, 109–10,
  116
propaganda value of, 104, 105
Red Cross boxes and, 92, 113,
  159
in Rheinhotel Dreesen,
  132–45
solitary confinement and, 94,
  106
as "special prisoner," 109,
  134
in Stalag XII-A, 87–88
treatment of, 73, 74–75, 76
in Trier, 76
in Wallendorf, 72–75
weight loss in captivity, 158
in Wittlich, 76–77
Legendre, Landine, 11, 42, 54–55,
  60–61, 127, 175, 197
Legendre, Morris, 33–38, 54, 56,
  59, 196
Legendre, Sidney, 4, 6, 11, 33–39
  Bronze Star received, 195
  death of, 196
  Gertie's fate and, 139

on Gertie's separation from
  their children, 60–61,
  65–66
hunting expeditions, 42–47
learns of Gertie's capture, 82
learns of Gertie's escape, 169
letters to Gertie, never received,
  109, 127, 139–40
Medway plantation and, 40–42,
  49, 195
portrait of, 197–98
reunited with Gertie, 195
secret life of, 59, 194–95
stationed in Hawaii, 4, 11, 51,
  54, 56–57, 58–59, 60, 127,
  139, 191, 194
as travel writer, 44
in U.S. Navy, 4, 11, 50–51
Leopold III, King of Belgium,
  133
Liebenau internment camp, 128
Life magazine, 100, 170, 179
"Lili Marlene" (song), 71, 78
Limburg an der Lahn, Germany,
  84, 103, 152, 179
  Stalag XII-A, 84, 87, 103
Lincoln, Abraham, 25
Lisbon, Portugal, 63
Lischka, Kurt, 115, 118
Little Prince (Saint-Exupéry), 62
London, England
  American PX in, 65
  blackout and bombings, 64
  black soldiers in, 66
  Eisenhower in, 63
  food coupons, 64–65
  Gertie at Osterley Park, 1928,
    33–34
  Gertie in, wartime, 5, 7, 10,
    63–71
  invasion of France and, 68–69
  little Blitz, 67
  OSS office in, 10, 63–71, 84,
    100
  U.S. embassy, 63

London, England *(continued)*
  V-1 or buzz bombs and, 69, 70,
    117
  wartime, 63–66
Lorraine American Military
    Cemetery and Memorial,
    Saint-Avold, France, 189
Lowman, Eleanor Barry, 48
Lowman, Larry, 48–49
Luckenwalde, Germany, 177, 179,
    183
Luftwaffe, 67, 87, 112
  interrogation center of, 107
Luxembourg, 11, 12–18, 118

MacLeish, Archibald, 34
Mainz, Germany, 154, 162
Majdanek concentration camp,
    184
Manon, Madame, 4
Marx, Harpo, 34
Maugham, Somerset, 34, 35
Mauthausen concentration
    camp, 95
May, Toni, 86
McCloy, John J., 82
Meade, George, 56
Mecklin, John, 10
Medway plantation, Charleston,
    S.C., 40–42, 49–51, 66, 195,
    196, 197
Meier, Frank, 3–4
Mellon, Andrew, 51
Menzies, Stewart, 84
Michael of Montenegro, Prince,
    144, 151, 173
Mombasa, Kenya, 30
Montgomery, Bernard, 180
Morton, Joseph, 95, 114
Moselle River, 76
Müller, Werner, 95, 116–17, 118,
    122, 125, 128, 157
Munich, Germany, 184
Murphy, Gerald and Sara, 34

Murrow, Edward R., 65
Mussolini, Benito, 26, 53

Nairobi, Kenya, 30
Nebe, Arthur, 114
"New Year's Sonnet" (Phelan), 93
New York City, 27, 191
New York Times, 36, 38
  Gertie's wedding covered,
    38–39
  report on Gertie's capture, 108
Nimitz, Chester W., 54
Noland, Charlotte, 42
Nuremberg, Germany, 48
  trials, 122

Oberpleis, Germany, 151, 152
Office of Strategic Services
    (OSS), 4–5, 52–53, 55
  acting chief, London, 84
  Bern office, 171
  Bruce and, 7, 51–52, 53, 60
  capture of Gertie, Jennings,
    Papurt and, 81–82, 107–8,
    172
  counterintelligence branch,
    X-2, 13, 14, 84, 100
  Dungler affiliated with, 142
  eclectic mix of characters in,
    49, 55
  German capture of Anglo-
    American team in Slovakia
    and, 94–95, 114
  German ignorance about, 100
  Gertie and secrets of, 81–82, 95
  Gertie gets message to, 106
  Gertie in, 4, 5, 6, 51, 53–61
  Gertie leaves on good terms,
    192
  Gertie's escape learned by,
    168–69
  Gertie's fate and, 139
  Gertie's papers confiscated, 174,
    192

Gertie's release questioned by, 172

hiring a "league of gentlemen," 55

interrogation of interpreter, 157

London office, 5, 10, 63–71, 84, 100

Lowman in, 48

Papurt and, 13–14, 69–70, 82–84, 99–100

Paris office, 4, 6–7, 8, 97, 174, 182

postwar questioning of Zieschang, 124

search for Gertie and others, 81

Washington office, 55–61

women working for, inequity and, 59

Office of the Coordinator of Information (COI), 52

Oliver, Lunsford E., 16–17

Orwell, George, 69

Osborn, Henry Fairfield, 36

Pansa, Mario, 53, 196

Papurt, Jerry, 13–18, 81–83, 84, 101, 106, 179

ambush, wounding, and capture of, 18–22, 72, 73, 74, 75, 108

Bourke-White and, 14, 83, 100–103

death of, 103, 145, 172

Gertie and, 14, 83, 85, 97

Gertie's letter to his brother, 189–90

grave of, 189

incriminating papers on, 73, 83

interrogation of, 94, 99

as Jewish, 99, 110

in London X-2, 13–14, 69–70, 82, 84

OSS concern about capture of, 82–84

SCI document and, 83, 84, 85, 97, 98, 213n84

secrets known by, 14–15

SHAEF pass, 83

in Stalag XII-A, 84, 87

trip to Wallendorf, 15, 17–18

Ultra and, 83, 84, 100

Papurt, Sol, 189

Paris

Allied Expeditionary Force Club, 108

Americans in, 3, 5, 9

Arc de Triomphe, 7

Gertie in, 3–4, 6–8, 174

liberation of, 3, 7–10, 70, 136

OSS office in, 4, 6–8, 97, 182

Patton, George S., 8, 11, 13, 105, 117, 119, 122, 159

advance into Germany, 146, 154

Bourke-White and, 180

crosses the Rhine and emulates William the Conqueror, 180

Gertie and, 161

Gertie leaves word for, 147

Gertie's note interceding for the Griemes to, 161, 180

at Oppenheim, Germany, 180

Pearson, Norman Holmes, 84, 100

Peking, China, 43

Pétain, Philippe, 135, 185

Phelan, Larry, 93

"New Year's Sonnet," 93

Picasso, Pablo, 34

Prague, Czechoslovakia, 104, 116

prisoners of war, 77

Allied bombing and deaths of, 179

American Jewish prisoners, 99

angry German mobs and, 112

as bargaining chips, 134

crossing at Constance and, 162–63

prisoners of war *(continued)*
  death rate for POWs in
    Germany, 88
  in Flamersheim, Germany,
    78–80, 84–87
  food and, 92–93
  Geneva Convention and, 86
  German defeat and violence
    against, 149
  German soliciting to fight,
    177–78
  German starvation of, 93
  German torture and execution
    of, 95, 114, 130, 136,
    148–49, 185
  Gertie as first American woman
    in uniform captured by the
    Nazis, 22, 108
  Goebbels's retaliation planned
    for Allied bombardment,
    178–79
  Himmler given authority over,
    110
  liberation of, 183, 186
  Nazi's system for high-ranking
    prisoners, 133–34
  news correspondents as, 95,
    104, 111–12
  noncombatants exchanged,
    74, 78
  Red Cross and, 92, 105, 139
  Russians as German prisoners,
    88, 177
  solitary confinement and, 94,
    106, 107
  Vatican delivering messages to,
    103
Promised Land School,
  Strawberry, S.C., 41–42
Purple Heart Valley (Bourke-
  White), 100
Putzell, Edwin, 81

Raggenbass, Otto and Risa, 168,
  170, 173

Red Cross, 8, 50, 52, 92, 74, 105,
  110, 113, 138, 139, 159
Reisdorf, Luxembourg, 81
Remagen, Germany, 154
Reuters, 168–69
Reynaud, Paul, 134, 185
Rheinhotel Dreesen ("special and
  honored" prisoner camp),
  137, 138, 185
  air raids at, 143–44
  Cailliau de Gaulle at, 135–36,
    140, 144
  cigarettes as money, 144
  Couiteas de Faucamberge at,
    143
  daily life at, 140–42
  English books at, 141
  food, tobacco, and alcohol
    for prisoners at, 138, 139,
    140
  Germain as prisoner leader,
    136–37
  Gertie at, 132–45
  "Godesberg" poem, 141–42
  Hitler and the *Führersuite,* 134,
    137
  Nazis' code name for, 135
  prisoners removed, 147–48
  religious services at, 140
  special prisoners, 133–34, 136,
    143, 144
  war progress monitored at,
    142–43
Rockefeller, John D., Jr., 58
Rockefeller, Nelson, 57
Rocque, François de La, 185
Roosevelt, Franklin Delano, 4, 55,
  178
  COI spy service of, 52–53
  unconditional surrender policy,
    159

Sachsenhausen concentration
  camp, 133
Saigon, Vietnam, 44–45

St.-Étienne, France, 135
Saint-Exupéry, Antoine de, *Little Prince*, 62
Saint-Jean-Cap-Ferrat, France, 38
Saint-Quentin, France, 12
Sands Ceased to Run, The (Legendre), 192, 221n166
Sanford, Ethel, 25–28
Sanford, Gertrude DuPuy, 25
Sanford, Henry Shelton, 25
Sanford, Jane, 26, 28, 34, 53, 196
Sanford, John, 25–28, 39
Sanford, Sarah Jane Cochran, 25
Sanford, Stephen, 25, 26
Sanford, Stephen "Laddie," 26, 28, 30, 31, 32, 53
Sauer River, 16, 17, 72
Schuschnigg, Kurt, 133
Sebald, W. G., 130–31
Sebastian, Frau, 115, 126, 129, 132, 192
Selassie, Haile, 4, 36
Siegburg, Germany, 149
Siegfried Line (Westfall), 15–16, 76
Silesia, Germany, 176
Slovakia, 94–95, 114
Smolensk, Russia, 101
Soviet Union (Russia), 63, 67
    advance into Germany, 146, 176
    eastern front, advance on, 75
    German advance on, 56
    POWs in German captivity, 88
    troops entering Poland, 10
Spaatz, Carl, 70, 105
Special Counter-Intelligence (SCI), 83
    Papurt's paper and, 84, 85, 97, 98, 213n84
SS (SchutzStaffel), 94, 115–16, 118, 163
    Gertie and, 128, 151, 162, 221n166
    Itter Castle and, 184, 186

Rheinhotel Dreesen and, 133, 138, 139, 145, 147, 151
SD (intelligence arm), 112
Stalin, Josef, 178
Stargardt, Nicholas, 124
Stravinsky, Igor, 34
Strok, Michael, 102
Strong, Kenneth, 84
Sunset Pass (Grey), 92
Supreme Headquarters Allied Expeditionary Force (SHAEF), 6
Switzerland, 161–71

Talbott, Harold, 28, 29, 30
Talbott, Peggy, 28, 30, 31, 33
Tender Is the Night (Fitzgerald), 34
T-Force, 14, 84
Transocean news agency, 108
Trier, Germany, 76

Uganda, 29, 32
Ulm, Germany, 162
Ultra, 15, 83, 84, 100
United Press, 10, 183
U.S. Army
    1st Army, 146
    3rd Army, 8, 146, 180
    5th Armored Division, 16
    5th Armored Division, Combat Command R, 16–17
    5th Army, Italian campaign, 100
    12th Army Group, 14
    Counterintelligence Corps, 14, 84
U.S. Army Air Forces, 10, 121
U.S. Marines, 56
U.S. Navy
    Battle of Midway, 56
    Joint Intelligence Center, Hawaii, 57
    Morris Legendre in, 54, 56
    Sidney Legendre in, 4, 11, 51, 54, 56–60, 127, 139, 191, 194

U.S. Navy *(continued)*
Pacific Fleet, 4
spouses barred, Hawaii, 58, 60,
194

Vanderbilt, Bill and Anne, 57

Wallendorf, Germany, 15, 16,
17–18, 72–75, 81, 108,
207n16
Warsaw, Poland, 10, 104–5
Washington, D.C., 54–61
Washington Goes to War
(Brinkley), 54
Wehrmacht, 89, 121, 154, 176
control of Gertie and, 110, 119
decimation of, 178
Foreign Ministry, 110, 119
interrogation center, Diez,
88–98
Papurt interrogated by, 99
prisoners of war and, 96
surrender of, 186–87
Weiter, Eduard, 185
Wetzlar prisoner of war camp, 181
Weygand, Maxime, 185
When Next I See Paris (film), 70
"Wien" (song), 78
Wiesbaden, Germany, 48, 154,
158
Wimmer, Sebastian, 184
Winant, John G., 70, 117
Windsor, Edward, Duke of, 117
Witsell, Edward F., 187, 188
Wittlich, Germany, 76–77
Women's Army Corps (WAC), 4
World War I, 27, 120
World War II, 146
Aleutian Islands and, 10
Allied advance, 9, 15, 75, 83,
122, 146–50, 154, 162, 180
Allied bombing of Germany, 8,
111, 112, 130–31, 143, 154,
158, 162, 178
Allied unconditional surrender
policy, 159–60
Battle of Midway, 56
Battle of the Atlantic, 62
Battle of the Bulge, 122
bombing of Britain, 67
Casablanca Conference, 159
casualties, 56, 121, 180, 187
D-Day landings, Normandy,
7, 68
eastern front, 56, 75, 178
fears of attack on the U.S., 50
France falls to the Nazis, 56
German aggression in Europe,
104–5
German attack at Ardennes,
121–22
German invasion of France,
67, 68
German seizure of
Sudentenland, 138
German U-boats and, 62
Guadalcanal, 56
Hitler's secret weapon
rumors, 67
Italy and, 56
Japan's bombing of Pearl
Harbor, 49
Japan surrenders, 195
Munich Conference, 137–38
North Africa, 56
Siegfried Line (Westfall),
15–16, 76
Soviet advance, 146, 176
summer/fall 1942, 56
Yalta Conference, 178

Zieschang, Ursula, 116–18,
122–26, 128–29, 134, 192,
216n110, 217n111

A NOTE ABOUT THE AUTHOR

Peter Finn is the national security editor at *The Washington Post.* He is also the co-author of *The Zhivago Affair: The Kremlin, the CIA, and the Battle over a Forbidden Book,* a finalist for the National Book Critics Circle Award for nonfiction and a finalist for the Pushkin House Russian Book Prize. *The Zhivago Affair* has been translated into eight languages.

A NOTE ON THE TYPE

The text of this book was set in Plantin, a typeface first cut in 1913 by the Monotype Corporation of London. Though the face bears the name of the great Christopher Plantin (ca. 1520–1589), who in the latter part of the sixteenth century owned, in Antwerp, the largest printing and publishing firm in Europe, it is a rather free adaptation of designs by Claude Garamond made for that firm. With its strong, simple lines, Plantin is a no-nonsense face of exceptional legibility.

Composed by North Market Street Graphics,
Lancaster, Pennsylvania
Printed and bound by Berryville Graphics,
Berryville, Virginia
Designed by Soonyoung Kwon

Gertie's Europe, 1944–45

NETHERLANDS

BELGIUM

•DÜSSELDORF

•COLOGNE

BONN
BAD GODESBERG• •OBERPLEIS
FLAMERSHEIM• •KÖNIGSWINTER

LIMBURG AN DER LAHN
DIEZ•
KRONBERG•
FRANKFURT•

WITTLICH•
•WALLENDORF
ARLON• LUX. •TRIER
★LUXEMBOURG CITY

SAINT-QUENTIN•

★PARIS

FRANCE

CONSTANCE

KREUZLINGEN
ZURICH•

BERN★
SWITZERLAND